I0706593

The bane of humankind is the malignant lie, employed by the malevolent liar for depraved self-interest, in politics and families. The ability to initiate and sustain the lie takes no special talent nor intellect, only the capacity to abandon personal integrity and character.

When good people try to correct the mendacity, the liar gets angry and vindictive. So the question is, in politics and families: Roll over in silent acquiescence or stand up for truth and take the hit?

TRUMP'S LAST YEAR IN OFFICE:

Two Impeachments and 400,000 Funerals

TOM ERSIN

GraniteWord.com
Troy, Michigan

Print Edition ISBN: 9798439604586

Written and edited by Tom Ersin (tom@graniteword.com)

Printed in the United States of America

Front Cover Image ("D. J. Trump silhouette"): GDJ/Pixabay.com

Cover Design by: Tom Ersin

20240307

GraniteWord.com
Troy, MI

<div align="center">~~~</div>

Please Make This Author Happy

I hope you get as much of a kick out of reading this book as I did writing it. I'd be forever appreciative if you would post a review on Amazon. Just a sentence or two and a rating would be great. Reviews are lifeblood for authors and they help readers find my books.

(https://www.amazon.com/dp/B09WHSGVG1)

Thanks a lot,
Tom

The Series

This is the third in my subseries comprising the three books:

> *Trumpism: Why Traditional Republicans Should Withdraw Support [2017-2021: A Primer]*

> *Trump's First Year in Office: The Awakening*

> *Trump's Last Year in Office: Two Impeachments and 400,000 Funerals*

All three books listed above are carve-outs from my exhaustive 1,400-page history:

> *Trump's Presidency: A Real-Time Commentative History [2017-2019]*

> *Trump's Presidency: A Real-Time Commentative History [2019-2021]*

This book, *Trump's Last Year in Office: Two Impeachments and 400,000 Funerals,* is the third book in the subseries, all drawn from the perspective of a long-time avid political observer. Think of the histories as an in-depth every-Thursday recap of all the news you were too busy to consume because you had a life and didn't realize the gravity of the dysfunction and disinformation. When you see my opinion you'll know it. Much more often, when you see facts, quotations, and details, I'm assuring you that I've backed up their accuracy with careful research and citation.

TABLE OF CONTENTS

IBATR: YOUR CRITICAL THINKING PRIMER

This book resides on a foundation of *critically thoughtful communication.* This is communication that consistently incorporates the principles of critical thinking and best supports the ethical, accurate transfer of information.

It does not involve intellectual hoop-jumping or mental gymnastics that only lawyers, philosophers, or Mensa members understand. It's a simple form of critical thinking that anyone should use to cut through the adult male bovine excreta and get to the most accurate possible version of the truth regarding any given issue or question.

IBATR (pronounced *"EYE-batter"*) is the acronym representing the five legs of our critically thoughtful communication table. When even one leg is broken — or missing — the table wobbles. Milk spills.

I) Information — Carefully consider the communicated information or question at hand, ensuring you understand it clearly. Assign no immediate favoritism toward information sources and no immediate judgment about accuracy or inaccuracy of the information.

B) Biases — Examine all biases you or the sources might have surrounding the communicated information or question at hand.

A) Assumptions — Examine all assumptions you or the sources might have surrounding the communicated information or question at hand.

T) Truth — Maintain a commitment to truth and honesty, and consider the level of this commitment for each communication or information source.

R) Response — Carefully draw a conclusion and formulate a response. And always remember that this might require modification based upon new analysis, new communication, or new information-source evaluation.

IBATR is the Holy Grail of successful communication. Granted, perfection is not possible. But applying one's best intentions *is* possible. Applied IBATR best intentions means that we try to follow the steps to the best of our ability. And the last one, Step "R," always allows for the reexamination of information, sources, and personal motives.

Critically thoughtful communication and IBATR constitute the trunk of the communications tree. When this trunk is weakened, branches break or die — or get misquoted. This acronym represents the foundation of accurate, ethical information exchange. Make this acronym your best friend. Put aside time for it. When it is speaking to you, give it your full attention as if it were the most important acronym on Earth. Compliment it now and then on a new hypothesis (or hairstyle). Surprise your acronym occasionally with an intimate rendezvous at home. And never, *ever*, dispute your acronym when the two of you are with friends.■

Introduction

Unlike the rom-com film *Four Weddings and a Funeral*, the story in this book, *Trump's Last Year in Office: Two Impeachments and 400,000 Funerals*, was a preventable tragedy, a national apocalypse. From Mr. Trump's extortion of Ukraine's president, to the intentional venal mishandling of the coronavirus pandemic, to fomenting a violent takeover of Congress and then implementing a literal coup attempt to retain power after his reelection loss, it was all preventable. How? By promoting a more critically thoughtful electorate. By nurturing a more empathetic population, less susceptible to selfish white grievance and more conscious of humanity as a whole.

Instead, through a convergence of electoral anomalies and populist gullibility, we got the antithesis of humanitarianism, a President Donald J. Trump.

Thinking observers know that Mr. Trump did more damage to the presidency, American governmental institutions, and the rule of law in his first three years as president than likely any U.S. chief executive before him. But fortunately he had been confronted with no serious global crises, at least no crises he himself hadn't created.

But in Donald's last year in office, he smashed his personal record for corruption, incompetence, and amorality set during his first three years. He was tried by the Senate for shaking down Ukrainian leader Volodymyr Zelenskyy: President Trump tried to extract nonexistent dirt on his likely presidential opponent by withholding desperately needed, congressionally authorized military aid from our ally. He was tried again for prompting followers to violence in an attempt to overturn his reelection loss.

And in early 2020 the crisis hit. A deadly pandemic brought the world to its knees. Donald didn't cause the plague, but his jackleg response produced a conservatively estimated 200,000 needless COVID-19 deaths, half the U.S. total during his administration (based on documentation from leading nonpartisan health and disease research organizations).

How? The president wanted only to project optimism in the election year. He thought leading on pandemic prevention guidelines, messaging, and medical equipment production and its supply chain would interfere with national optimism, so Donald took the lead on none of those things. Doing so, he believed, would hurt his economy, cost him reelection, and remove the presidential immunity that had been shielding him from myriad legal and financial investigations and prosecutions including Mueller probe charges.

Instead he took the lead on playing down, ignoring, and politicizing the crisis. He interfered with federal officials and governors who tried to take up his leadership slack. He made opposition to pandemic prevention and science a measure of political support for him, a badge of honor. On his watch, 400,000 people died from coronavirus infection, half of those needlessly.

The story of President Trump's last year in office also includes the obsequious enabling of his crimes and other depravity by almost all elected Republicans in Congress. They protected him in committees. They defended him in the media. And they shielded him with their impeachment acquittal votes in spite of the deadliest and most despicable atrocities ever committed by an American president.

Finally, Trump was put out of office by the people. This book was written to educate, not gloat. Forty percent or so of Americans still believe Donald Trump was a great president. In fact, they believe his "big lie" that he won the most votes in 2020 and still should be president. He's still a suffocating, controlling force in the GOP. He could come back.

Vote, don't gloat.■

01/02/20 — Happy Holidays to Anti-Trump, Anti-War Republicans

Thank Jesus for the anti-Trump Republicans who have given us Christians permission to say "Happy Holidays" again.

During Donald's War Against the War on Christmas, we were not allowed to combine Christmas and New Year's greetings into one concise salutation representing the love for humankind many people feel during the period starting in mid-December and ending shortly after Jan. 1. Instead we were forced to delineate exactly which holiday we were offering greetings for: either "Merry Christmas" or "Happy New Year." Any attempt at merging the two into "Happy Holidays" was considered blasphemy and an affront to religious (read: Christian) freedom.

But now that President Trump has lost his War on the War Against Christmas, he might be looking for conflagrationist opportunities in Iran and Iraq. That certainly would take the nation's focus off impeachment.

What is killing 25 Iranian militia members in retaliation for the death of one American contractor? A good start.

With our religious freedom now restored (including the right to secularism), and the "Happy Holidays" over with, it's time to return to the business of saving our country.

Perhaps the holiday flirtation with love for humanity has touched some GOP legislators. Perhaps the rising tensions in Iran and Iraq are scaring the bejesus out of them, knowing the inept, self-dealing Trump is pulling the levers of foreign policy.

It's telling to note the long list of prominent Republicans who put country over party. Now juxtapose those with the long list of Republican invertebrates in Congress who, solely for seat-preservation, have decided to hold their noses, look the other way, and let a perverse president continue to degrade the presidency, endanger American democracy, and threaten foolish wars.■

01/09/20 — One More Time: Trump Starts Fire, Takes Credit for Dousing It

In the past two weeks some stuff has happened:

— Iranian-backed militia forces killed an American contractor in Iraq

— In retaliation U.S. forces killed 25 Iranian-backed militia troops in Iraq and Syria

— In further retaliation Trump shook world order with the military assassination of Iran's top general (equivalent to our secretary of defense), claiming Quds Gen. Qasem Soleimani was an "imminent threat," though he's caused havoc, American deaths for years

— (By an amazing turn of events, Trump concurrently is facing an impeachment trial)

— Trump drew a clear red line by tweet-threatening Iran devastation, Iranian cultural site destruction (a violation of international law) if it responds to our assassination of its military leader

— U.S. Secretary of State Mike Pompeo announced Trump did *not* threaten Iranian cultural sites (also said up is down)

— Trump immediately undercut his secretary of state, tweeted that destroying Iranian cultural sites (a violation of international law) is fair game

— Iran pulled further out of U.S.-Iran nuclear deal, will resume nuclear weapons development if U.S., other signatories don't recommit

— Iraqi parliament voted to expel U.S. troops

— Pentagon publicly agreed to leave Iraq, laid out detailed departure plans

— White House ordered DOD to say, "Oops," Pentagon was wrong, U.S. is *not* leaving Iraq

— By the way, Pentagon said it will *not* attack Iranian cultural sites (which would be a violation of international law)

— Iran attacked two U.S. military sites in Iraq with ballistic missiles; no casualties so far

— Iran announced they were good now; as long as U.S. does not respond, they don't want to escalate

— Trump tweeted, "All is well," made no mention of his red line threats

— After Iran's retaliatory attack, Trump spoke to nation: declared victory and retreated; falsely blamed Obama for providing money to fund Iranian missiles

Decisions, Decisions

I don't claim to know the proper response when a foreign adversary kills one of our military contractors in a foreign war zone. I imagine it involves complicated discussions and decisions depending upon changing circumstances. I *do* know that I don't want a corrupt, incompetent, amoral commander in chief making those decisions for my country.

If I were in charge:

I *do* know I should think through carefully my decision to commit an act of war by assassinating our adversary's top general (the equivalent of our secretary of defense).

I *do* know I should hesitate in drawing a clear red line if that adversary responds (which it's sure to do), especially if I had criticized my predecessor mercilessly for doing the same thing.

I *do* know I shouldn't threaten a violation of international law (destroying Iranian cultural sites) without consulting the Pentagon, the State Department, and my legal team.

I *do* know I should coordinate with my secretary of state before he publicly denies that I *did* threaten a violation of international law (destroying Iranian cultural sites).

I *do* know I would look stupid undercutting my secretary of state by reemphasizing my threat to violate international law (by destroying Iranian cultural sites) — especially after my staff informed me what international law is.

I *do* know I would look stupider by not having coordinated with "my" Pentagon before it announces that it would *not* violate international law (by destroying Iranian cultural sites).

Speaking of my Pentagon, I *do* know I would look galactically stupider after it announces detailed military departure plans to honor Iraq's vote to expel our troops, but then I order my Pentagon to say, "Oops, I guess we're staying; we made a mistake."

And after said adversary indeed crosses my red line and conducts a measured response to my assassination of its top general (the equivalent of our secretary of defense), I *do* know I would look weak — *and* stupid — by tweeting, "All is well."

Come to think of it, I would know that it's stupid, juvenile, incompetent, and counterproductive to be *tweeting* foreign policy — or *any* policy — announcements at all.

Finally, I *do* know that I would look colossally petty and likely certifiable 1) by conjuring up the non sequitur-ious lie during my speech to the nation that Barack Obama funded Iran's missile system through the "foolish" Iran nuclear deal (from which my pulling out has caused this entire foreign policy debacle), and 2) by demonstrating that (as pundit Chris Matthews, *MSNBC,* noted) I have a "kind of Tourette's when it comes to Obama" — I can't get through a day without some crude, false criticism of the former president, whom good and smart people wish were still in office and to whom I could never hold a candle.

"Look at you — even David Crosby thinks you let yourself go!" *(— Triumph the Insult Comedy Dog, to a rotund Rob Reiner at a 2000 N.Y. Friars Club roast)*

On Tuesday Democratic presidential front-runner Joe Biden criticized President Trump's handling of the growing tensions with Iran as employing a "haphazard" decision-making process and offering "tweets, threats, and tantrums" that expose Donald to be "dangerously incompetent and incapable of world leadership."

Of course Democrats will criticize Trump.

But wait: Even the usually reliably MAGA-supporting Sen. Rand Paul (R-Ky.) forcefully has denounced Donalds "feckless" Iran policy:

> "Republican Kentucky Sen. Rand Paul slammed President Donald Trump's strike on Iranian Gen. Qasem Soleimani during an appearance on Fox News Tuesday. 'I hate this. I hate that this is where we are going,' Paul said on air. … '[T]here was much less killing [and] violence after the Iran agreement. In fact, there was a lull, a period in which I think we were headed towards a much more stable situation with Iran, and now I think that's gone. And I think it may be gone for a lifetime. … [It's] much more likely [Americans will be attacked.]'

> "The Kentucky senator also said that while he disagreed with the Iran deal, the Trump administration could have tried to build on it[:] 'It wasn't perfect … however, I think it was a big mistake to pull out. … [W]e placed an embargo where Iran was not allowed to sell any goods internationally, including their main export of oil. An active embargo is like an act of war. To top that off, we've now killed one of their major generals.'

"This comes after Paul criticized 'feckless intermittent eruptions of violence w/ no clear mission for our soldiers' on Twitter following the strike."

> (Caruso, Justin; "'I Hate This': Rand Paul Slams Trump's Iran Escalation"; *Daily Caller*; 1/7/2020.)

Ouch.■

01/16/20 — Hillary Cleared of EVERYTHING by Trump's DOJ, Nobody Cares

You might have missed the *real* news of this week.

No, it wasn't Trump's reckless unwarranted assassination of an Iranian top leader and the aftermath: Iran's accidental killing of 176 civilians aboard a Ukrainian airliner, which never would have happened except for the aforementioned reckless unwarranted assassination of an Iranian top leader. No, it wasn't House Speaker Nancy Pelosi's (D-Calif.) game of impeachment chess with Senate Majority Leader Mitch McConnell (R-Ky.). (Pelosi won.) No, it wasn't Donald's most recent lie justifying the Gen. Soleimani assassination: that Soleimani was planning attacks on four U.S. embassies — never mind that Trump's own defense secretary said he had seen no intelligence to this effect and the embassies never were warned.

No, it wasn't the new evidence that Russia hacked the Ukrainian company Burisma Holdings in an attempt to help the Trump campaign get dirt on Joe and Hunter Biden. No, it wasn't the release of a trove of new evidence (if you really needed more) connecting Donald directly to the Trump-Ukraine extortion plot: Rudy Giuliani's indicted associate Lev Parnas' phone and document contents apparently contain "damning" evidence further implicating Mr. Big (aka "No. 1," aka "The Donald") by elucidating his (small-) hands-on direction of the illegal scheme.

No, it wasn't the House vote to end its holdup and send impeachment articles over to the Senate after having achieved the following through delay: 1) blocked GOP Senate Leader McConnell's attempt to have the lame-duck Senate vote for an immediate dismissal of articles; 2) provided time for several GOP senators to become ready to vote for witnesses; 3) allowed John

Bolton time to agree to testify; and 4) allowed time for the emergence of more damning evidence against Trump with the likelihood of more down the road.

Finally, no, it wasn't even the blockbuster Rachel Maddow (*MSNBC*) interview with the aforementioned indicted Giuliani associate Lev Parnas. Lev shook the Trumpian universe last night attesting to these allegations: 1) he worked directly for Giuliani who worked directly for Trump, and Trump knew everything every step of the way about Parnas' efforts to get Ukraine to announce a Biden investigation or it would get no aid, no visits, and no U.S. relationship or support; 2) as Ukraine resisted Donald's strong-arming, its aid was held up, it lost a planned Trump meeting in Poland, and it lost VP Pence's attendance at the new Ukrainian president's inauguration; 3) all the many meetings Parnas had with Ukrainian officials started out with Giuliani on speakerphone confirming that Parnas spoke directly for Trump; 4) VP Mike Pence, AG Bill Barr, and NSA John Bolton all knew the illegal extortion plot was going on; 5) Rep. Devin Nunes (R-Calif.) was involved in the scheme; 6) Parnas personally witnessed Trump ordering the firing of ambassador to Ukraine Marie Yovanovitch.

Yes, that is all news. But not *the* news.

Real News of the Week

No, the biggest news of the week, which you likely missed in the avalanche of other political headlines, was that Hillary Clinton was cleared of all legal charges and (transparently false) accusations from Trump World related to her infamous emails, so-called Uranium One scandal, Clinton Foundation hanky-panky, and anything else ever thrown at her.

"Who cleared her, the ACLU?" you might be thinking with snotty, holier-than-thou indignation and MAGA disbelief. Look no further than the Trump administration Department of Justice under Attorney General Bill Barr:

"A Justice Department inquiry launched more than two years ago to mollify conservatives clamoring for more investigations of Hillary Clinton has effectively ended with no tangible results, and current and former law enforcement officials said they never expected the effort to produce much of anything. …

"[Attorney General Jeff Sessions initiated the investigation in March 2018 with this directive to his prosecutors:] 'Your recommendations should include whether any [Hillary Clinton] matters not currently under investigation warrants the opening of an investigation, whether any matters currently under investigation require further resources or further investigation, and whether any matters would merit the appointment of a special counsel.'"

(Barrett, Devlin & Zapotosky, Matt; "Justice Dept. Winds Down Clinton-Related Inquiry Once Championed by Trump. It Found Nothing of Consequence."; *The Washington Post*; 1/9/2020.)

Lest you think the deep state is so strong, so insidious that it can manipulate the career professionals at Justice and the FBI, note that this open-ended, catch-all investigation was prompted by Trump and his allies and initiated by Attorney General Jeff Sessions (R-Ala.). At that time Sessions was under fire from Trump for recusing himself from the Russia investigation. Trump's AG would've bent over backward, sideways, or forward to get back in the boss' good graces.

Then the investigation came under the auspices of an interim attorney general and hand-picked Trump puppet, the galactically unqualified Matt Whitaker, who pushed the Hillary investigators to be more aggressive under his three-month watch.

Finally, oversight of the Clinton investigation fell to new Attorney General William Barr who is believed widely to be the (deceased shady former Trump-protecting lawyer) "Roy Cohn" Donald always has pined for in an AG. Barr has come under intense scrutiny for lack of independence from, and total deference to, the Trump White House. Barr long has thought Clinton was culpable in the made-up Uranium One scandal. Ultimately even AG Barr would not, could not stop the exculpatory report by his investigators that declared Hillary Clinton innocent of everything. Everything.

(By the way, Trump's own State Department already had cleared Hillary in October 2019 of any wrongdoing or intended wrongdoing surrounding her email brou-ha-ha while she was secretary of state.)

Upshot

Hillary Clinton has been cleared of all charges and accusations — ever made by Trump World — by Donald's own Justice Department.

It infuriates me that this is not big news. It infuriates me that it will not change the false beliefs of MAGA cultists or independent low-information voters who bought it hook, line, and comb-over. They've heard the lies so often and for so long, "There must be something to it."

For all you low-information voters who never looked beyond the Trumpian disinformation — the incessant, voluminous high-volume disinformation — How would your 2016 presidential vote have changed knowing (and accepting) Donald had lied?

For all you independents who believed "both sides are just as bad so let's shake things up and vote for an outsider" — How would your 2016 presidential vote have changed knowing he had lied?

For all you apathetics who chose to stay home "out of principle" or voted third party because neither candidate "excited" you — How would your 2016 presidential voting behavior have changed knowing he had lied?

For all you deplorables that simply liked the guy who spits in the eye of competence, intelligence, experience, and morality — well you're still a lost cause.

How Did He Do It?

It takes a colossal ethical deficit to lie brazenly and unceasingly. Many people can't accept that someone could be that morally bereft, so they believe the lies or at least attribute equal weight to them. Donald Trump and his Republican Party *are* that morally bereft. Now that you know, What are you going to do about it?

The simple fact is that Democrats, as a group, don't have the ethical paucity to pull off the obvious, unceasing mendacity it takes to support a confidence artist as their party leader. And that kind of mendacity is near-impossible to combat, especially in the digital media age. It's not that Trump and the current GOP are brilliant manipulators of message. No, any idiot with a media platform can do it. It only requires a hole in your soul where character is supposed to live.■

01/23/20 — "A Trial by Any Other Name ..." (Nice Play, Shakespeare)

> "Do you solemnly swear that in all things appertaining to the trial of the impeachment of [Donald John Trump], president of the United States, now pending, you will do impartial justice according to the Constitution and laws, so help you God?"

> (1798 oath administered to U.S. senators by Supreme Court Chief Justice John Roberts; followed by senators confirming their oath via signature in Senate oath book; 1/16/2020.)

There are 100 affirmative signatures in the Senate oath book.

But there is a prominent anti-oath theme running through the Senate Republican caucus appertaining to the impeachment trial of President Donald John Trump. Trump World wants no witnesses, no documents, and Leader Mitch McConnell (R-Ky.) is doing his damnedest to keep his caucus together to oblige. Mitch even tried to exclude the existing House evidence, but that was a GOP bridge-for-sale too far. Team Trump, of course, wanted *no trial* if they could get away with it. They had hoped to prompt a motion to dismiss the whole thing on Day 1 without any arguments.

But pity the fate of poor GOP senators. They fear tough impeachment trial decisions. They're terrified of possible tough procedural votes — you know, the ones on which they'll have to vote "no" to save their seats but every ethical person in America knows they should have voted "yes." Their problem with Trump, of course, is they can't live with The Donald and they can't get reelected without him. Most of them secretly loathe him and much of what he stands for, but they're deathly afraid of his cultist

Twitter-base of supporters. Republican senators have sold their souls to keep their jobs, but one school-yard-put-down tweet could end it all in a primary.

"I Don't Wanna Know"

The Trump Republican Party theme for the impeachment trial is: "I don't wanna know."

The only thing getting in the way of a 100% cover-up, i.e., no trial, no House evidence, not even a remote chance of witnesses and documents, is the handful of moderate Republican senators who must present the appearance of fairness to appease their ideological mix of constituents. These moderates still care only about reelection (and future business opportunities with GOP buds), but their constituent base requires a slightly different calculus.

So McConnell has to settle for a 97% cover-up.

There has been much said about the complaints from Democrats, independents, and ethical Republicans that a real trial cannot be conducted without witnesses and documents. But just look at the classic TV courtroom drama *Law and Order*. Faithful viewers remember these were the same rules Asst. District Attorney Jack McCoy had to play by in each episode. There never were any witnesses. There never were any documents submitted as Exhibits 1, 2, and 3. There simply were opening and closing arguments all rolled into one. Then the jury voted. Oh yeah, the jury always was comprised of mostly the defendant's friends, and they could leave the courtroom, do crossword puzzles, or talk to each other during the trial.

Not.

But that's what the GOP would have you think.

> "Senator McConnell, I watched Jack McCoy (question witnesses). I knew Jack McCoy (submitted evidentiary documents). Jack McCoy was a (fictional) friend of mine.

Senator, you're no Jack McCoy." *(— apologies to 1988 vice presidential candidate Lloyd Bentsen)*

Not a Criminal Trial

On a lighter note: Trump supporters and other observers like to remind us that an impeachment trial is not a criminal trial. There are House managers instead of prosecutors. The presiding judge, the chief justice of the Supreme Court, has almost no power compared to a criminal trial judge. Senators are the jurors, and all of them have a bias for or against the president. Senators can ask questions but they must be fed through the chief justice who reads them. Yes, impeachment is a *political* exercise, not a criminal one.

But this doesn't mean there are *zero* similarities between an impeachment trial and a criminal trial. Here are the primary parallels:

— They're both supposed to be an impartial process.
— They're both supposed to seek the truth.

We also could say they both involve a bunch of lawyers.

It's well known in political circles that the Constitution says little about impeachment guidelines. The House sets its own rules to do the indictment-like part. The Senate sets its own rules to do the trial part. That's about it. The framers wrote it this way because no set of laws can regulate every possible contingency or historical development. The Constitution was written as a living, breathing document to accommodate adjustments such as amendments (notwithstanding Justice Antonin Scalia's 2013 declaration that the Constitution is "dead, dead, dead"). The Constitution is the *bend-don't-break* defense in the Super Bowl of democratic republic football. *(Excuse my tedious metaphorical overkill.)*

Simple Question

But our Founding Fathers did take certain things for granted. When Madison texted Hamilton at 2 a.m. and asked, "u up?" the night before the Constitutional Convention's 1787 vote, they didn't hook up to hash out final arguments over the term *try*, as in "The Senate shall have the sole Power to *try* all Impeachments." To intend that it would be a *trial* never was in doubt. There was no other concept for the event they envisioned as a remedy to remove a corrupt president. They accepted that there is and always will be certain connotations that accompany the word *try* in the new republic:

> — A trial is supposed to be an impartial process.
> — A trial is supposed to seek the truth.

Yeah, "high crimes and misdemeanors" could have been sussed out a little more. But no founder doubted the definition of *try*, as in *trial*.

Which leaves us with a simple question: Do the Senate's impeachment proceeding rules reflect the two givens that every honest rhetor can agree appertain to the term *trial*?

> — Do the Senate rules reflect an impartial process?
> — Do the Senate rules support seeking the truth?

With his opening introductory presentation of the House case against Donald Trump Wednesday night, lead House impeachment manager Adam Schiff scared the absolute hell out of me. He laid out the facts of the crime. He laid out Donald's complete inculpation from top to bottom. And he laid out the consequences for our republic if this corrupt president is not held accountable.

No senator doing "impartial justice according to the Constitution and laws" could have been unmoved.∎

01/30/20 — Cult of the Senate: Lawlessness Amok

Trump defense team lawyers wrapped up their initial presentation to the Senate Tuesday using only about half their total allotted 24 hours.

Critics have issued their pull-quote reviews: "Feel-good impeachment of the year!" "Magical (not in a good way)." "Irrelevant." "Hypocritical." "Ironic (not in a good way)." "Highly hypocritical." "Dangerous." "Stupid (there is no good way)." "Galactically stupid." "Farcical." "Laughable (in all ways)."

The defense's only full day, Monday, provided a star-studded performance by an array of lawyers critical thinkers love to hate including: 1) Jay Sekulow ("Trump held up aid for several other countries," "There is no proof of a quid pro quo," "You can't impeach a president over policy differences"); 2) Pat Cipollone ("The president committed no crimes, but just in case he did, they're not impeachable"); 3) Jane Raskin ("Rudy Giuliani is just a minor player in Trump's Ukraine scheme"); 4) Ken Starr ("Impeachment is too divisive for the country, and it's becoming too common, too arbitrary"); 5) Pam Bondi ("Look at the *Bidens*"); and 6) Alan Dershowitz ("A crime is needed to impeach, abuse of power and obstruction of Congress are not crimes, therefore not impeachable").

Day 8, Wednesday, began the first half of 16 hours of questions asked by senators (submitted to, and read by, the chief justice) and answered by House managers and defense team members.

Here's what you need to know:

> "If a president does something which he believes will help him get elected in the public interest, that cannot be the kind of quid pro quo that results in impeachment."
>
>> (Dershowitz, Alan, Trump defense team member; Senate impeachment trial of President Donald John Trump; 1/29/2020.)

> "Mere [damaging] information [from a foreign government] is not something that would violate the campaign finance laws. And if there is credible information, credible information of wrongdoing by someone who is running for a public office, it's not campaign interference for credible information about wrongdoing to be brought to light."
>
>> (Philbin, Patrick, Trump defense team member; Senate impeachment trial of President Donald John Trump; 1/29/2020.)

> "We've witnessed over the course of the last few days, and the long day today, a remarkable lowering of the bar to the point now where everything's OK as long as the president believes it's in his reelection interest."
>
>> (Schiff, Adam, D-Calif., lead House impeachment manager; Q&A with reporters; outside Senate chambers; 1/29/2020.)

GOP Arguments

The president's defense team has argued the following in the Senate impeachment trial:

— A president shouldn't be impeached in his first term, when the people can vote him out in the next election, even if he's conspiring to rig that election.

(Which defeats the purpose of the impeachment clause.)

— Even if guilty of all articles of impeachment, the president cannot be impeached for *any* abuse of power that is not a statutory crime.

(This is antithetical to all evidence of framer intent and historical impeachment standards.)

— As long as the president believes his reelection is in the public interest, anything he does to that end is not impeachable.

(This brings up the laughable hypotheticals that the president could give the Russians our nuclear codes, take a yearlong nonworking vacation, or shut down "fake news" media outlets and not be threatened with impeachment — as long as he believes these actions help his reelection, which will be in the country's best interests.)

— Soliciting, accepting, or using damaging foreign information against a presidential electoral opponent is perfectly acceptable as long as it does not violate campaign finance law.

(This is laughable on its face — foreign interference in our elections was a primary concern of the founders. Additionally the illegality of using

foreign dirt against an electoral opponent was reestablished by the DOJ after special counsel Robert Mueller found that top Trump team members had engaged in that very offense in the 2016 election campaign.)

— No witness testimony or documentation should be subpoenaed no matter how obvious it is that this evidence would address the heart of the impeachment articles, because the House "didn't do its job" (didn't prove its case), it will "take too long," and it will not change the outcome (i.e., acquittal was preordained anyway).

(The Senate is refusing to call John Bolton, knowing what he has to say: that the president did the crime and told Bolton personally. As I wrote last week, everyone, including the framers, knows what a trial is, though Senate Republicans are changing its definition. It's long been held that House impeachment is the equivalent of a grand jury indictment and the Senate conducts the trial. Trial evidence expands on grand jury evidence. Moreover witnesses and documents were called in every one of 50-some U.S. impeachments that have gone to trial since 1797.)

It is an insane political climate in which the Republican Senate majority almost certainly will accept these arguments and vote, first, to hear no witnesses, and second, to acquit President Trump. The insanity is ignored by the vast majority of the electorate because they're numb to it.

Trump Republicans have become a lawless party run amok by cult force.

The country is in real danger.

I am sick to my stomach.■

02/05/2020 — Impeachment No. 1 (Extorting Ukraine): Senate Acquits

02/06/2020 — COVID-19: First U.S. Death Occurs

02/06/20 — Trump Impeachment and the Legend of Mitt Romney

On Feb. 5, 2020, the Senate voted to acquit President Donald John Trump of the impeachment charges against him related to Ukraine.

Last Thursday night (Jan. 30), after Sen. Lisa Murkowski (R-Alaska) announced she would not be the hoped-for third GOP vote to allow witnesses and documents in the impeachment trial, Sen. Sheldon Whitehouse (D-R.I.) went on cable news to explain the atomic bomb that just had been dropped on American democracy.

Fix Is In

In 2010 the Supreme Court decided the case of Citizens United v. FEC in favor of the plaintiffs. This was the decision that uncapped previous limits on political spending. It also allowed money sources to remain unidentified (i.e., *dark money*). Sen. Whitehouse explained how this has resulted in approximately six to 10 super-rich anonymous Republican donors coming together to move hundreds of millions of secretly sourced dollars.

Here's the kicker: These donors have organized, funneling the bulk of their donations through the sole discretion of Senate Majority Leader Mitch McConnell (R-Ky.). He controls which of his senators receive what share of these dark money funds. And the way the system is set up, senators are dependent upon these funds to run a successful reelection campaign. Ergo Leader McConnell is able to use this tremendous financial power to keep his caucus members in line, totally beholden to him.

So what explains Sen. Mitt Romney's (R-Utah) "yes" vote with the Democrats on witnesses (and ultimately to convict)? What explains Sen. Susan Collins' (R-Maine) "yes" vote? Romney is a reluctant maverick who holds enough Utah-ian constituent support that he is functionally immune to McConnell's threats. Susan Collins? According to Mr. Whitehouse she was given a "hall pass" by McConnell. This means Mitch allowed her to vote "yes" on witnesses and documents because she is in a tight 2020 Maine reelection race in which she must show a modicum of independence from Trump. But she only received the hall pass because McConnell knew he had all other GOP senators besides Romney prostrate with his majority-leading foot up their posteriors. Note that Collins voted to acquit in the end.

Also note that Romney held firm. We've seen Mitt Romney break with his past (wishy-washy, flip-flopper) reputation and exhibit attributes during this impeachment trial that neither Susan Collins nor any other Republican senator has exhibited: integrity and character.

Why Are Ex-Trump Employees Still Afraid of Him?

Now you might ask: Why don't *retiring* GOP legislators like Sen. Lamar Alexander (R-Tenn.) stand up to Trump, especially when we know most of them secretly loathe Donald? And what about *former* Cabinet members, senators, and top White House aides like Secretary of Defense Jim Mattis, national security adviser H. R. McMaster, chief of staff Gen. John Kelly, Sen. Bob Corker, Secretary of State Rex Tillerson, et al.? Why are they remaining mostly mute while the country and government are declining rapidly due to Trump's shenanigans (i.e., crimes)?

My good friend, long-lost cousin, and history-teacher-lawyer-all-'round-smart-guy, Larry R., explained something to me a while back. Since then I've seen it reiterated by a few keen political pundits. Even if Republicans-no-longer-in-government don't need Trump's approval to get reelected or appointed anymore, the majority still depend on their Republican buds to make tons of money after they leave office. If they defy Donald they lose their social standing. They'll be shut out of investment opportunities. They will be denied the lucrative corporate board memberships and lobbyist positions they had counted on. They'll never get GOP support again if they have any future hope of elected office. And they'll be shunned at *the* (country) *club*.

In this way, the Republican Party of Trump has become ethically depleted, morally spent.

Lesson Learned

But don't worry. President Trump will be a good boy from now on according to Sen. Susan Collins (R-Maine) in this *CBS News* interview:

> *[SEN. SUSAN COLLINS (R-MAINE):]* "I believe that the president has learned from this case."

> *[NORA O'DONNELL (CBS):]* "What do you believe the president has learned?"

> *[SEN. SUSAN COLLINS (R-MAINE):]* "The president has been impeached. That's a pretty big lesson. I'm voting to acquit because I do not believe that the behavior alleged reaches the high bar in the Constitution for overturning an election and removing a duly elected president."

> *[NORA O'DONNELL (CBS):]* "But the president says he did nothing wrong. Why do you think he learned something?"

> *[SEN. SUSAN COLLINS (R-MAINE):]* "He was impeached. And there has been criticism by both Republican and Democratic senators of his call. I believe that he will be much more cautious in the future."

> *(CBS Evening News; 2/4/2020.)*

Remember that the pro-choice Sen. Collins explained she voted to confirm the rabidly pro-life Supreme Court nominee Brett Kavanaugh because of his assurance that he considered Roe v. Wade "settled law" and he never would vote to overturn that "precedent."

Sen. Collins suffers from Brooklyn-Bridge-for-sale syndrome.

But wait. GOP Senators Joni Ernst and Lamar Alexander also are confidant Donald has learned his lesson:

> "I think that he knows now that, if he is trying to do certain things — whether it's ferreting out corruption there, in Afghanistan, whatever it is — he needs to go through the proper channels."
>
> (Ernst, Joni, R-Iowa, U.S. senator; *CNN's State of the Union*; 2/2/2020.)

> "[Sen. Lamar] Alexander was asked on NBC's 'Meet the Press' whether Trump might see his upcoming acquittal as an exoneration and a license to do it all again. 'I don't think so,' Alexander said. 'I hope not. I mean, enduring an impeachment is something that nobody should like. Even the president said he didn't want that on his résumé. I don't blame him. So if a call like that gets you an impeachment, I would think you would think twice before you did it again.'

> "Then host Chuck Todd asked a fair question: 'What example in the life of Donald Trump has [shown that he has] been chastened?' Alexander conceded after a beat, 'I haven't studied his life that close.'"
>
> (Blake, Aaron; "Susan Collins Says Trump Will Be 'Much More Cautious' After Impeachment. The Evidence Suggests Otherwise."; *The Washington Post*; 2/4/2020.)

Check the Google for other Republican senators who believe Donald has learned his lesson.

Remember that this is the president who — one day after his 2016 campaign's Russian collusion and obstruction of justice was exposed by special counsel Robert Mueller in his congressional testimony — got on the phone to extort dirt on Joe Biden from the new Ukrainian President Zelenskyy in return for military aid and a coveted White House visit.

SOTU

President Donald Trump delivered his State of the Union address in the people's house Tuesday night, the night before his impending Senate impeachment vote. He opened by refusing to shake Speaker Nancy Pelosi's (D-Calif.) hand. Pelosi closed by ripping a paper copy of his speech in half as he was finishing.

It essentially was a campaign event. Republicans chanted "Four more years" and cheered his every Democratic slight. Democrats chanted House bill numbers that Senate Majority Leader Mitch McConnell has refused to bring to a vote. They heckled Trump's Trumpian lies.

And there were many.

The "Jeff Bezos Amazon Washington Post" compiled at least 31 whoppers that the president loves to repeat repeatedly. Redundantly. Over and over. I'll mention just a few.

In his never-ending quest to gain approval while standing in Barack Obama's long dark shadow, Donald perpetuated his lies about the economy: He has created more job growth. He's lowered unemployment more. He has raised wages more. He's made us energy independent. America was a sh*thole until he took over Obama's failed reign.

But Steve Rattner, former Obama Treasury official, manager of Michael Bloomberg's personal and philanthropic assets, and national economics expert, had a different story to tell on

Wednesday's morning cable news. Citing Trump's own U.S. Bureau of Labor Statistics, Steve made these comparisons between Obama's last three years in office and Trump's last three years in office:

> — Average monthly job growth numbers: Obama, 227,000; Trump, 191,000

> — Lowering of the unemployment rate: Obama, by 2.0%; Trump, by 1.2%

> — Real wage growth adjusted for inflation: Obama, 1.1%; Trump, 0.6%

In other news, though Trump bragged that he has made America energy independent, U.S. oil and gas independence largely occurred well before Donald took office, under Obama's watch.

To be fair, under the comparable three-year periods, GDP average annual growth was 2.4% under Obama, 2.5% under Trump — a hair better but essentially a statistical tie. Weigh this against statements Trump has made at any given time that he has increased GDP to 4%, 5%, 6%, or whatever he feels at the moment.

These are the facts.

Never Forget

Essentially most of Trump's achievements have come upon the huge shoulders of Barack Obama including all Donald's bogus claims about the economy and the energy revolution.

But it's Trump's failures we need to keep in mind: backtracking on climate change solutions, rolling back lifesaving safety regulations in industry and society, continuing to manipulate financial regulations and tax cuts in favor of his ultra-rich brethren, promoting his embarrassing and dangerous foreign policy, weakening alliances, endangering national security, buddying up to dictators, separating families and putting immigrant children in cages, and forcing parents to direct their kids *not* to act like the president.

Most importantly we need to keep his crimes in mind: obstruction of justice, witness tampering, bribery of foreign governments, numerous ongoing emoluments clauses violations, campaign finance violations ("Individual-1"), fraud (Trump Foundation, Trump University, inaugural committee, etc.), voter suppression, and more.

And the incompetence — don't forget the incompetence.

And failures. And crimes. It's that simple.

The Legendary Mitt Romney

Of course the big takeaway from the Senate impeachment trial now that it's over is Mitt Romney's (R-Utah) vote to convict the president on the abuse of power article (I).

Trump loves records and firsts. His impeachment represents the first time in American history that a senator of the president's own party — a senator *and* former presidential candidate and party leader no less — ever voted to remove that president from office. *And* Donald's impeachment trial was the first ever, out of 50-some Senate impeachment trials for presidents, judges, etc. since 1797, to close without hearing any witnesses or documentary evidence — because the president's party controlled the Senate and the majority voted against evidence, effectively changing the definition of the word *trial.* In other words it was an empty acquittal.

Romney's vote to convict, along with several vulnerable red-state Democratic senators, robbed Trump of bragging rights to a "bipartisan acquittal." Only four senators — one Republican, three Democrats — were in the chamber the afternoon before the final vote to hear Romney's 10-minute speech that explained his vote and rocked the White House. But it was the speech heard 'round the world. It left a glimmer of hope for the American democratic system. The Republican lawmaker in attendance walked out of the chamber in silence. Two of the Democratic legislators sat with eyes moistened, all three feeling profound reverence for the senator from Utah.

Mitt occasionally has been accused of waffling insincerity in the past, especially during his 2012 presidential run. But there can be no doubt about the depth of poignancy, good faith, and integrity that ran through Mr. Romney's words yesterday.

> "Is there one among you who will say: 'Enough'?"
>
>> (Schiff, Adam, D-Calif., House Intelligence Committee chair, lead House impeachment manager; closing arguments, impeachment trial of President Donald John Trump; 2/3/2020.)

Yes there is.

Excerpts of Sen. Mitt Romney's Speech Explaining His Vote to Convict

> "The allegations made in the articles of impeachment are very serious. As a senator-juror, I swore an oath, before God, to exercise 'impartial justice.' I am profoundly religious. My faith is at the heart of who I am. *(12-second pause to regain composure)* I take an oath before God as enormously consequential. I knew from the outset that being tasked with judging the president, the leader of my own party, would be the most difficult decision I have ever faced. I was not wrong. …

> "This verdict is ours to render. The people will judge us for how well and faithfully we fulfilled our duty. The grave question the Constitution tasks senators to answer is whether the president committed an act so extreme and

egregious that it rises to the level of a 'high crime and misdemeanor.'

"Yes, he did.

"Accordingly, the president is guilty of an appalling abuse of public trust. … Corrupting an election to keep oneself in office is perhaps the most abusive and destructive violation of one's oath of office that I can imagine. …

"I have voted with [the president] 80% of the time. But my promise before God to apply impartial justice required that I put my personal feelings and biases aside. …

"I acknowledge that my verdict will not remove the president from office. … But irrespective of these things, with my vote, I will tell my children and their children that I did my duty to the best of my ability, believing that my country expected it of me. … [W]hat the president did was wrong, grievously wrong.

"We're all footnotes at best in the annals of history. But in the most powerful nation on earth, the nation conceived in liberty and justice, that distinction is enough for any citizen."

    (Romney, Mitt, R-Utah, U.S. senator; floor speech; 2/5/2020.)∎

02/13/20 — Censorship Through Noise

"Safeguard or surrender. You choose."

> (Rosenberg, Chuck, former U.S. attorney, former senior FBI official, former acting DEA administrator; "This Is a Revolting Assault on the Fragile Rule of Law"; *The Washington Post;* 2/12/2020.) *(referring to current attacks on DOJ independence through illicit influence by the president and attorney general to help Trump friends, persecute Trump enemies)*

The Donald Trump presidential freak show in the days after his impeachment acquittal has decent, critically thoughtful citizens terrified and MAGA cultists jubilant. Completely contrary to GOP senators' empty assurances that after being impeached, "President Trump has learned his lesson," Donald is more emboldened than ever to abuse the presidency and commit crimes to get reelected.

The president is firing administration employees who did nothing more than testify truthfully, under subpoena, before Congress. Many others have resigned in protest or out of fear. He's drawn his protector Attorney General William Barr ever closer, directing Barr to take hands-on control of all formerly independent Department of Justice investigations and cases concerning Trump and Trump enemies. Multiple Justice prosecutors have resigned, objecting to Barr's interference to favor the president. Note that the separation of White House and DOJ has been sacrosanct since the Nixon-Watergate-Attorney-General-John-Mitchell suite of crimes was uncovered in the 1970s.

The unimaginable horror of a Trump reelection is becoming imaginable.

Trump's primary weapon is disinformation — $1 billion worth — and character-assassination-retaliation against anyone, friend or foe, who deviates from the White House disinformation script. According to journalist McKay Coppins, communications scholars call it *censorship through noise*. The autocrat no longer needs to repress the heretical truth-teller. He simply drowns her out with wave after wave of disinformative noise. Thinking people know how the process works and see through it. But this weapon still could reelect Donald and damage functional understanding of knowledge for many decades. How do we fight it?

We might not have the complete solution to this quandary yet. But all who care about ethical government and truth must commit to supporting both. They must speak. They must participate in the rhetorical fight or lose what they hold dear, what many take for granted.

"Safeguard or surrender. You choose."

Mr. Coppins has written a comprehensive piece in *The Atlantic* explaining the origins and mechanics of the Trump propaganda machine. I've decided a good use of my efforts this week is to offer excerpted sections of his article for educational purposes. It certainly enlightened me. Coppins tosses around various Democratic strategists' ideas for overcoming insidious, enormous disinformation campaigns. He writes that it appears the best hope in the long run is forcing social media companies to take legal responsibility for accuracy in political posts, as they already must with standard corporate advertising. But obviously this won't happen under a Trump GOP administration.

VERBATIM: Excerpts From "The Billion-Dollar Disinformation Campaign to Reelect the President" (McKay Coppins; *The Atlantic;* 2/10/2020)

VERBATIM Excerpt: Censorship Through Noise (McKay Coppins; "The Atlantic"; 2/10/2020)

What I was seeing [from the Trump campaign] was a strategy that has been deployed by illiberal political leaders around the world. Rather than shutting down dissenting voices, these leaders have learned to harness the democratizing power of social media for their own purposes — jamming the signals, sowing confusion. They no longer need to silence the dissident shouting in the streets; they can use a megaphone to drown him out. Scholars have a name for this: censorship through noise.

After the 2016 election, much was made of the threats posed to American democracy by foreign disinformation. Stories of Russian troll farms and Macedonian fake-news mills loomed in the national imagination. But while these shadowy outside forces preoccupied politicians and journalists, Trump and his domestic allies were beginning to adopt the same tactics of information warfare that have kept the world's demagogues and strongmen in power. …

Both parties will have these tools at their disposal. But in the hands of a president who lies constantly, who traffics in conspiracy theories, and who readily manipulates the levers of government for his own gain, their potential to wreak havoc is enormous.

The Trump campaign is planning to spend more than $1 billion, and it will be aided by a vast coalition of partisan media, outside political groups, and enterprising freelance operatives. These pro-Trump forces are poised to wage what could be the most extensive disinformation campaign in U.S. history. Whether or not it succeeds in reelecting the president, the wreckage it leaves behind could be irreparable.

VERBATIM Excerpt: War on the Press (McKay Coppins; "The Atlantic"; 2/10/2020)

[I]n the Trump era, an important shift has taken place. Instead of trying to reform the press, or critique its coverage, today's most influential conservatives want to destroy the mainstream media altogether. "Journalistic integrity is dead," [*Breitbart* editor Matthew] Boyle declared in a 2017 speech at the Heritage Foundation. "There is no such thing anymore. So everything is about weaponization of information."

It's a lesson drawn from demagogues around the world: When the press as an institution is weakened, fact-based journalism becomes just one more drop in the daily deluge of content — no more or less credible than partisan propaganda. Relativism is the real goal of Trump's assault on the press, and the more "enemies of the people" his allies can take out along the way, the better. …

VERBATIM Excerpt: Powers of Incumbency (McKay Coppins; "The Atlantic"; 2/10/2020)

It doesn't require an overactive imagination to envision a worst-case scenario: On Election Day, anonymous text messages direct voters to the wrong polling locations, or maybe even circulate rumors of security threats. Deepfakes of the Democratic nominee using racial slurs crop up faster than social media platforms can remove them. As news outlets scramble to correct the inaccuracies, hordes of Twitter bots respond by smearing and threatening reporters.

Meanwhile, the Trump campaign has spent the final days of the race pumping out Facebook ads at such a high rate that no one can keep track of what they're injecting into the bloodstream.

After the first round of exit polls is released, a mysteriously sourced video surfaces purporting to show undocumented immigrants at the ballot box. Trump begins retweeting rumors of voter fraud and suggests that Immigration and Customs Enforcement officers should be dispatched to polling stations. "ARE ILLEGALS STEALING THE ELECTION?" reads the *Fox News* chyron. "ARE RUSSIANS BEHIND FALSE VIDEOS?" demands *MSNBC*. The votes haven't even been counted yet, and much of the country is ready to throw out the result. …

VERBATIM Excerpt: Nothing Is True (McKay Coppins; "The Atlantic"; 2/10/2020)

There is perhaps no better place to witness what the culture of disinformation has already wrought in America than a Trump campaign rally. …

After the [November 2019 Tupelo, Mississippi,] rally, I loitered near one of the exits, chatting with people as they filed out of the arena. Among liberals, there is a comforting caricature of Trump supporters as gullible personality cultists who have been hypnotized into believing whatever their leader says. The appeal of this theory is the implication that the spell can be broken, that truth can still triumph over lies, that someday everything could go back to normal — if only these voters were exposed to the facts. But the people I spoke with in Tupelo seemed to treat matters of fact as beside the point.

One woman told me that, given the president's accomplishments, she didn't care if he "fabricates a little bit." A man responded to my questions about Trump's dishonest attacks on the press with a shrug and a suggestion that the media "ought to try telling the truth once in a while." Tony Willnow, a 34-year-old maintenance worker who had an American flag wrapped around his head, observed that Trump had won because he said things no other politician would say. When I asked him if it mattered whether those things were true, he thought for a moment before answering. "He tells you what you want to hear," Willnow said. "And I don't know if it's true or not — but it sounds good, so f*** it."

The political theorist Hannah Arendt once wrote that the most successful totalitarian leaders of the 20th century instilled in their followers "a mixture of gullibility and cynicism." When they were lied to, they chose to believe it. When a lie was debunked, they claimed they'd known all along — and would then "admire the leaders for their superior tactical cleverness." Over time, Arendt wrote, the onslaught of propaganda conditioned people to "believe everything and nothing, think that everything was possible and that nothing was true."

Leaving the rally, I thought about Arendt, and the swaths of the country that are already gripped by the ethos she described. Should it prevail in 2020, the election's legacy will be clear — not a choice between parties or candidates or policy platforms, but a referendum on reality itself.

    (Coppins, McKay; "The Billion-Dollar
    Disinformation Campaign to Reelect the President";
    The Atlantic; 2/10/2020.)■

02/20/20 — Trump Persecutes Patriots, Pardons Pals, Pressures Prosecutors

There are three primary topics of news coverage this week: 1) Trump-Barr DOJ interference; 2) Trump's indiscriminate, politicized pardons; and 3) the Democratic primary. Let's touch on each.

Trump-Barr DOJ Interference

By Monday, President's Day, over two thousand former Department of Justice prosecutors and other officials had affixed their names to a letter calling for Attorney General William Barr to resign over his unethical interference in DOJ matters related to the president. That's *thousand* — with a "T"! This is unprecedented. The AG's most recent protest-letter-precipitating conduct comprised quashing the work of four prosecutors involved in the case of presidential bud Roger Stone. After they presented their sentencing recommendation (seven to nine years in prison, based on long-standing, tougher Trump Justice Department guidelines), which Donald then tweet-bashed, Barr intervened to lower that recommendation drastically. The four attorneys resigned the case in protest — one quit the DOJ outright. Hence the letter with two thousand-plus signatures.

This is only the latest outrage. Thank God for dedicated investigative journalists who have exposed Barr's Trump-protecting corrupt interference in DOJ matters since he was confirmed a year ago Valentine's Day: 1) sabotaging and falsely discrediting the Mueller investigation; 2) shutting down the Michael Cohen, Trump Organization hush-money probe into keeping Donald's paramours quiet before the 2016 election; 3) shutting down the investigation into fraudulent spending and other financial funny business by the Trump Inaugural Committee; 4) aborting the probe of Trump attorney Rudy Giuliani after Giuliani associates Lev Parnas and Igor Fruman were indicted for campaign finance fraud and other crimes; 5) changing (lowering) the sentencing recommendation for convicted former Trump national security adviser Michael Flynn.

And the many we don't yet know about.

On a lighter note it appears Sen. Susan Collins (R-Maine) might have erred when she said, "I believe that the president has learned from [his impeachment.] … I believe that he will be much more cautious in the future."

That's two *thousand* — with a "T"!

> "During his Senate impeachment trial, Democrats repeatedly asserted that President Trump is 'not above the law.' But since his acquittal two weeks ago, analysts say, the president has taken a series of steps aimed at showing that, essentially, he is the law. …

> "More than 2,000 former Justice Department employees signed a public letter this week objecting to Trump's public intervention in the case of his longtime friend Roger Stone, and urging Barr to resign. The head of the Federal Judges Association has called an emergency meeting to address growing concerns about political interference in the Stone case. And four prosecutors resigned from the case last week after Trump publicly decried their recommended prison sentence of seven to nine years for Stone, and the Justice Department reversed course to lobby for a lower sentence."

> (Olorunnipa, Toluse & Reinhard, Beth; "Post-Impeachment, Trump Declares Himself the 'Chief Law Enforcement Officer' of America"; *The Washington Post;* 2/19/2020.)

Trump's Indiscriminate, Politicized Pardons

> "You know oftentimes, pretty much all the time, I really rely on the recommendations of people that know them."
>
> (Trump, Donald, R-Fla., U.S. president; Q&A with reporters; outside *Air Force One*; 2/18/2020.) *(referring to how he determines pardon recipients)*

Donald added *(not really but could have)*, "Of course an appearance on *The Apprentice* (Rod Blagojevich), a $10 million Trump fundraiser haul (Michael Milken), or $200,000 in donations to me and my party (Paul Pogue) can't hurt. And I've got a soft spot for fellow corrupt businessmen and politicians — especially the poor bastards who got caught." *(— writer's embellishment)*

Last Tuesday President Trump pardoned or bestowed clemency to a few more high-profile, white-collar, white-male rich corrupt politicians and businessmen: guys like him. And if you appeared on his "reality" TV show, all the better.

> "By this point, it's no secret that President Trump's pardons have been significantly more self-serving than those of other presidents. While his predecessors have lodged controversial pardons — no question — Trump is simply on another level. Not only has he pardoned his allies, but he has often pardoned people who cozy up to the powerful people around him, whether via Fox News or some other method. But there's another key aspect of Trump's pardons that shouldn't get lost: In many cases, there are significant similarities between the pardon recipient and Trump — or at least Trump's depiction of himself.

> "Trump suggested that the phone call on which [Gov. Rod] Blagojevich was caught talking about selling an appointment to the U.S. Senate wasn't actually bad. 'He's been in jail for

seven years over a phone call where nothing happens — over a phone call which he shouldn't have said what he said, but it was braggadocio, you would say,' Trump said in early August. 'I would think that there have been many politicians — I'm not one of them, by the way — that have said a lot worse over the telephone.' The irony of that comment wasn't known at the time, but it practically slaps you in the face today. …

"[T]he Blagojevich commutation and the dual billionaire pardons Tuesday drive home the idea that Trump may sometimes see himself in these pardons. That's too much coincidence for one day. Trump has maintained before that he has the 'absolute right' to pardon himself if need be. He kind of already has."

(Blake, Aaron; "Trump Keeps Pardoning Himself";
The Washington Post; 2/19/2020.)

And get this: The day after he was released from prison, the corrupt former Illinois governor showed zero remorse for attempting to sell — for cash — Barack Obama's old Senate seat in 2009. Rod Blagojevich (D-Ill.) called himself a "political prisoner" and now a "Trumpocrat" who will vote for Donald if he's allowed to vote. Can the Trump-pardon circus get any more disgusting? Can one's stomach be turned any further?

On a lighter note, the president continues to persecute patriots like Lt. Col. Alexander Vindman and other administration officials who answered their subpoenas and spoke the truth before Congress. And the whistleblower. And Joe Biden. And Mitt Romney. And any former administration official who speaks truth about Donald's corruption, incompetence, and amorality.

Democratic Primary

Yeah, I'm worried. I love Bernie Sanders who has surged to the lead. But can he beat Trump? I like Michael Bloomberg's commitment to spend some of his billions to elect a Democratic president even if it's not him. But should a former Republican New York City mayor be able to buy a Dem nomination? And can *he* beat Trump, especially now that past misogynistic and racist remarks are out? I also love Elizabeth Warren but she's slumping in the polls. And speaking of slumping polls, I continue to believe Joe Biden's our best shot. But does he still have it? He looked good at last night's debate but so did all the others (except Mike).

I'll keep up my civic engagement by reading, speaking, writing, donating, and voting. After that: que será, será. All I can do is speculate and hope that the universe could not be so cruel as to give us a second Trump term.

Here's a snapshot of the race:

> "Sen. Bernie Sanders (I-Vt.), on the strength of his performances in Iowa and New Hampshire, has surged nationally and now holds a sizable lead over all of his rivals for the Democratic presidential nomination, according to a Washington Post-ABC News poll.

> "Former Vice President Joe Biden, who led Sanders in a Post-ABC national poll in January, has seen a sharp drop in his support after finishing fourth in the Iowa caucuses and fifth in the New Hampshire primary. Biden is now in a battle for second place with former New York mayor Mike Bloomberg and Sen. Elizabeth Warren (D-Mass.). Former South Bend, Indiana, Mayor Pete Buttigieg, who won the state-delegate-count battle in the Iowa caucuses and came a close second to Sanders in New Hampshire, is in single digits nationally, roughly even with Sen. Amy Klobuchar (D-

Minn.), whose surprise third-place finish in New Hampshire further scrambled the Democratic contest. …

"Looking ahead to November, the poll tested six Democrats in hypothetical general-election matchups. Biden, Sanders, and Bloomberg fare best, edging Trump by five to seven points, with Trump receiving 45% support against each. Buttigieg, Klobuchar, and Warren are within the margin of error of Trump in these measures. Across all matchups, Trump is in a similar position as January but better off than last October."

> (Balz, Dan & Clement, Scott; "Sanders Surges Into National Lead in New Post-ABC Poll"; *The Washington Post*; 2/19/2020.)

In other prominent polls, the numbers in key battleground states show Biden beating Trump by the largest margins, peaking at 8%. The other four top Democrats also beat the president, though by lesser margins. Many analysts believe these states are the key to Trump's defeat and that a non-Biden candidate might not sufficiently drive enthusiasm and turnout.

Yeah, I'm worried.

Notwithstanding that whole que será, será crap.■

02/27/20 — Trump Doesn't Own the CDC – Yet

[TOPICS: pandemic]

President Trump purports huge bragging rights for U.S. stock market performance. In his mind the stock market *is* the economy. Never mind that myriad economic experts believe the market has questionable effect on the economy. Never mind that in measuring the last three years of each president's time in office, Barack Obama beats Donald Trump on several primary economic indicators including: 1) average monthly job growth; 2) unemployment rate decrease; and 3) real wage growth. And never mind that about half of all Americans are disconnected from the market by virtue of no 401(k) or 403(b) participation or other stock investments. But to Donald, the daily Dow Jones Industrial Average is his identity, his plea for us to believe he is a good president in spite of reality.

Donald's lies are an obvious joke. They're a pathetic device to prop up a small man. And often they have the potential to cause great harm (notwithstanding their greatest inherent harm: they put and keep him in office.) The coronavirus pandemic is steering Trump's presidential lies in a deadly direction. He's already dissembling about the effects of the virus on America, to try to stop his precious market numbers from falling. He's already backed himself into a corner with indiscriminate cuts to the National Institutes of Health and other government health and science departments including firing the U.S. pandemic response team in 2018. Lives will be lost.

Holding Firm

Fortunately the doctors, experts, and scientists at the Centers for Disease Control and Prevention have not gone Trump prostrate. So far, against Trumpian prevarication, the CDC is holding its own, telling the truth. The question remains, Who will win the ultimate rhetorical tug of war: David or Goliath?

Trump has become a virtual cult leader. No individual or entity in his party dares cross him, dares tell the emperor he has no pants on, because of the power he's amassed through his followers' blind emotional loyalty. As an elected official, stray one inch from the party line and you'll risk being primary-ed. As a rich supporter, disrespect or disagree with The Donald and you'll be shut out of money-making opportunities and shunned at *the club* after the tweet-attacks.

Donald Trump owns the Senate, Justice Department, Environmental Protection Agency, Education Department, Energy Department, and other Cabinet agencies. He's buying up much of the intelligence community by installing non-experienced sycophants at the top. The Trump HR department has been ordered to seek out and cleanse the administration of anyone neutral about the president, let alone not pathologically loyal.

Fortunately he does not own the CDC — yet.

Party Line

> "We have [the coronavirus] totally under control ... We have it under control. It's going to be just fine."
>
> (Trump, Donald, R-Fla., U.S. president; speaking to *CNBC* reporter Kernen, Joe; World Economic Forum, Davos, Switzerland; 1/22/2020.)

Donald already was getting nervous about his stock market numbers, which he lives and dies by, which *are* his political identity.

"[T]he coronavirus is very much under control in the USA … Stock Market starting to look very good to me."

(Trump, Donald, R-Fla., U.S. president; Twitter post; 2/24/2020.)

The previous tweet came about an hour after the U.S. stock market closed Monday, by which time the Dow Jones Industrial Average had plunged 1,032 points (3.56%), its second-largest one-day point drop in 124 years of existence. The drop was near-unanimously attributed to the current news of a coronavirus pandemic and specifically to fears that the Trump administration is incapable of managing it in this country. As mentioned, Donald fired the U.S. pandemic response team in 2018 and consistently has cut funds to agencies dealing with health and science.

If we didn't already know what a fabulist he is, the following tweet would have caused Trump's mental stability to come under heavy scrutiny. (Oh wait — it is already.)

"[The coronavirus outbreak is] under control [and is going to] go away. We have very few people with it. The people are getting better, they're all getting better. … I think that the whole situation will start working out."

(Trump, Donald, R-Fla., U.S. president; news conference; New Delhi, India; 2/25/2020.)

The Dow dropped another 879 points the day of that last tweet.

"The rosy sheen that Trump, [Larry] Kudlow, and other White House officials have tried to express about the economic impact of the coronavirus outbreak has now collided with reality: The coronavirus is spreading, quickly, to more countries. The death toll is rising, and the outbreak is wreaking havoc on global supply chains. …

"The White House's assurances also fell flat on Capitol Hill, as lawmakers from both parties expressed outrage at the Trump administration's seeming unfamiliarity with facts about the scale of the problem."

> (Stein, Jeff & Dawsey, Josh; "White House Struggles to Contain Public Alarm Over Coronavirus"; *The Washington Post*; 2/26/2020.)

The administration is doing everything possible to protect the stock market, Donald's self-perceived report card, even at the expense of public safety.

Are You Serious?

"This White House may already be in danger of losing the capacity to be seen as serious."

> (Sperling, Gene, top [Clinton, Obama] economic adviser; as cited in Stein, Jeff & Dawsey, Josh; "White House Struggles to Contain Public Alarm Over Coronavirus"; *The Washington Post*; 2/26/2020.)

No argument here. And this doesn't apply only to the coronavirus threat. To paraphrase what many pundits have declared: We're not "in danger" of having a White House that can't be taken seriously. We're there. We've been there for a long time.

"President Trump on Wednesday attacked CNN and 'MSDNC (Comcast)' — a reference to MSNBC — for 'doing everything possible to make the Caronavirus look as bad as possible, including panicking markets, if possible.'

(He misspelled coronavirus in his tweet.) 'Likewise their incompetent Do Nothing Democrat comrades are all talk, no action,' Trump added. 'USA in great shape!'"

> (Taylor, Noack, McAuley, & Denyer; "Live Updates: Coronavirus Fears Spook Markets as Outbreak Spreads; Trump Calls News Conference, Accuses Media of 'Panicking Markets'"; *The Washington Post*; 2/26/2020.)

Finally we have the inevitable. You have to ask, What took him so long? The president now is blaming the media and Democrats for stoking coronavirus fears to hurt him and his stock market.

> "Now there are more than 50 people in the United States with coronavirus, and health officials believe the number will continue to grow. On Tuesday, as the stock market began its second day of a precipitous slide, Nancy Messonnier, a top CDC official, told reporters that the coronavirus' impact on the United States 'may seem overwhelming and that disruption to everyday life may be severe.' She said that it was inevitable the virus would spread more broadly in the United States and that people needed to begin taking precautions. …

> "Now, White House officials' efforts to contain the economic fallout from the coronavirus have created new political hazards, as they publicly play down the threat while other federal officials with a background in health and diseases are warning of more severe consequences for inaction. The administration also risks creating new health hazards, should the pressure to assure investors of economic stability undercut its public health message about the mounting threat."

(Ibid.; Stein & Dawsey; 2/26/2020.)

So far Donald doesn't own the CDC.

Journalist Greg Sargent in Trump's Brain

> "We already know Trump views the markets as a kind of backup gauge of his chances of reelection. But now, with markets tumbling, Trump has persuaded himself that warnings from *his own administration's health officials about the public threat it poses to Americans* are to blame for those market travails. … The core absurdity of Trump raging at the media for hyping coronavirus is that his own officials are describing it in terms Trump won't acknowledge. He doesn't want them to publicly do this, because it influences his leading gauge of his political health. …
>
> "If the media reports facts about coronavirus that Trump fears will damage him politically, or if officials follow procedures ensuring accountability in government — as the whistleblower and officials who testified to Congress about the Ukraine scheme did — [Trump purports] these things can only constitute corruption in their own right, that is, corrupt plots against Trump. All this justifies any and all [of his] efforts to corrupt government [that] Trump undertakes on his own behalf. [His assumption is] everyone is corrupt. All that matters is who wins or loses."

> (Sargent, Greg; "As the Virus Spreads, Trump Rages Over the Markets. That's Alarming."; *The Washington Post;* 2/26/2020.)

Trump doesn't own the CDC.

"I think the financial markets are very upset when they look at the Democrat candidates standing on that [primary debate] stage making fools out of themselves."

> (Trump, Donald, R-Fla., U.S. president; news conference; White House; 2/26/2020.) *(blaming Democrats' Wednesday debate comments for the previous Monday-Tuesday market crash)*

Last night President Trump took to the podium for only his second formal White House news conference. He stated the following, among other things:

> — The coronavirus outbreak probably will not affect the U.S., which is "very, very ready" for it.

> — The U.S. only has about 15 infected people *(this is a lie; the U.S. has over 60 cases)*, most of them are recovering nicely, and soon we'll be at zero.

> — Mike Pence *(someone with no public health experience, and even a negative record of reacting to the HIV outbreak while Indiana governor)* will be placed in charge of coordinating the government's response to the coronavirus outbreak.

> — The Democratic candidates' Wednesday debate comments time-traveled to cause the stock market's 2,000-point crash over the previous Monday and Tuesday.

Meanwhile the CDC speaks.

> "It's not so much a question of *if* this will happen anymore, but rather more a question of exactly *when* this will happen — and how many people in this country will have severe illness."

(Messonnier, Nancy, MD, National Center for
Immunization and Respiratory Diseases director,
CDC; 2/25/2020.)

"We do expect more cases."

(Schuchat, Anne, MD, CDC principal deputy
director; news conference; White House;
2/26/2020.)

"It's possible this could be an instance of community spread
of COVID-19."

(CDC media statement; 2/26/2020.)

Trump doesn't own the CDC — yet.■

03/05/20 — Thank You, Selfless Democrats

In the midst of the coronavirus pandemic, President Trump's corruption, incompetence, and amorality have been front and center, characterizing his response to the world health crisis.

Pandemic Response

Donald has been *corrupt* and *amoral* in his dissemination of information about the pandemic's progression, falsely playing down the danger. He called the coronavirus story a "Democrat hoax" (then denied video evidence of his statement). He called the World Health Organization's stated current mortality rate of 3.4% "false" and said, "Personally, I would say the number is way under 1%."

He's deliberately misled the country, putting preparedness and lives at risk specifically to prop up U.S. stock market performance, which has been rocked by the crisis. He believes a humming market protects his reelection chances. And if he's not reelected, he faces indictment on multiple crimes for which he currently is immune as president (notwithstanding the old saw about "no one is above the law"). Plus he won't be able to make the big emoluments-clauses-violation money anymore by gouging foreign diplomats and political allies on Trump property convention fees, room rates, and drink prices.

Donald has been too *incompetent* to learn even basic information about virology and vaccination development. His experts informed him multiple times that research and trials take 12 to 18 months at minimum. But at his gathering of drug company CEOs, he was pestering them to do it in "a few months," attempting to have them bid against each other for the shortest development time.

Additionally the administration dropped the ball on test kit production, resulting in a huge current shortage. It sent a team of untrained health workers to receive 14 infected Americans from overseas, resulting in unnecessary exposure. Ultimately the core incompetence has been systematically to cut health and science professionals from the government since Inauguration Day.

Selflessness

Also in the midst of the coronavirus pandemic, there is a Democratic presidential primary season underway. A funny thing happened on the way to the nomination. Viable moderate candidates have shown tremendous selflessness and patriotism by exiting the race just days before Super Tuesday to clear the way for Joe Biden. In a normal primary season, even weak candidates would have stayed in longer — at least *48 more hours*, which wouldn't have cost them any more effort or money — hoping for an unexpected boost or at least to continue delivering their message and building name recognition for the future.

But this year we have a sitting president who must — must — be defeated. In the course of four days, Biden, with strategic help, has pulled off one of the most amazing turnarounds in American political history after being left for dead following the Iowa Caucuses and New Hampshire Primary. He's emerged as the only Democrat to beat the democratic populist, Bernie Sanders (an *Independent* running as a Democrat), and therefore beat the Trump GOP (phony) populist, Donald Trump.

I say *Trump GOP* because the Republican Party now is wholly owned and controlled by the president. It has abandoned most of its core values and now stands for Trumpism, that is, cold, venal avarice and power.

I continue to like Bernie. His values probably align more closely with mine than Biden's do. But as many pundits have said, the country doesn't need another revolution right now, albeit a progressive one. It needs and wants a return to boring, competent, moral, humane, sane leadership — to steer a government of integrity, to have our nation resume its status as a trustworthy international neighbor and dependable free-world ally.

Above all, Bernie Sanders can't win the general election. Donald would eat Bernie's "democratic socialism" for breakfast, lunch, dinner, and two scoops for dessert. I've always said Sanders should have softened his ideological label to "social Democrat." But he didn't ask me.

Joe Biden's Comeback

President Trump's response to the pandemic has been but the latest example of why Democrats must choose the person best qualified to beat him, for no other reason than to beat him.

Joe Biden's candidacy was in the tank a week ago after beyond-disappointing finishes in Iowa, New Hampshire, and Nevada. Then last Saturday South Carolina happened, a state much more ethnically representative of the country. After a must-have pre-primary endorsement from influential Rep. James Clyburn (D-S.C.), Biden creamed Sanders 48% to 20%. The billionaire Tom Steyer dropped out that night. Pete Buttigieg dropped out Sunday and endorsed Joe. Amy Klobuchar dropped out Monday and endorsed Joe.

Three days later Super Tuesday happened with 14 states holding primaries. Joe stunned even his supporters and staff by winning 10 of those states, several decisively. On Wednesday the other billionaire, Michael Bloomberg, dropped out of the race and endorsed Joe.

After Super Tuesday it's essentially Joe Biden versus Bernie Sanders, with Biden holding a substantial delegate lead and the overall edge. This was not the case last week. But Uncle Joe clearly has the momentum now.

Many pundits have explained that this Democratic development is exactly what the 2016 Republican presidential primary candidates did *not* do. Most of them stayed in the race way too long splitting the "reasonable" Republican vote. This allowed a jackleg confidence artist to take over their party, become president, and continue to hold the entire GOP hostage.

Selflessness. Tom Steyer, Pete Buttigieg, Amy Klobuchar, and Michael Bloomberg deserve our deepest gratitude no matter what one thinks of their views or perceived shortcomings. Running a presidential campaign takes over your life. It commands monumental commitment. It is extremely difficult to let go, to call it quits. These four Democrats are true patriots. They saw what it's going to take to rid the country of a reprobate president and they did their duty.

Thank you.∎

03/12/20 — "I Don't Need to Have the Numbers Double Because of One Ship"

Donald Trump lies. It is not exaggeration. It's not "truthful hyperbole," as he characterizes his rhetoric in a book he "wrote." If only it *were* just truthful hyperbole. If only he knew the meaning of *hyperbole*. If only he knew the meaning of *oxymoron* — a truthfully hyperbolic *oxymoron*. Trump is a fabulist whose lies are now costing lives.

The U.S. is experiencing a disastrous shortage of coronavirus testing kits because Trump lies. We had two months to gear up production — as many other countries did — but Donald kept playing down the crisis. He declined testing help offered by the World Health Organization in January. And how convenient that a shortage of test kits keeps the confirmed-cases count artificially low.

Trump consistently has contradicted and muddled his health experts' analyses, counsel, and public guidance. He blew up privately after the CDC's Dr. Nancy Messonnier said Feb. 25 that protective measures "will be disruptive to people's day-to-day lives." Next thing you know, Dr. Nancy is sidelined and targeted for condemnation by the right-wing press.

The CDC recently wanted to put out a nationwide recommendation that senior citizens and those in fragile health should not travel by airline. The White House, fearing a hit to business, overruled that recommendation, watering it down — again muddling the danger.

As some experts and pundits have pointed out, Trump gives snapshots of the crisis with no context, in effect telling us it's always worse somewhere else: "We're fine." While it's bad enough he's ignoring the deadly trend, he wants us to believe the opposite of reality: that people are getting better and the victim number is trending toward zero.

Why is the president suppressing accurate information and disputing his own health experts? Why is he callously playing with American lives? It's all about the stock market. Coronavirus concerns have rocked the market with two weeks of record-setting losses. Donald views a healthy stock market (unencumbered by bothersome bad news about pandemic infections) as integral to his reelection. If he loses in 2020, thereby losing presidential immunity, he faces multiple indictments. You do the math.

Art of the Downplay

"We think we have it very well under control. We have very little problem in this country at this moment — five. And those people are all recuperating successfully. ... [W]e think it's going to have a very good ending for us — that I can assure you."

(Trump, Donald, R-Fla., U.S. president; speech;
Dana Inc. [formerly Detroit Arsenal Tank Plant],
Warren, Mich.; 1/30/2020.)

"[W]hen you have 15 people, and the 15 within a couple of days is going to be down to close to zero, that's a pretty good job we've done."

(Trump, Donald, R-Fla., U.S. president; press
briefing; White House; 2/26/2020.)

"As they get better, we take them off the list, so that we're going to be pretty soon at only five people. And we could be at just one or two people over the next short period of time. ... And again, if you look at some countries, they are coming down. It's starting to go in the other direction."

(Ibid.; Trump; 2/26/2020.)

"[W]e're testing everybody that we need to test. And we're finding very little problem. Very little problem."

(Ibid.; Trump; 2/26/2020.) *(this is a lie; there's a massive shortage of test kits in the U.S.)*

"It's going to disappear. One day it's like a miracle, it will disappear."

(Trump, Donald, R-Fla., U.S. president; African American History Month reception; White House; 2/27/2020.)

"The Democrats are politicizing the coronavirus. … This is their new hoax."

(Trump, Donald, R-Fla., U.S. president; campaign rally; North Charleston, S.C.; 2/28/2020.)

"'And how long would that [vaccine] take?' Trump asked. The [drug company] CEO said it would take months and then head into phase three. 'All right. So you're talking within a year[,' Trump said.] 'A year to a year and a half,' [government infectious disease expert Dr. Anthony] Fauci again clarified. 'Well, but, Lenny is talking about two months, right?' Trump said, incorrectly referring to [Regeneron CEO Leonard] Schleifer's August estimate. 'A little — a little longer,' Schleifer again clarified. … 'A couple of months, right?' Trump pressed. 'I mean, I like the sound of a couple of months better, I must be honest with you[,' Trump said.] …

"What's remarkable about these exchanges is that Fauci has explained all of this — in front of Trump and publicly: … '[The vaccine] would not be applicable to the epidemic unless we really wait about a year to a year and a half.'"

(Blake, Aaron; "Trump's Baffling Coronavirus
Vaccine Event"; *The Washington Post*; 3/3/2020.)

"I think the [stated WHO mortality rate of] 3.4% is really a false number … Because a lot of people will have this and it's very mild. They'll get better very rapidly. They don't even see a doctor. … So if, you know, we have thousands or hundreds of thousands of people that get better just by, you know, by sitting around and even going to work — some of them go to work, but they get better. … I think the number — personally, I would say the number is way under 1%."

(Trump, Donald, R-Fla., U.S. president; *Fox News'
Hannity*; 3/5/2020.)

"I would rather [keep those infected and exposed passengers *on* the cruise ship anchored near San Francisco] because I like the [current U.S.] numbers being where they are. I don't need to have the numbers double because of one ship that wasn't our fault. … I'd rather have them stay on [the ship], personally."

(Trump, Donald, R-Fla., U.S. president; Q&A with
reporters; CDC; 3/6/2020.) *(ignoring the advice of all his
health experts, after a similar situation exploded with
infections)*

"The [questionable CDC coronavirus] tests are all perfect like the letter was perfect. The transcription was perfect. Right? This was not as perfect as that but pretty good."

(Ibid.; Trump; 3/6/2020.) *(comparing the CDC's troubled COVID-19 test development efforts to his impeachment-worthy phone call with Ukrainian President Volodymyr Zelenskyy)*

"Mr. Trump started Monday playing down the virus, reminding Americans that tens of thousands of people die of the ordinary flu every year. 'Nothing is shut down, life & the economy go on,' he wrote on Twitter. 'At this moment there are 546 confirmed cases of CoronaVirus, with 22 deaths. Think about that!' He dismissed the effect of the outbreak in fueling Monday's market meltdown. 'Saudi Arabia and Russia are arguing over the price and flow of oil,' he wrote. 'That, and the Fake News, is the reason for the market drop!'"

(Baker, Peter & Haberman, Maggie & Karni, Annie; "Trump Floats Economic Stimulus in Response to Coronavirus"; *The New York Times;* 3/9/2020.)

"We will not delay. I will never hesitate to take any necessary steps to protect the lives, health, and safety of the American people. I will always put the well-being of America first."

(Trump, Donald, R-Fla., U.S. president; national address; Oval Office; 3/11/2020.)

Upshot

The problem with these Oval Office Donald-come-lately assurances is this: Who can believe the president now after months of downplaying the crisis for personal, partisan, corrupt reasons. He is not leading. He's being dragged against his will because the tsunami of factual information is drowning his attempts to spin the problem.

Yesterday the World Health Organization officially designated the novel coronavirus spread as a *pandemic*. Yesterday Trump's own director of the National Institute of Allergy and Infectious Diseases, Dr. Anthony Fauci, warned that the U.S. could have a *problem* or it could have a *catastrophic nightmare* — it's the government's choice, depending upon its response.

Finally, yesterday, the Attending Physician of the United States Congress told a congressional committee in private session that the country could experience 70 to 150 million novel coronavirus infections before the crisis is over.

Only after these dire warnings has the president apparently decided to — at least appear to — take the pandemic seriously. But still: 1) he has yet to reassemble fully the U.S. pandemic response team he fired in 2018 because it had Obama's fingerprints on it; 2) Dr. Fauci has had to warn him — through the media — to stop comparing COVID-19 benignly to the flu; 3) he got several crucial points wrong in his Oval Office address, causing intensified market turmoil (which he was trying to suppress) because investors fear his incompetent leadership; and 4) after two months of wasted lead time, only now has he ordered a push for coronavirus test kit production.

> "The Democrats are politicizing the coronavirus. … This is their new hoax."

> (Ibid.; Trump; 2/28/2020.)

> "[T]hat governor is a snake. OK. Inslee [(D-Wash.)] … who is not a good governor, by the way."

> (Ibid.; Trump; 3/6/2020.) *(referring to Democratic Gov. Jay Inslee of Washington state, whose state has suffered the most COVID-19 infections and deaths by far)*

"We must put politics aside, stop the partisanship, and unify together as one nation and one family."

(Ibid.; Trump; 3/11/2020.)

As of this writing, March 12, 2020, 8:18 a.m. EST, the U.S. has 1,323 confirmed coronavirus cases and 38 deaths spread across 45 states. Earth has 127,749 confirmed cases and 4,717 deaths across 116 countries.■

03/19/20 — The Boy Who Cried "No Wolf" – Wait … "WOLF!"

The Boy Who Cried "No Wolf"

Regarding the novel coronavirus pandemic, President Trump is the boy who cried "No Wolf."

For two months he's played down the crisis consistently to calm the markets for self-serving purposes. He said there will be a "very good ending for us — *that* I can assure you." He said the number of cases, "15, within a couple of days is going to be down to close to zero." He said, "We're finding very little problem, very little problem." He reassured, "It's starting to go in the other direction." He fantasized, "One day it's like a miracle, it will disappear."

And he politicized, saying the coronavirus story is the "Democrats' new hoax." He said the World Health Organization's numbers are wrong and turned down its January offer of help with testing. He callously preferred to keep 21 infected — and thousands of in-danger-of-being-infected — Americans holed up on a virus-growing petri dish of a cruise ship anchored off San Francisco rather than be transferred home: "I don't need to have the numbers double because of one ship that wasn't our fault."

Now that reality has slapped him upside the head and he's realized he can't tweet-intimidate a virus into submission with junior high school ad hominems, the boy has been forced to cry "Wolf!" Forced finally to get serious. Because the boy is supposed to be the leader of the free world. And because the wolf now is snarling at his feet, tearing away the boy's chances for reelection. And the boy knows reelection loss equals presidential immunity loss equals multiple indictments slapped on him after Jan. 20, 2021.

The COVID-19 pandemic has been a dual-track story from the beginning. The first track is the fear and devastation of a plague the likes of which has not been seen in a century.

The second track is Donald Trump's handling of the disease in this country — the corrupt and incompetent response of a piss-ant (an underrated ad hominem), pompous, maybe-billionaire who woke up one day to find himself an accidental president.

What He Said Before

"It's going to disappear. One day it's like a miracle, it will disappear."

> (Trump, Donald, R-Fla., U.S. president; African American History Month reception; White House; 2/27/2020.)

"The Democrats are politicizing the coronavirus. ... This is their new hoax."

> (Trump, Donald, R-Fla., U.S. president; campaign rally; North Charleston, S.C.; 2/28/2020.)

The Historical Rewrite

"This is a pandemic. I felt it was a pandemic long before it was called a pandemic. ... No, I've always viewed it as very serious. There was no difference [in my tone] yesterday from days before. I feel the tone is similar, but some people said it wasn't."

> (Trump, Donald, R-Fla., U.S. president; news conference; White House; 3/17/2020.)

"It's a war. ... [I'm] a wartime president."

(Trump, Donald, R-Fla., U.S. president; news conference; White House; 3/18/2020.)

No Wait — *"WOLF!"*

Even *Fox News* and *Breitbart* have followed Trump's lead in his 180-degree reversal on the seriousness of the pandemic, including his decision to "shut down" the country (i.e., urge national prevention guidelines, non-essential business closures, and shelter-at-home practices) for 15 days starting March 15. Of course they've also replicated the fawning derriere-kissing of Dear Leader's vice president, Cabinet members, and aides in praising his "leadership" in the face of this now-crisis. Before now, they have one real thing to point to: Donald's repeated claims that he presciently stopped travel to and from China six weeks ago in the face of widespread opposition; therefore he always took the virus "seriously." But here's the deal, folks (to channel Joe Biden): 1) There was little resistance to the travel ban; and 2) U.S. airlines already had announced a halt to China service.

The Buck-Passing

"Yeah, no, I don't take responsibility at all [for the lack of testing kits] because we were given a set of circumstances and we were given rules, regulations, and specifications from a different time."

(Trump, Donald, R-Fla., U.S. president; news conference; White House; 3/13/2020.)

[YAMICHE ALCINDOR (NPR):] "You did disband the White House pandemic office, and the officials that were working in that office left this administration abruptly. So what responsibility do you take to that, and — the officials

that worked in that office said the White House lost valuable time because that office was disbanded. What do you make of that?"

[PRESIDENT TRUMP:] "Well, I just think it's a nasty question, because … we saved thousands of lives because of the quick closing [of China travel]. And when you say 'me,' I didn't do it. We have a group of people, I could ask perhaps, in my administration … because I don't know anything about it. I mean, you say we did that, I don't know anything about it. Disbanding, no, I don't know anything about it."

[YAMICHE ALCINDOR (NPR):] "You don't know about the reorganization that happened at the National Security Council?"

[PRESIDENT TRUMP:] "It's the administration, perhaps they do that, let people go. You used to be with a different newspaper than you are now, you know, things like that happen."

(news conference; White House; 3/13/2020.)
(Alcindor's mic was cut during her next follow-up question)

The Piling On

Trump enablers and lemmings lament the "piling on" of presidential criticism from opponents at a time when we should all be coming together. You know — like the president has urged since Inauguration Day, for all Americans to "come together," like The Beatles at their favorite ashram.

But it's not piling on if the criticism is warranted. One need only peruse any credible media source over the past two months to understand the enormous failings of this administration in responding to the pandemic — let alone most other issues facing a presidency — while the president tries to blame his way out of responsibility.

> "The Obama administration made a decision on testing that turned out to be very detrimental to what we're doing, and we undid that decision a few days ago. ... That was a decision we disagreed with. ... But we've undone that decision."
>
> (Trump, Donald, R-Fla., U.S. president; meeting with airline executives; White House; 3/4/2020.)

> "[E]xperts and laboratory trade organizations say there was no 'decision [on testing],' and they don't know what Trump is referring to. 'We aren't sure what rule is being referenced,' [said] Michelle Forman, a spokeswoman for the Association of Public Health Laboratories. ... '[W]e are not aware of anything that changed.'"
>
> (Wilkie, Christina & Mangan, Dan; "Trump Blames Obama for Lack of Coronavirus Tests: 'I Don't Take Responsibility at All'"; *CNBC.com;* 3/13/2020.)

Moreover the so-called piling on serves a legitimate purpose. Trump has not led. But he has been *dragged* to a position in which he must get serious about the crisis. For example he finally declared a national emergency this past Friday, which most experts say is several weeks too late. He would not be there yet without the full force of legitimate, accurate, deserved criticism. It only seems like a piling on because he's performed so poorly.

Donald still hasn't picked up the ball fully on vital medical hardware and personal protection equipment production, test kit production, test reporting, federal-state prevention guideline coordination, and message consistency. This is why the *piling on* needs to continue, to drag him toward some semblance of leadership and to call him out on the mendacious blame-shifting to hide his failings.

> "If you go back to the swine flu, it was nothing like this, [the Obama administration] didn't do testing like this, and they lost approximately 14,000 people. They started thinking about testing when it was far too late."
>
> (Ibid.; Trump; 3/13/2020.)

> "The Obama administration tested 1 million people for H1N1 [flu] in the first month after the first U.S. diagnosed case. The first U.S. coronavirus case was 50+ days ago. And we haven't even tested 10,000 people yet."
>
> (Klain, Ron, [Obama] Ebola response coordinator, 2014-2015; Twitter post; 3/12/2020.)

Some media sources, even so-called liberal ones, have held back on some of the criticism because of a sense of false equivalency, i.e., the assumption that both sides — Trump World and its critics — should get equal time and equal condemnation. But this is wrong. It's simple: Trump should get more criticism, more condemnation because of his galactic ineptitude as a leader.

Sometimes failure and incompetence are not equal opportunity.

The Delusional Chutzpah

> "I'd rate it a 10."
>
> (Trump, Donald, R-Fla., U.S. president; news conference; White House; 3/16/2020.) *(when asked how he would rate his response to the pandemic on a scale of 1 to 10)*■

03/26/20 — Disbelieve This President Like Your Life Depends on It – It Does

[PETER ALEXANDER (NBC):] "Is it possible that your impulse to put a positive spin on things [including on the unproved-to-be-effective-on-COVID-19 antimalarial drug hydroxychloroquine] may be giving Americans a false sense of hope and misrepresenting preparedness right now?"

[PRESIDENT TRUMP:] "Such a lovely question. No, I don't think so. Look, it may work, may not work. … I feel good about it. That's all it is, just a feeling. I'm, you know, a smart guy." …

[PETER ALEXANDER (NBC):] "What would you say to Americans who are scared, though? I guess nearly 200 dead, 1,400 who are sick, millions, as you witnessed, who are scared right now. What do you say to Americans who are watching right now who are scared?"

[PRESIDENT TRUMP:] "I say that you are a terrible reporter, that's what I say. I think it's a very nasty question, and I think that it's a very bad signal that you are putting out to the American people. The American people are looking for answers and looking for hope, and you're doing sensationalism. And the same with NBC [which is owned by] *Concast*. I don't call it Comcast, I call it *Concast*. Let me just tell you something. That's really bad reporting. … You ought to be ashamed of yourself."

(press briefing; White House; 3/20/2020.)

Yes, students in 2040 or 2050 American History class (if I'm so rewarded to have you reading my work), there once was a United States president who spoke like this in public. And not just the occasional slip of tongue or flare of misplaced, disingenuous passion. President Donald Trump spoke in this shocking, emotionally immature manner near-daily — even to political allies who dared stray at all from Trump doctrine. And this is how he handled the 21st century COVID-19 plague, which killed so many of your grandparents. By the dawn of the 2020 pandemic, however, Trump's fourth year in office, Americans had become desensitized to the middle school ad hominem attacks and were no longer shocked by his galactic, pathological narcissism.

An Observation

> "Mr. Trump's performance on the national stage in recent weeks has put on display the traits that Democrats and some Republicans consider so jarring — the profound need for personal praise, the propensity to blame others, the lack of human empathy, the penchant for rewriting history, the disregard for expertise, the distortion of facts, the impatience with scrutiny or criticism. For years, skeptics expressed concern about how he would handle a genuine crisis threatening the nation, and now they know."
>
> (Baker, Peter & Haberman, Maggie; "Used to Meeting Challenges With Bluster and Force, Trump Confronts a Crisis Unlike any Before"; *The New York Times;* 3/21/2020.)

Yes, this is an observational piece by Baker and Haberman. But virtually all critically thoughtful observers have seen enough to know it's accurate. Let me just describe the observation this way: "At least, I feel good about it. That's all it is, just a feeling. I'm, you know, a smart guy." *(— thanks to Donald Trump)*

President Trump wanted to "reopen" the country for business after his administration's 15-day social distancing guidelines ended around April 1. When that idea met too much public flak, he touted an Easter Sunday (April 12) emergence from the suggested national isolation, for which he's still pushing in press briefings and tweets. Meanwhile his task force scientists, Dr. Anthony Fauci and Dr. Deborah Birx, are performing a finely tuned balancing act of contradicting and correcting Donald's self-serving fantasies as much as they can without getting canned.

Disregard for Expertise

If Doctors Fauci and Birx go, there will be almost zero trustworthy information coming from the White House. Fauci's appearances at briefings already have become intermittent, reportedly because the president is unhappy with the attention and respect Tony is garnering from the press — and because Dr. Fauci has contradicted Trump's statements in these briefings moments after Trump made them. If it weren't a true national medical crisis, and if Fauci hadn't already ingratiated himself with the public, he would be long gone.

The U.S. infection curve still is arcing skyward as multiple cable news graphs illustrate. The World Health Organization is warning that the virus is spreading faster, especially in the lower 48. Speaking of curves, those same graphs clearly show the U.S. now is where Italy, Spain, China, et al. were several weeks ago. Every credible health and science expert says the crisis is growing and there's no way to predict its denouement. The only sane response is for governments, including ours, to do everything in their power to impede viral spread.

> "We really, really need everyone to stay at home. ... As the nation's doctor I'm here to help America understand how we need to respond to this, and where I come down is that every single day counts. Every single second counts, and

right now there are not enough people out there taking this seriously."

> (Adams, Jerome, U.S. surgeon general; *NBC's Today*; 3/23/2020.)

"We're not going to let the cure be worse than the problem. … Our country was not built to be shut down. … We're going to be opening up our country, and we're going to be watching certain areas. We're going to be watching this very closely but can't keep it closed for the next, you know, for years. … I'm not looking at months [either], I can tell you right now. … America will again and soon be open for business. Very soon. … Probably more death [will result from job losses] than anything we're talking about with respect to the virus."

> (Trump, Donald, R-Fla., U.S. president; press briefing; White House; 3/23/2020.)

Boy Who Finally Cried Wolf — Maybe

No wonder "there are not enough people out there taking this seriously," Surgeon General Adams. The president doesn't want us to. Well, he does and he doesn't.

The president is corrupt. Thinking people know this. But he is, "you know, a smart guy." As I wrote last week, Trump knows his presidential reelection chances lay squarely upon American economic performance, specifically the stock market. I'll say it again: He believes poor market performance equals reelection loss equals presidential immunity loss equals multiple indictments coming his way after Jan. 20, 2021 — not to mention no more bilking of influence-seeking foreign governments and lobbyists for (more than usually) overpriced Trump hotel services and embedded restaurants.

Donald wants the country to get back to work even if it risks lives. But he doesn't want you to know that last part. So sometimes he appears to take the pandemic seriously. He had everyone fooled last week or so when he appeared to shed his carefree attitude ("It's going to disappear. One day it's like a miracle, it will disappear.") and held a news conference to announce his newfound seriousness:

> "This is a pandemic. I felt it was a pandemic long before it was called a pandemic. … No, I've always viewed it as very serious."
>
> (Trump, Donald, R-Fla., U.S. president; press briefing; White House; 3/17/2020.)
>
> "It's a war. … [I'm] a wartime president."
>
> (Trump, Donald, R-Fla., U.S. president; press briefing; White House; 3/18/2020.)

Even the "failing, Trump-hating" *New York Times* and the "Jeff Bezos Amazon" *Washington Post* assailed us with multiple headlines about the president finally getting serious.

But they were fooled, too. It was a scam. Let me use the dreaded *Peanuts* metaphor: Schroeder promised to play "Beethoven's Ninth Symphony" but instead … No, wait — Pigpen promised to take a bath, but once again … No, WAIT! — Lucy pulled the football on Charlie Brown's kick attempt one more time.

Full-on Half-Measures

Every valid expert says the U.S. government should take all possible measures to curb the virus' spread. But this president is taking full-on half-measures.

He won't implement the Defense Production Act to meet needed personal protection equipment and ventilator production because he's afraid Democrats will turn his "socialism" ad hominem back on him. ("I'm not blaming [Gov. Cuomo but] he's supposed to be buying his own ventilators.")

He won't kick-start necessary expansive test kit production because it will increase the positive-test numbers. ("We're not a shipping clerk. It's up to the governors.")

Donald continues the happy talk. He lied about test kit shortages. ("I'm not hearing it.") He lied about two Navy hospital ships being deployed, about millions of masks in transit, about private companies manufacturing ventilators, about drugs near approval for COVID-19 treatment. He blames the media (no, really) for "overblowing" the crisis, including a reporter who offered up a softball question to give the president a chance to show some humanity. ("What would you say to Americans who are scared?" *[TRUMP:]* "I say that you are a terrible reporter.")

Disbelief

A president's word influences the country, especially his supporters. But this president has corrupted his influence. He equivocates, tacitly winking as he recites lukewarm social distancing warnings. He strengthens the conspiracy theories — already abounding that the pandemic is an exaggerated danger perpetuated by his opponents to hurt Trump — which he, himself, started. ("The Democrats are politicizing the coronavirus. … This is their new hoax.")

Donald held another bifurcated press briefing yesterday. The bifurcation? Trump fantasy juxtaposed with careful-not-to-offend-the-emperor scientific analysis. Trump tried to draw in Dr. Fauci to back up his assertion that the WHO is biased toward China. Fauci expertly declined to weigh in on the politics: "I'm a scientist." Trump continued spewing the pabulum about "reopening" America by Easter, saying Tuesday, "You'll have packed churches all over our country. I think it'll be a beautiful time." But his scientists said there is no predicting when it will be safe to let down our guard. Trump said the U.S. has tested "far more" than any other country.

But his scientists mentally edited and qualified that statement: U.S. per capita testing is 10% of other afflicted developed countries.

Donald still refuses to nationalize testing and production of test kits, PPE, and ventilators, leaving crucial presidential power on the table, and states to fend for and fight among themselves. He wasted two months of precious prep time while consistently playing down and denying the novel coronavirus threat while it spread in U.S. hot spots. But yesterday he was proud to crow, "It's hard not to be happy with the job we're doing."

President Trump's middle name is *Mendacity*. This is well known. Most of us have learned long ago to blow off his male bovine excreta. We know he's desperate to be reelected for corrupt reasons. But now there is a pandemic going on. Now you must disbelieve this president like your life depends on it. Because it does.■

04/02/20 — President Learns a New Word: "Aspirational"

COVID-19 Deaths

2/06/2020 — U.S.: 1 | World: 2,976
3/05/2020 — U.S.: 12 | World: 3,293
3/12/2020 — U.S.: 38 | World: 4,717
3/19/2020 — U.S.: 150 | World: 9,115
3/26/2020 — U.S.: 1,046 | World: 22,030
4/02/2020 — U.S.: 5,137 | World: 48,284

(COVID-19 Dashboard by the Center for Systems Science and Engineering at Johns Hopkins University; approximately 8 a.m. each day)

[JONATHAN KARL (ABC):] "[A]re you able to guarantee, to assure these states, these hospitals that everybody who needs a ventilator will get a ventilator?"

[PRESIDENT TRUMP:] "Here's what I will tell you. We are in good shape. I think we are in great shape. I think that number one, we have distributed — ventilators are a big deal, we are distributing vast numbers and we are in great shape."

[JONATHAN KARL (ABC):] "So everyone that needs one will be able to get a ventilator?"

[PRESIDENT TRUMP:] "Don't be a cutie pie. Everyone who needs one — Nobody has done what we have been able to do, and everything that I took over was a mess. It

was a broken country in so many ways. In so many ways other than this. We had a bad testing system. We had a bad stockpile system, we had nothing in the stockpile system. So I would not tell me what you're telling me, like, being a wise guy."

(press briefing; White House; 3/27/2020.)

President Trump learned a new term this week. No, not *cutie pie*. He learned the word *aspirational*. We know this is a new word for him because we can find no one who ever has heard him use it before. But his aides and media gurus floated the word in the days before his open-by-Easter-retraction press briefing March 29, and they prompted *him* to say *aspirational* several more times Sunday for good measure.

History of *Aspirational*

"We're opening up this incredible country because we have to do that. ... [Easter]'s such an important day for other reasons, but I'd love to make it an important day for this. ... [I want the nation] opened up and just raring to go by Easter."

(Trump, Donald, R-Fla., U.S. president; *Fox News;* 3/24/2020.)

"More than 800,000 doctors across the United States sent a letter to President Donald Trump, urging him to reinforce social distancing after he suggested the economy could reopen by Easter. ... [The doctors said, 'This could] gravely jeopardize the health of all Americans.' ... [T]hey said medical staff are risking their lives to treat coronavirus patients and ask that the Trump administration support 'science-based recommendations' on social distancing."

(Edmonds, Lauren & Griffith, Keith; "More Than 800,000 Doctors Plead With Trump NOT to Reopen the Country by Easter Because It Will 'Gravely Jeopardize the Health of All Americans'"; *Daily Mail;* 3/28/2020.)

After pushing for an Easter Sunday (April 12) reopening, to "get our country back to work," the president finally had to back down. In the week or so before his March 29 back-down presser, Trump came as close as he could to telegraphing the Easter reopening without guaranteeing it. His business buddies had gotten to him, leading him to favor the economy (read: profits).

But then science went where it never had gone before: into the black hole of Donald's consciousness. The doctors of his coronavirus response team showed him numerical projections (read: political truths) that even he could not spin or tweet-attack away: If he did not get serious about the pandemic now, untold higher numbers of Americans would die and he would be blamed (i.e., not reelected). So President Trump extended his administration's virus-prevention guidelines and shutdown (non-essential business closures, shelter-at-home directives) for another month to April 30.

But to rewrite the history of his incessant Easter projection — and the folly and colossal irresponsibility of it — the White House came up with *aspirational.* As I said, his advisers started tossing the word around in the days before the president debuted it, either to influence him through his favorite reference source — TV — or to provide him a soft landing after he finally had agreed to rescind the happy talk of churches filled on Easter.

"Top White House economic adviser Larry Kudlow says President Donald Trump's hopes to reopen the country by Easter was an 'aspirational target,' and insisted the president would not rush efforts to stem the spread of the coronavirus."

(Reyner, Solange; "Kudlow Calls Trump's Easter
Timeline an 'Aspirational Target'"; *NewsMax;*
3/25/2020.)

"Dr. Anthony Fauci, the nation's top infectious disease expert, said President Donald Trump's recent calls for the nation to 'open up' again by Easter were 'aspirational,' saying now was 'no time to pull back' as COVID-19 continues to spread around the country."

(Visser, Nick; "Fauci Says Trump's Call for Country
to Open Up by Easter Is 'Aspirational'"; *HuffPost;*
3/27/2020.)

"The president expressed really an aspirational goal as we continue to follow the data."

(Pence, Mike, R-Ind.; U.S. vice president; *CNBC;*
3/27/2020.)

Then finally the man, himself:

"Trump rejected on Sunday that publicly setting the Easter timeline was a mistake, calling it 'aspirational.' 'No, that was aspirational,' he said. 'We had an aspiration of Easter, but when you hear these kinds of numbers and you hear the potential travesty, we don't want to do anything where — we don't want to have a spike up.'"

(Samuels, Brett & Chalfant, Morgan; "Trump Shifts,
Says Distancing to Go to April 30"; *The Hill;*
3/29/2020.)

Aspirational or incomprehensible, pushing this false hope encouraged Americans to drop their guard, especially MAGA supporters who already believe the pandemic has been overblown to hurt Trump. Dropping their guard translates to increased cases and deaths — and not just in MAGA supporters. There's no legitimate defense for the president's corrupt leadership and decision-making.

Sorry Truth

> "The idea that Easter was simply aspirational is politically convenient — the president doesn't want to be seen as backing down — but difficult to take seriously. After touting the holiday target date nearly a week ago, Trump had multiple opportunities to downplay its significance. He did largely the opposite. It's unfortunate that at this point in the crisis, what passes for good news is when the president comes up with a ridiculous idea and then abandons it."
>
> (Benen, Steve; "Retreating From Easter Deadline, Trump Extends Distancing Guidelines"; *MSNBC.com*; 3/30/2020.)

***Aspirational* Redux**

Just for fun, an aspirational blast from the past:

> "Sen. Susan Collins (R-Maine) on Wednesday acknowledged that her stated belief that President Trump had learned a lesson from impeachment was 'aspirational,' saying that she 'may not be correct on that.'"
>
> (Wise, Justin; "Collins Admits Comments About Trump Learning a Lesson Are 'Aspirational'"; *The Hill*; 2/6/2020.)

Never Forget

"There was good news and bad news emanating from the White House on Sunday. First, the bad news: a deadly pandemic is apparently gaining steam and killing more Americans. The good news? The ratings for President Donald Trump's near-daily briefings are beating *The Bachelor* and *Monday Night Football*, at least according to a boastful series of tweets from the commander in chief.

"[Trump tweeted,] 'Because the "Ratings" of my News Conferences etc. are so high, "Bachelor finale, Monday Night Football type numbers" according to the @nytimes, the Lamestream Media is going CRAZY. "Trump is reaching too many people, we must stop him." said one lunatic. See you at 5:00 P.M.! — Donald J. Trump (@realDonaldTrump) March 29, 2020'"

(Haring, Bruce; "White House COVID-19 Briefings Are Beating 'The Bachelor' in Ratings, President Trump Boasts"; *Deadline.com;* 3/29/2020.)

So his television ratings are *way* up.

President Trump continues to favor business and political expediency over human life. This is not hyperbole. He refuses to nationalize fully the pandemic response because it hurts industry, contradicts GOP states' rights dogma, and presents the risk of the dreaded "socialism" label being turned back on him. He refuses to issue a national stay-at-home order and fully implement the Defense Production Act — compelling U.S. companies to manufacture desperately needed PPE and ventilators — for the same reasons. He has dragged his presidential feet on implementing widespread testing, for which experts have begged, because he wants to keep his numbers down: Fewer tests mean fewer cases counted.

But his TV ratings are up.

Don't ever forget the smallness of this president — the smallness of his intellect, his judgment, his integrity. This small, incompetent, corrupt man is costing American lives.■

04/09/20 — For the Love of GOD! Donald, Please Resign

COVID-19 Deaths

2/06/2020 — U.S.: 1 | World: 2,976
3/05/2020 — U.S.: 12 | World: 3,293
3/12/2020 — U.S.: 38 | World: 4,717
3/19/2020 — U.S.: 150 | World: 9,115
3/26/2020 — U.S.: 1,046 | World: 22,030
4/02/2020 — U.S.: 5,137 | World: 48,284
4/09/2020 — U.S.: 14,808 | World: 89,435

(COVID-19 Dashboard by the Center for Systems Science and Engineering at Johns Hopkins University; approximately 8 a.m. each day)

Every move he makes is about reelection. President Trump's reprobate leadership is costing many thousands of American lives through corrupt responses and nonresponses to the novel coronavirus pandemic.

Let Me Count the Ways

1) *He discounted the virus for two months, squandering critical preparation time, and still downplays it when he can.* He had January intelligence reports with explicit warnings of an impending pandemic. One of his favorite aides, Peter Navarro, warned in a Jan. 29 White House memo (and again in a Feb. 23 memo) that America could suffer 500,000 deaths if it didn't prepare properly. President Trump said he missed that memo. His HHS secretary tried in vain to get the president to take the virus seriously, but Donald called him an "alarmist." Trump balked at taking earnest action for fear of the

"numbers" (infections, deaths) going up and the markets being spooked. He did call for an exception-laden ban on China travel — *after* U.S. airlines and 38 other countries already had acted. He still is selectively silencing aides and government scientists, promoting his "the cure can't be worse than the problem" theme, and again pushing for a deadly premature reopening of the country.

2) *He won't nationalize the medical policy of his own scientists, specifically their social distancing order recommendations.* This puts the entire country at higher risk. He's allowing about 10 venal GOP governors to use their "best judgment." He refuses to overrule them because it would hurt his reelection chances: A) he doesn't want to alienate business; B) he doesn't want to alienate Republican governors he needs to win; C) he wants to keep the country open and markets up at any cost; D) he doesn't want to oppose GOP "states' rights" doctrine; and E) he's afraid opponents will turn the "socialism" tag back on him in November. The only reason he's taken the minimal actions he has is because advisers have convinced him that too many deaths will cost too many votes. Rather than saving every American life possible, Mr. Trump callously is calculating a kind of benefit-loss ratio: balancing how much human death is acceptable to maintain stock market performance (read: reelection chances).

3) *He won't nationalize the supply chain, refusing to interfere with private business.* ("We're not a shipping clerk.") Meanwhile all 50 states and FEMA are forced to bid against each other for scarce PPE and precious ventilators, driving up prices, while opportunist profiteers, domestic and foreign, are exploiting the desperation. The president blames states for not being prepared, essentially saying the shortages are their tough luck.

4) *He won't sufficiently nationalize supply production (by using the Defense Production Act) to produce desperately needed medical supplies and ventilators* (even though affected companies would be compensated fairly).

Again this refusal is for reelection reasons: to keep markets up, economic fear down, and the "socialism" accusations at bay.

5) *He won't fully compel needed mass test kit production because fewer tests mean lower "numbers."* His failed leadership and continued corrupt decision-making — by refusing foreign help, putting business concerns over lives, etc. — is killing thousands of people unnecessarily. This is not hyperbole. Virtually all experts point to widespread testing as the way out of this crisis, and medical personnel across the country are screaming about the frightening, demoralizing shortages.

6) *He won't sufficiently deploy military medical personnel to the most desperate large-city hospitals.* Yes, Saturday he finally did call up 1,000 military staff to help out in New York hospitals after weeks of Gov. Cuomo begging him. But there are tens of thousands of doctors and nurses in the armed forces. A majority of those could be redeployed temporarily to the worst-hit areas of the country. This is part of the military's purpose. Civilian medical staffs are pleading, praying for help because they are overwhelmed.

Add to All That These Nuggets:

> — He continues to disparage certain Democratic governors. He blames governors who are not loyalists and rewards those who are with favorable supply shipments.

> — He's turned his daily near-two-hour press briefings into low-key campaign rallies, complete with persistent journalist invective and free-for-all mendacity.

The largest elephant in the Trumpian herd of pachyderms in the room (sounds cerebral but I don't know what it means) is the consistent, colossal obliquity, the willingness to fabricate corruptly at every turn. Now it's producing unnecessary death and will produce more. Donald lies about the numbers, lies about the testing, the supply chain, the DPA, responsibility, favoritism, journalism, drugs, reopening the country by Easter.

But what *really* irks me is the prevarication about his hand-size and BMI.

Partisan Pandemic

Historian and presidential biographer Jon Meacham recently characterized the crisis as the first "partisan pandemic" in history. What he meant was that beliefs about the cause of, effects of, and response to the pandemic fall into two camps: the science and reason camp, and the Trump-supporter camp. Because of this president's corrupt influence, the Trump-supporting camp — cult — refuses to believe science, i.e., truth, because Donald has inculcated in its members the precept that science — truth — is out to hurt its leader. The overriding problem is that the cult comprises 40% or so of America, which has morally paralyzed invertebrate Republican legislators, separating them from all ethical clarity.

Meacham's simile is this: "It's like The Enlightenment itself is on trial."

I'll sign off on Jon Meacham's analogy the way many MAGA lemmings love to close their social media entries after posting an article purporting that Nancy Pelosi starves her grandchildren while voting to feed illegal alien children no matter what planet they're from:

"Let that sink in." ∎

04/16/20 — I Got Your "Metrics" Right Here

COVID-19 Deaths

2/06/2020 — U.S.: 1 | World: 2,976
3/05/2020 — U.S.: 12 | World: 3,293
4/02/2020 — U.S.: 5,137 | World: 48,284
4/16/2020 — U.S.: 30,985 | World: 138,008

> (COVID-19 Dashboard by the Center for Systems Science and Engineering at Johns Hopkins University; approximately 8 a.m. each day)

Metrics Are in His Head

> *[REPORTER:]* "Can you say, sir, what metrics you will use to make that decision [to reopen the economy]?"
>
> *[PRESIDENT TRUMP:]* "The metrics are right here *(points at head)*. That's my metrics. That's all I can do."
>
> (press briefing; White House; 4/10/2020.)

In response to the dreadful lack of U.S. coronavirus testing, the president said this:

> "There's not a lot of issues with testing. … We're leading the world now in testing, by far."
>
> (Trump, Donald, R-Fla., U.S. president; press briefing; White House; 4/10/2020.)

But he's wrong. Or for the more cynical among you: He's lying.

> "During Wednesday's briefing, Vice President Pence said more than 1.2 million tests have been performed on Americans. Given the population of the U.S. (about 327 million), that's roughly 1 in every 273 people [0.3%], as of April 2."

> (Sprunt, Barbara & Montanaro, Domenico; "FACT CHECK: Trump Claims U.S. Testing for Coronavirus Most per Capita — It's Not"; *NPR.org*; 4/2/2020.)

The U.S. per capita testing rate is dangerously, embarrassingly low.

Unfortunately we know all too well about the metrics in President Trump's head.

"Empty Chair"

A White House-designated "thought leader" on Donald's own Great American Economic Revival Industry Groups — a panel of experts and CEOs the administration has assembled this week to determine how and when to reopen the U.S. economy — said this:

> "Larry Lindsey, a former economic adviser to President George W. Bush … was invited by House Minority Leader Kevin McCarthy (R-Calif.) to give an overview of the U.S.-China trade war. Lindsey also [brought] research on Trump's character, telling Republican lawmakers that he had asked two psychologists to evaluate the president from afar. The professionals found that Trump was a '10 out of 10 narcissist.' … 'That's what he scored.' Lindsey said … Trump's behavior [was] a symptom of his upbringing and a mother who didn't pay enough attention to him. … Lindsey

also compared Trump's long-term planning ability to that of an 'empty chair.'"

(Itkowitz, Colby & DeBonis, Mike; "Former Bush Official Puts Trump on the Couch: A '10 out of 10 Narcissist'"; *The Washington Post*; 5/15/2019.)

OK, former George W. Bush adviser Larry Lindsey saying Trump has mommy issues might have been inaccurate. Clearly we know it's the *daddy* issues that are much more consequential to Donald's pathology.

"10 out of 10 narcissist"? Old news.

Calling the president an "empty chair" in characterizing his long-term planning ability, however, is just wrong. *Empty chair* implies no planning, no action. But we would be so much better off if Donald simply did nothing while in office. To the contrary, he's done tremendous damage through most of his actions. And his long-term planning has been *spot on* (as the kids like to say): He continues to enrich himself corruptly, and he's stayed out of prison despite numerous felonies.

Total Authority

"When somebody's president of the United States, the authority is total."

(Trump, Donald, R-Fla., U.S. president; press briefing; White House; 4/13/2020.)

President Trump said this as he was (mistakenly) articulating his complete control over when governors will reopen — or not — their states' economies. Even Liz Cheney (R-Wyo.) said in response, "The federal government does not have absolute power." Even the conservative *National Review* and *Fox News'* Brit Hume called this statement "reckless." Even David Crosby says Donald has let himself go *(— apologies to Triumph the Insult Comedy Dog, aka Robert Smigel).* (And apologies to Mr. Crosby whom I understand has reaped the benefits of positive lifestyle changes since the time of the original Triumph quote dissing Rob Reiner at a *Friar's Club* roast.)

WHO's on First *(I couldn't resist)*

> "President Trump announced Tuesday that he will suspend payments to the World Health Organization in response to the United Nations agency's handling of the coronavirus pandemic, as the organization is in the midst of combating a global outbreak that has killed thousands and crippled world economies. Trump's announcement was expected, as he seeks to deflect blame for his early dismissal of the virus as a threat to Americans and the U.S. economy. … 'We have not been treated properly,' Trump said."
>
> > (Gearan, Anne; "Trump Announces Cutoff of New Funding for the World Health Organization Over Pandemic Response"; *The Washington Post*; 4/14/2020.)

> "Halting funding for the World Health Organization during a world health crisis is as dangerous as it sounds. Their work is slowing the spread of COVID-19, and if that work is stopped, no other organization can replace them. The world needs WHO now more than ever."
>
> > (Gates, Bill, Microsoft co-founder, world health advocate, second-largest WHO donor [through his and Melinda's foundation] after U.S.; Twitter post; 4/15/2020.)

Don't just take Bill's word for it. U.N. Secretary General António Guterres, the American Medical Association, and Brett D. Schaefer, conservative Heritage Foundation expert and member of the U.N.'s Committee on Contributions, all have deeply criticized the move as wrong, dangerous, and galactically damaging to pandemic health care efforts in underdeveloped *and* developed countries.

Several prominent virologists and medical pundits called it "insanity" to cut WHO funding during a pandemic.

Keep the Criticism Up

The criticism of President Trump's pandemic response is not to bash him and hurt his reelection chances (well, maybe a little). The primary purpose for keeping up the criticism is because it's the only reason he's taken any of the minuscule right action he *has* taken. Look no further than the administration's cockamamie move Friday to stop auxiliary funding for state and local coronavirus testing sites.

Virtually every independent medical expert on the planet avers that testing, testing, testing (to be able to trace and quarantine) is the only way out of this crisis, to achieve the goal Donald, himself, wants: the reopening of world economies. The U.S. is dangerously, embarrassingly near the bottom of per capita testing among developed nations. But the White House decided to cut funding support for the relatively few state and local testing sites in operation.

Until they reversed that cockamamie move after ferocious public backlash.

Why would the White House make such a stupid, callous decision in the first place? Many speculate. We might never know why. But it might be Oscar's razor — you know: The simplest explanation is usually the right one. Maybe the administration is simply that stupid. Maybe Oscar always sports a nice, clean shave because he's got a good razor.

What we *do* know is that legitimate, blistering criticism is the only thing that got Donald to change his mind, to correct his colossal blunder.

"In Unprecedented Move, Treasury Orders Trump's Name Printed on Stimulus Checks" (*The Washington Post* headline, April 15, 2020)

President Trump initially wanted his lie-detector-graph of an over-sexed-Sharpie signature on each government Economic Impact Payment check. But the law says a president is not authorized to sign Treasury payments. So he settled for having his name printed on the memo line, the spot where Aunt Evelyn writes "Congratulations!" on your high school graduation gift check.

Connecting in the language of the common woman and man, U.S. Treasury Secretary Steven Mnuchin assured struggling out-of-work Americans that their "bridge liquidity" remittance of $1,200 per adult will be disbursed as planned and that it's intended to hold them over for 10 weeks.

This transparent presidential promotion thing never has been done before in the history of IRS refunds or government stimulus/reimbursement checks. The president believes he can fool people into thinking the money comes from, or because of, him. And he gets the free advertising benefit for his reelection campaign. It likely will delay checks at least several days for desperate citizens who need them.

This is all you need to know about Donald J. Trump.■

04/23/20 — Amid Pandemic Malfeasance, Don't Forget: Trump Is Still a Literal Criminal

COVID-19 Deaths

2/06/2020 — U.S.: 1 | World: 620
3/05/2020 — U.S.: 12 | World: 3,293
4/02/2020 — U.S.: 5,137 | World: 48,284
4/23/2020 — U.S.: 46,785 | World: 184,372

> (COVID-19 Dashboard by the Center for Systems Science and Engineering at Johns Hopkins University; approximately 8 a.m. each day)

Intro

During this time of pandemic anxiety and death it's easy to forget the nightmare presidency that has led up to this crisis and enormously exacerbated its effects. Some pundits like to proclaim now is not the time to analyze how we got here. I say evaluating and loudly criticizing this president's incompetence and corruption is the only thing pushing him anywhere near right action.

Remembering that Donald is a literal criminal multiple times over can mitigate tragedies of this magnitude in the future. You know the old saying: Those who fail to learn from redundancy are doomed to repeat it. Again. *(— thanks to Rob E., long-time friend of the show, 21ˢᵗ century American philosopher)*

Besides being willing to allow tens of thousands of Americans to die needless, lonely viral deaths, President Trump also, still is guilty of myriad provable crimes. He is the unindicted co-

conspirator, "Individual-1," in the Michael Cohen campaign finance investigation. His inaugural committee took illegal foreign money and still can't account for most of it. During the Mueller investigation, he obstructed justice at least 10 times including secretly *and* openly dangling pardons to keep the rats quiet. He openly witness-tampered. He committed perjury. He has profited illegally from the presidency. He's likely a serial sexual predator with multiple criminal and civil cases pending. His keep-hidden-at-any-cost tax records widely are believed to buttress evidence of financial crimes.

And he shook down Ukraine, extorting its president to get illegal, false dirt on his presidential opponent. But his invertebrate GOP buds in Congress thought that one should slide.

Unindictable Crimes Against Humanity

> "[Television's Dr. Phil] acknowledged that the novel coronavirus is killing Americans — more than 33,000 as of early Friday — but also wondered why the economy would shut down over the pandemic but continues to function as people die from lung cancer, car crashes, and pool drownings. (Unlike coronavirus, none of the causes of death listed by Dr. Phil are contagious.) 'We don't shut the country down for that,' said Dr. Phil, after he cited inaccurate statistics on accidental deaths. 'Yet we are doing it for this.'"
>
> (Shepherd, Katie; "After Fauci Urged Caution in Reopening the Economy, Fox News Turned to Dr. Phil for a Second Opinion"; *The Washington Post;* 4/17/2020.)

Note that another infamous non-virologist expert and TV doctor, Mehmet Oz, said in the same week that getting American children back in school to make the most out of their lives "may only cost us

2% to 3% in terms of total mortality [and] that might be a trade-off some folks would consider.”

Presidential Unindictable Crimes Against Humanity

“President Donald Trump urged supporters to [protest] against stay-at-home restrictions. … A day after laying out a road map to gradually reopen the crippled economy, Trump tweeted the kind of rhetoric some of his supporters have used to demand the lifting of the orders that have thrown millions of Americans out of work. ‘LIBERATE MINNESOTA!’ ‘LIBERATE MICHIGAN!’ ‘LIBERATE VIRGINIA,’ he said in a tweet-storm in which he also lashed out at New York Gov. Andrew Cuomo for criticizing the federal response. Cuomo ‘should spend more time “doing” and less time “complaining,”’ the president said.”

(Miller, Zeke & Sedensky, Matt; “Trump Urges Supporters to ‘LIBERATE!’ States With Coronavirus Restrictions a Day After Unveiling Guidelines to Gradually Reopen Economy”; *The Associated Press;* 4/17/2020.)

Never mind that the administration’s own doctors, scientists, and infectious disease experts believe the presidential tweets (there’s an oxymoron) are undermining the White House’s own pandemic recommendations, thereby likely causing increased, unnecessary death.

Lies …

“[President Trump accused] the World Health Organization of ‘covering up the spread of the coronavirus’ and … was cutting off funding for the world’s public health body in the middle of a pandemic. … [But] 15 officials from his

administration were embedded with the WHO in Geneva,
working full time, hand-in-glove with the organization on
the virus from the very first day China disclosed the
outbreak to the world, Dec. 31. ... Everything that the
WHO knew, the Trump administration knew — in real
time."

(Milbank, Dana; "Trump Tells a Damnable and
Murderous Lie"; The Washington Post; 4/17/2020.)

Damn Lies ...

"For years, President Trump has derided the assessment by
American intelligence officials that Russia interfered in the
2016 presidential election to assist his candidacy, dismissing
it without evidence as the work of a 'deep state' out to
undermine his victory. But on Tuesday, a ... three-year
review by the Republican-led Senate Intelligence Committee
unanimously found that the intelligence community
assessment, pinning blame on Russia and outlining its goals
to undercut American democracy, was fundamentally sound
and untainted by politics."

(Fandos, Nicholas & Barnes, Julian E.; "Republican-
Led Review Backs Intelligence Findings on Russian
Interference"; The New York Times; 4/21/2020.)

Let me repeat that: "The Republican-led Senate Intelligence
Committee *unanimously* found that the intelligence community
assessment, pinning [election interference] blame on Russia ... *was
fundamentally sound and untainted by politics.*"

> "A new NBC News-Wall Street Journal poll this weekend showed that fully 65% of Americans say Trump did not take the coronavirus 'seriously enough at the beginning.' That echoes a Pew Research Center poll from late last week that showed the same number (65%) said Trump was 'too slow to take major steps' to address the situation. In that poll, even one-third of Republicans and GOP-leaning voters conceded that Trump didn't react quickly enough."

> (Blake, Aaron; "The One Poll Number That Could Haunt Trump on Coronavirus"; *The Washington Post*; 4/20/2020.)

The Connection

President Donald J. Trump fears indictment, financial downfall, and prison if he's not reelected.

His sole hope for reelection has been the admittedly booming (at least for the stock market and the rich) economy, however much he had to stand on Barack Obama's shoulders to take credit for it.

Now the economy has entered a colossal crash. It took the blink of an eye for COVID-19 to sink it, but the stock market, unemployment rate, and consumer confidence numbers will take years to recover, certainly not until well beyond Election Day 2020.

The genesis of the pandemic occurred through no fault of Donald's. But the deadly, corrupt perpetuation of the devastation falls squarely at his feet. Two weeks ago I enumerated his unindictable crimes of nonaction, and the highlights bear repeating:

> 1) *He discounted the virus for two months and still downplays it*, pushing to reopen the economy prematurely.

2) *He won't nationalize social distancing policy recommendations* because he favors business over lives.

3) *He won't nationalize the medical supply chain*, fearing the "socialism" label, while leaving profiteers to gouge states.

4) *He won't sufficiently nationalize production* for desperately needed ventilators, PPE, and other supplies, again fearing the "socialism" label.

5) *He won't sufficiently deploy military medical personnel to desperate private hospitals* because he won't admit it's necessary.

6) *He won't compel needed national testing production and implementation* because more tests mean higher reported case numbers.

These six points lay out the *corruption* aspect of Trump's pandemic response leadership. Now add in the *incompetence* component: The president and his appointees lack the management skills, intelligence, and compassion necessary to respond. Finally, consider the third leg of the Trumpian stool: *amorality*. This president is willing to cause many thousands of unnecessary deaths in his gamble to shore up the economy and be reelected.

Of course any first-term president wants to be reelected. This first-termer also is concerned with staying out of prison.

Remember:

— He is the unindicted *"Individual-1"* in the preelection campaign finance law violation (specifically hush money paid to Trump paramours) for which Donald's former personal attorney-fixer, Michael Cohen, is serving (part of) three years at the Federal Correctional Institution in Otisville, New York.

— The exhaustive Mueller report (on Russian interference into the 2016 U.S. election) detailed at least 10 instances of *presidential obstruction of justice.* Thousands of former attorneys general, former U.S. attorneys, and constitutional and legal scholars across the country have signed letters stating they believe at least half of those instances are impeachable offenses and would be indictable if Mr. Trump did not enjoy DOJ OLC presidential immunity — meaning the indictments are possible when he's no longer president.

— The Mueller report also exposed several instances of *presidential perjury* in Donald's written answers to investigators' questions about conspiring with Russians. Set aside his refusal to give in-person testimony because his lawyers convinced him he'd be inherently incapable of avoiding oral perjury. And set aside his refusal to answer even any written questions related to obstruction of justice.

— The president has several significant *emoluments clauses* cases pending (illegal foreign and domestic self-enrichment from the presidency). The number of White House conflicts of interest is astonishing.

— The president has over 20 pending credible accusations of *sexual assault and misconduct,* and several of those are making their way through the courts.

— The president is deathly afraid of his *tax records* becoming public. Among speculative reasons: 1) he's worth far less than he has boasted about for decades; and 2) his tax returns will provide or corroborate evidence of financial crimes.

— The *Trump Inaugural Committee still is under investigation* for facilitating and accepting illegal foreign contributions, missing funds, and financial malfeasance.

— Finally, we could all have fun chalking up the things like *extorting Ukraine* for dirt on Trump's likely 2020 presidential opponent, and the many other crimes he's gotten away with.

Outro

Now that his pandemic response poll numbers are upside down by 2:1, President Trump is upping the defensive lies and prompting even more unnecessary death.

This week he said his CDC director was misquoted in *The Washington Post* saying the pandemic will resurge more harshly in the fall combined with the seasonal flu outbreak. Donald did this to create false hope. He wants the electorate to ignore his own White House health recommendations and get back to work so his economic numbers will rise by Election Day. Minutes after Donald's press briefing lie, Director Robert Redfield answered a reporter's question: "Yes, I was quoted accurately."

Trump tried again: "But there might not even be a second wave."

White House Coronavirus Task Force top doctor Anthony Fauci responded, "What Dr. Redfield was saying ... that we will have coronavirus in the fall: I am convinced of that."

This week President Trump fired the government's *Tom Brady* (arguably the best NFL quarterback ever) of vaccine development, Rick Bright, director of the Biomedical Advanced Research and Development Authority. Bright's crime? Quietly following medical science standards. You might have heard about the president's (and *Fox News'*) push to use the drug hydroxychloroquine for COVID-19 treatment even though it has not been tested for this. Trump has been pushing it as false hope and also is suspected of pushing it for profit (you know, for his compadres in the pharmaceutical business). Mr. Bright has filed a whistleblower complaint alleging he was removed for internally resisting White House efforts to "provide an unproven drug on demand to the American public."

You might also have heard that Donald and *Fox* have gone radio-silent on hydroxychloroquine since recent studies show its experimental treatment with COVID-19 patients has resulted in more deaths than the use of placeboes.

President Trump blamed the World Health Organization last week for all the malfeasance for which he has been guilty. To back up this public relations charade, he's cutting funding for the WHO, the only worldwide organization that is slowing the viral spread.

To prop up his lies, Trump is causing more unnecessary deaths around the world and in his own country.

Don't forget that he also is a literal criminal.◼

04/30/20 — Trumpism Is Lethal – Literally

COVID-19 Deaths

2/06/2020 — U.S.: 1 | World: 620
3/05/2020 — U.S.: 12 | World: 3,293
4/02/2020 — U.S.: 5,137 | World: 48,284
4/30/2020 — U.S.: 60,999 | World: 228,057

(COVID-19 Dashboard by the Center for Systems Science and Engineering at Johns Hopkins University; approximately 8 a.m. each day)

Trump Presidency Is Deadly

The astonishing deadly circus that is the Trump presidency is like the Grand Canyon. Standing at the abyss, one person's two eyes are incapable of comprehending the vastness. It overwhelms the consciousness.

The staggering state of Trumpian havoc can be perceived only through the big picture of reading books and consuming media reports throughout his tenure. Sadly the average person can't or won't do this. So the lethal clown show lumbers on.

With spray-on tan, million-dollar comb-over, and both raccoon eyes focused firmly upon reelection — and only reelection — President Trump needlessly is allowing Americans to die in the following ways:

1) He's forcing heavily infected meat plants to reopen or stay open while refusing to order workplace safety rules enactment and enforcement.

2) But he's (still) refusing to mandate national testing production and implementation. He wants to keep the "numbers" down. (After declaring a national emergency 48 days ago, and 77 days after his partial China travel ban, the U.S. per capita testing rate is still at the bottom among developed nations.)

3) He's castrated the CDC and OSHA, stifling their influence and rule-making authority that would enforce life-saving safety measures at U.S. workplaces.

4) He's openly and tacitly influencing states to reopen their economies prematurely, "rapidly," almost guaranteeing a second deadly wave of the pandemic.

5) He's threatening to withhold aid to states with Democratic governors and has played favorites with PPE shipments.

6) He's telling dangerous lies saying "experts say the worst is behind us," the virus will "soon just go away," and that the U.S. has done sufficient testing. This provides fodder for the Diamond-and-Silk, anti-deep-state crowd pushing for premature reopening and elimination of social distancing.

7) He's refusing to extend the White House social distancing guidelines — even though they're only weak suggestions — past April 30, though U.S. deaths have exceeded 60,000 and still are climbing.

Trumpism Kills

"On Tuesday, Trump showed support for commentators Diamond and Silk after they were dropped by Fox News over their repeated nonsense about the virus: suggestions that the 'deep state' is to blame, that the virus is 'engineered' and that people should go 'out in the environment,' not shelter in their homes. Most recently, the pair hosted a scientist — part of the fire-Anthony-Fauci crowd — who argues that the coronavirus can be cured not with vaccines but with vitamin supplements.

"'I love Diamond & Silk, and so do millions of people,' Trump tweeted in their defense."

(Milbank, Dana; "Trump Tests His Most Promising Coronavirus Antidote: Lies"; *The Washington Post;* 4/28/2020.)

Complicating truth and reason are the president's tacit messages to his cult members. He states publicly that COVID-19 is a serious tragedy and he is doing more to fight it than anyone else on Earth could: We're doing a "beautiful job"; it's a "success story." Then he winks to MAGA devotees by tweeting his love for the ultra-right buffoonish comedy duo masquerading as political pundits, Diamond and Silk.

Donald's evil genius lies in his ability to send two completely conflicting messages simultaneously. This is apart from the galactic fire hose of patent mendacity. Trump can say in the same press briefing: 1) testing is important and that's why he's responsible for the U.S. conducting the most testing in the world; and 2) but it is states' responsibility to do testing and, besides, more testing is not that important to opening up the economy.

The result is that cultists hear one thing: The importance of testing is overblown, probably even a lie perpetuated by the deep state. Critics hear another thing: Trump is playing down the importance of testing while the U.S. per capita testing rate is dismally low. Then when they call him on it he can say, "Testing is important. Testing is not a problem. We're testing more — twice as much — as any other country in the world, combined."

Meanwhile every credible scientific and epidemiological expert in the country says that widespread testing is the only way out of this crisis and U.S. per capita testing still is woefully inadequate.

President Trump implies at his briefings: 1) there is no virus conspiracy, it's real; 2) people should continue social distancing; and 3) he has no intention of firing Dr. Fauci.

Then he tweet-throws love at Diamond and Silk — whom even *Fox News* thinks are over-the-top conspiracy nuts — who: 1) say the deep state has "engineered" the virus to topple Trump; 2) encourage people to ignore the safety guidelines and go "out in the environment"; and 3) host a fire-Anthony-Fauci-crowd scientist who advocates vitamins not vaccines.

Confession

I have a confession to make. I pose on Facebook as a liberal anti-Trump evangelical Caucasian man. (There are a few of "us.") I started this about a month ago and even I was shocked, thunderstruck at the venomous invective hurled by "my fellow Christians" as I respectfully pushed back on their phantasmagoric conspiracy theories and — still to this day — Hillary Clinton vitriol. Donald Trump is their man, a true Christian, and they will walk through rhetorical and maybe even literal fire for him. The cult mentality is frightening.

And while I was in a coma or something, Microsoft co-founder and world-class philanthropist Bill Gates has become a boogeyman for the right and Christian right. Instead of being lauded as a man donating 95% of his many billions of dollars to help citizens of Earth not die, he is pummeled falsely for 1) having decided the world is too populated, 2) conspiring secretly to engineer the coronavirus, and 3) spreading the virus to cull the herd and depopulate the planet. Oh, and Bill is the chief architect of the coming one-world government. White Christian ladies hate him the most.

Whatever happened to Ten Commandments enthusiasts?■

05/07/20 — Dog Bites Man: President Still Incompetent, Corrupt; Pandemic Response Still Horrendous

COVID-19 Deaths

2/06/2020 — U.S.: 1 | World: 620
3/05/2020 — U.S.: 12 | World: 3,293
4/02/2020 — U.S.: 5,137 | World: 48,284
5/07/2020 — U.S.: 73,431 | World: 264,189

(COVID-19 Dashboard by the Center for Systems Science and Engineering at Johns Hopkins University; approximately 8 a.m. each day)

Good Debate or Waste of Time

I love a raucous debate. I've been interested in political debate since my firebrand ninth grade social studies teacher, Gerald ("Gerry") Eggen, taught me how to be a respectful liberal always mindful that the other side has facts, too.

But the sad conclusion about most Trump supporters is that facts, reality, science, and expertise are out the window. Blind passion, inane fantasies, and dangerous idolatry are in — the last point being that much more surprising for Ten Commandments adherents.

Critically thoughtful discussion is possible between two groups of people who fundamentally disagree on issues. But it's not possible when one group dishonestly refuses to accept baseline facts that reasonable people on both sides of the argument do. It's not possible when one group engages in chronic projection and wholesale logical fallacy to disguise its critical weakness on the facts.

It's not possible when one group cites its arguments only from Trump World propaganda sources with few or no journalistic standards of critical analysis and credible corroboration.

When you deny things you know — but wish not — to be true, you are a waste of time. When you deny the veracity of legitimate information sources simply because your leader tells you to, you are a waste of time. When you ask for proof that the sun rises in the east, you're not an honest debater. By those standards of (noncritical) thinking, all truth is deniable and there is no reality except that which your leader deems to exist. Once this intellectual insincerity has been exposed about a person or group, any further attempt at critically thoughtful debate is a colossal waste of time.

Still, how can we get through to that group? A few stragglers might come around. There might still remain for them some Trumpian line of degradation not yet crossed. But for the majority of MAGA supporters there are no lines left, no bridges too far, no bottom too low.

On the other hand, somehow, some way, the middle must be educated and we must outvote the cult. American democracy depends upon it.

MAGA Fans

The sad state of affairs in America is that it remains business as usual at the top of government: President Trump still is depraved and inept; coronavirus testing still is widely unavailable; the White House still is demanding to reopen the U.S. economy at the expense of almost-certain dramatic increases in (second-wave) pandemic deaths; and Donald's "Little Monsters" *(— apologies to Lady Gaga)*, his legion of fans, still refuse to acknowledge his galactic transgressions, which now include MAGA-cide — red state citizens are dying, not just New York (pinko-commie) "reds."

While Trump's own Coronavirus Task Force head, Dr. Anthony Fauci, passionately urges states not to reopen too soon and to follow the White House's own guideline prerequisites for reopening, the president prevaricates as if the good doctor doesn't exist: "The country must reopen — rapidly." "The virus will disappear, with or without a vaccine." "More deaths occur from staying home than disease." "The story is a *Democrat* hoax." "If it's not a hoax, it's China's fault." "Anyone who wants a test can get one" (said months ago, *still* not true).

Models are showing red states — Donald's coveted flyover country — are about to explode with pandemic cases and deaths emanating from new hot spots at meat plants, nursing homes, and prisons. President Trump knowingly is sentencing tens of thousands of people to unnecessary death to prop up the economy for the sole — and I mean *sole* — purpose of getting reelected.

Revised CDC projections leaked by someone in the administration predict that daily COVID-19 deaths nearly will double to 3,000 in the coming weeks. Another prominent forecasting institution has revised its prediction, doubling total U.S. deaths to 135,000. The University of Washington's Institute for Health Metrics and Evaluation (which the White House formerly trusted until Trump didn't like its numbers) incorporated two disturbing factors into their updated projection: 1) poor White House leadership; and 2) poor adherence to social distancing guidelines due to that poor leadership.

Administration Insanity

Just to top off the insanity, note these additional developments. President Trump said Tuesday that he's preparing to disband the Coronavirus Task Force this month — as deaths are rising exponentially. He's blocked the CDC's release of guidelines — "overly specific instructions" — for the safe reopening of businesses because he wants businesses open as soon as possible looking totally normal. The president regularly refuses to wear a mask at pandemic-related photo ops, telling aides it "sends the wrong message." The administration is pushing to relax nursing home infection control regulations. And Donald vowed this week to put a complete end to Obamacare — during a pandemic — even in the face of vehement objections from his own top advisers.

The White House is blocking its entire pandemic-related staff from testifying before Congress. It already fired its top government vaccine development expert, Dr. Rick Bright, because he wouldn't succumb to corrupt pressure to push Trump's (unproved) pet drug, hydroxychloroquine. And Donald already has fired his Health and Human Services inspector general, a career health expert, because the IG issued a factual report the president didn't like.

> [BREAKING NEWS:] President Trump reversed himself a day after announcing plans to disband the White House Coronavirus Task Force. He said, "I had no idea how popular the task force is."

All these developments are efforts to achieve the appearance of pre-pandemic normalcy and jump-start the markets (stock, job, and retail) to get reelected.

Virtual homicide, betrayal of oath and country, and presidential larceny still are not enough to dissuade MAGA believers.

Though I retain hope. Let me reprise my open-mic-moment fantasy. In director Elia Kazan's prophetic 1957 movie, *A Face in the Crowd*, down-home media shyster Lonesome Rhodes (played by Andy Griffith) was riffing with his staff on the set just after bidding good night to the live audience of his wildly popular weekly TV show. While the production credits were rolling, his long-aggrieved, disillusioned manager (and long-suffering love interest) secretly turned the stage microphone back on for all the world to hear:

> "Those morons out there? Shucks, I could take chicken fertilizer and sell it to them as caviar. I could make them eat dog food and think it was steak. Sure, I got 'em like this. You know what the public's like? A cage of Guinea pigs. Good night you stupid idiots. Good night, you miserable

slobs. They're a lot of trained seals. I toss them a dead fish and they'll flap their flippers."

> (Lonesome Rhodes, played by Andy Griffith; Kazan, Elia: director; Schulberg, Budd: writer; *A Face in the Crowd* [motion picture]; 1957.) *(Lonesome saying what he really believed about his fans, unaware they could hear)*

Lonesome Donald. That's got a nice ring.■

05/14/20 — "This Is Why the Whole Concept of Tests Aren't Necessarily Great"

COVID-19 Deaths

2/06/2020 — U.S.: 1 | World: 620
3/05/2020 — U.S.: 12 | World: 3,293
4/02/2020 — U.S.: 5,137 | World: 48,284
5/07/2020 — U.S.: 73,431 | World: 264,189
5/14/2020 — U.S.: 84,136 | World: 297,569

(COVID-19 Dashboard by the Center for Systems Science and Engineering at Johns Hopkins University; approximately 8 a.m. each day)

This Week

This week several famous people produced utterances warranting our attention.

Also this week the United States passed the 80,000-pandemic-deaths marker. Contrary to MAGA supporters I wrestle with on social media, this *is* the news — the man-bites-dog news. The 329,647,808 Americans who have *not* died from COVID-19 are the dog-bites-man news — though good news nonetheless. Trump cultists accuse the media of sensationalizing the bad news and fearmongering to the masses: "Why don't you report all the people who have recovered!?! The *good* news!?!"

That "good" news is reported every day: You simply subtract current number of deaths (84,136) from current number of cases (1,390,764) and you have an approximate number of recoveries. There you go: the pandemic "good" news. Reported daily.

That reminds me of the other man-bites-dog bad news: A little more basic math produces a 6% U.S. mortality rate that has been holding. Additionally a growing number of recovered victims including many children are suffering severe aftereffects that are confounding doctors.

Trumpian Rhetorical Milestone

President Trump says a *yuge* number of galactically dumb things (along with the colossal list of cruel, racist, and mendacious statements). But this week he might have established a superlative milestone on even *his* rhetorical record:

> "She [Vice President Pence's press secretary] tested very good for a long period of time, and then all of a sudden today she tested positive. … [O]ut of the blue. … This is why the whole concept of tests aren't necessarily great. The tests are perfect but something can happen between a test where it's good and something happens."
>
> (Trump, Donald, R-Fla., U.S. president; meeting with congressional Republicans; White House; 5/8/2020.)

Other Trumpian Rhetorical Milestone

> "If we did very little testing, we wouldn't have the most cases. So, in a way, by doing all of this testing, we make ourselves look bad. … [W]e're going to have more cases because we do more testing. Otherwise, you don't know if you have a case."
>
> (Trump, Donald, R-Fla., U.S. president; meeting with Vice President Mike Pence, R-Ind., Gov. Kim Reynolds, R-Iowa; Oval Office; 5/6/2020.)

Cliché Alert: I'm going to use one here but it's (again) such a good one and so apropos: *Oops, he said the quiet part out loud.*

Donald has such an interesting way of framing the truth. If you missed it: He doesn't like coronavirus testing because it finds new cases.

Pundits, critics, experts, nonpartisans, doctors, epidemiologists, virologists, scientists, smart people, and avid news consumers like me have been saying this since February: Trump has been downplaying the pandemic and actively impeding a national testing strategy to keep the numbers down — because high pandemic numbers mean poor economic performance means reelection loss means indictment and possibly prison (or at least major expense and embarrassment).

Dr. Anthony Fauci: Smart, Reasonable

"If you think we have it completely under control, we don't. The consequences [of premature reopening] could be really serious. My concern is that if states or cities or regions … disregard to a greater or lesser degree the checkpoints that we put in our guidelines … there is a real risk that you will trigger an outbreak that you may not be able to control. [That] paradoxically will set you back, not only leading to some suffering and death that could be avoided, but it could even set you back on the road to trying to get economic recovery, because it would almost turn the clock back."

(Fauci, Anthony, Dr., National Institute of Allergy and Infectious Diseases head, White House Coronavirus Task Force medical lead; Senate Health Committee hearing; 5/12/2020.)

Note that Dr. Fauci couched his warnings about opening the U.S. economy prematurely in terms Trump can understand. First he warned of "suffering and death that could be avoided," specifically directed to those with humanity. Then the doctor framed it for the humanity-challenged, i.e., the president: "[I]t could even set you back on the road to trying to get economic recovery."

Self-dealing and corrupt is one thing. *Stupid* is another. Dr. Fauci is telling Trump, in secret code, that if he reopens too early he'll likely sabotage his own venal goal of economic-recovery-at-any-cost to win reelection.

It appears *stupid* still is winning out.

Sen. Rand Paul: Not Smart, Specious and Pompous

> "We ought to have a little bit of humility in our belief that we know what's best for the economy. And as much as I respect you, Dr. Fauci, I don't think you're the end-all. I don't think you're the one person that gets to make a decision. We can listen to your advice, but there are people on the other side saying there's not going to be a surge and [that] we can safely open the economy. And the facts will bear this out."
>
> (Paul, Rand, R-Ky., U.S. senator; Senate Health Committee hearing; 5/12/2020.)

Sen. Paul, sir, no one has ever — ever — argued that Dr. Fauci is the "end-all" decision-maker or *any* kind of decision-maker. This is borne out by the needless catastrophic sickness and death that already has occurred precisely because Donald has *ignored* so much of the doctor's and his team's guidance.

"People on the other side say there's not going to be a surge"? Yeah, "people on the other side" also said the news of the coming pandemic was a "*Democrat* hoax." "People on the other side" said the warnings of a pandemic totally were overblown. They said the virus simply would disappear. "People on the other side" still are saying Bill Gates and George Soros decided the world is too populated, conspired secretly to engineer the coronavirus, and are spreading it to cull the herd and depopulate the planet — "and the facts will bear this out."

Dr. Anthony Fauci Responds — Humbly

"[I] never made myself out to be the end-all and only voice in this. … [T]here are a number of [other officials.] … I'm a scientist, a physician, and a public health official. I give advice, according to the best scientific evidence. I don't give advice about economic things. … [Since] we don't know everything about this virus … we've really got to be very careful, particularly when it comes to children. … I think we better be careful [about opening schools in the fall as Sen. Paul advocates,] … not [be] cavalier, in thinking that children are completely immune to the deleterious effects. … I am very careful, and hopefully humble, in knowing that I don't know everything about this disease. And that's why I'm very reserved in making broad predictions."

(Ibid.; Fauci; 5/12/2020.)

Rand Paul, Even Liz Cheney Thinks You're too Right Wing

"Dr. Fauci is one of the finest public servants we have ever had. He is not a partisan. His only interest is saving lives. We need his expertise and his judgment to defeat this virus. All Americans should be thanking him. Every day."

(Cheney, Liz, R-Wyo., U.S. representative; Twitter post; 5/12/2020.)

If I wore one, my hat would be off to Liz Cheney. She is sure to get major blowback from the president and her party for this.

Stephen Colbert: Funny, Rhetorically Persuasive

"She tested positive, out of the blue. This is why the whole concept of tests aren't necessarily great." *(— President Trump)*

> "In the history of dumb things said by Donald Trump — and remember, there will one day be a library filled with them — that might be the dumbest thing he ever said, putting it in the running for the dumbest thing ever spoken by man. She was tested and didn't have it. Then she got it. Then the next test showed that she had it. Does Trump think the tests are good only if they tell you news you want to hear? *My girlfriend took a pregnancy test, it said she wasn't pregnant. Then we had a bunch of sex. Then, for some reason, all of a sudden, the test said she's having a baby. That's why these tests aren't so great. The tests should start wearing a condom.*"
>
> (Colbert, Stephen; *CBS' Late Show* with Stephen Colbert; 5/11/2020.)

Your White House at Work

In the week or so since President Trump mandated closed (due to virus outbreaks) meat producers to reopen, and open ones to stay open, a dozen or more major-meat-plant-virus-hot-spots have exploded with infections. These new outbreaks have pushed the U.S. confirmed cases number 19% higher over this time. The counties in which they're located have seen up to 40% increases in COVID-19 contractions.

In an attempt to bring the numbers down, Gov. Pete Ricketts (R-Neb.) ordered his state health officials to cease sharing figures about how many workers have been infected at each plant. The Nebraska data blackout covers four of the Top 10 U.S. counties with meat plant hot spots measuring the highest per capita infection rates.

Meanwhile Donald tweet-supports the "liberation" of Democratic states and tweet-loves his GOP governors.

[FUN FACT NO. 1:] After Dr. Fauci relayed his dire warnings to the Senate this week, President Trump became enraged. The next day he said the doctor was "playing both sides" and that he "didn't accept" the warnings.

[FUN FACT NO 2:] The White House has been pressuring the CDC to change their COVID-19 death-counting parameters, which would modify the numbers downward. This comes as Dr. Fauci is warning that the current numbers already represent a significant *undercount*.

[FUN FACT NO. 3:] *The Associated Press* reports the CDC's detailed guidelines for reopening the economy have been prepared and "signed off on by the director" for the last month. The White House, however, has blocked the release, quietly informing CDC officials their guidelines "would never see the light of day."■

05/21/20 — 2020 Grads: No Presidential Role Model (or Soup) for You

COVID-19 Deaths

2/06/2020 — U.S.: 1 | World: 620
3/05/2020 — U.S.: 12 | World: 3,293
4/02/2020 — U.S.: 5,137 | World: 48,284
5/07/2020 — U.S.: 73,431 | World: 264,189
5/21/2020 — U.S.: 93,439 | World: 328,565

(COVID-19 Dashboard by the Center for Systems Science and Engineering at Johns Hopkins University; approximately 8 a.m. each day)

Looking Back

Last Saturday night I watched the national virtual graduation ceremony for 2020 high school seniors. Their literal ceremony, prom, and standard end-of-year senior shenanigans were preempted by a once-in-a-century deadly pandemic. Didn't recognize half the performing artists. To be expected. Did recognize the keynote speaker (Barack Obama). So nice to see his comforting face and hear his reassuring tone.

As those of us born before 2002 approach the anniversary of our own high school graduation, I can't help but review the time gone by. Contrary to the universal admonition not to beat oneself up over past mistakes and poor decisions, I still find myself nursing self-inflicted bruises and aching bones over taking the wrong forks in the roads *(— thanks to Yogi Berra, New York Yankees)*. So many things I would've done differently except for meeting and marrying my tremendous partner of 38 years who has kept me and the family as steady as possible.

But I'm where I am now. Don't you wish you could grab those 2020 seniors by the throat and point them in the right direction? No, I know. Most will find their own right direction. And as several parents on the show averred, they've learned more from their graduating offspring than vice versa.

So this is my goal going forward: to resist set-in-my-ways age inertia, to keep learning from others, especially young adults, and to keep strengthening my empathy muscle. I might not have recognized the artists H.E.R. and Bad Bunny, but I'm up on Malala.

Role Models

Many of the graduating 2020 seniors will be role models in the years to come. In the meantime they *need* good role models now. Sadly the current president is not one.

In 1993 NBA star Charles Barkley, then a Phoenix Sun, famously proclaimed:

> "I'm not paid to be a role model. I'm paid to wreak havoc on the basketball court."

Barkley had been embroiled in several un-role-model-like incidents including attempting to spit on a racial-slur-slinging heckler sitting courtside during a game. Charles' celebrity spittle found its way onto an innocent young girl's blouse. The incident made news at the time. To his credit Mr. Barkley later tracked down the girl and her family, apologized, and befriended them with complementary Suns tickets.

Shortly after Charles Barkley's not-a-role-model declaration, a fellow NBA star, "The Mailman" (he delivered on the court), Utah Jazz power forward Karl Malone, responded in a June 14, 1993, *Sports Illustrated* column titled "One Role Model to Another":

"Charles … I don't think it's your decision to make. We don't choose to be role models, we are chosen. Our only choice is whether to be a good role model or a bad one."

Ultimately Barkley role-modeled behavior to which we all wish our kids would aspire: He made a mistake, owned it, apologized for it, and made amends. In the years since, Charles Barkley has been a mixed role-modeling bag, a sometimes brawler but known as a man of humor and honesty.

It has been noted famously, even by supporters, that President Trump is not a role model mothers and fathers want their kids to look up to. In fact many parents of juveniles rush to change the television channel if the president is speaking and their children are in the room.

My contention is that you can't think a president's policies are good if you also don't think he or she is a good role model for kids. The two are inextricably intertwined, joined at the hip, and several other redundant phrases meaning *tightly connected*. I'm with Karl Malone. To paraphrase: "Presidents don't choose to be role models, they are chosen. Their only choice is whether to be a good role model or a bad one."

Graduating seniors of 2020 here's a list of presidential Trumpian behaviors *not* to emulate.

The List

— Don't make up lies about where your non-Caucasian adversaries were born.

— Don't disparage the judge overseeing your company's fraud trial because of where his parents were born.

— Don't disparage a prisoner-of-war hero's service to our country simply because that hero criticized your policies.

— Don't make numerous, disparaging remarks about the opposite gender even if the remarks *aren't* being recorded.

— Don't call a woman a "fat pig" or accuse her of having "blood coming out of her wherever" if she asks you a tough but fair question.

— Don't kiss, grope, or make other sexual overtures toward members of the human race without their permission.

— Don't disparage the grief of Gold Star parents (those who have lost a daughter or son fighting for the U.S. military) simply because those parents disagree with your policies.

— Don't call for the death penalty for five exonerated-beyond-a-DNA-doubt innocent young men simply because they are non-Caucasian.

— Don't lie more than 18,000 times in three and a half years.

— Don't assign every adversary or critic a public, ad hominemistic junior-high-school-put-down nickname, then shower them with additional disparaging remarks (accurate or not) about their appearance and career success.

— Don't call countries that have populations comprising ethnicities you don't like "sh*thole countries."

— Don't consistently revert to disparaging any news source information you don't like as "FAKE NEWS!"

— Don't consistently pressure your friends to lie and cheat for you, then chastise them when they refuse.

— Don't say, "Why was there a Civil War? Why could that one not have been worked out?"

— Don't say, "Many of them are fine people" when referring to neo-Nazis marching with torches and chanting "Jews will not replace us!" at a Confederate statue-supporting counterprotest.

— Don't lie about the popular vote that you lost. Demonstrate good sportsmanship by being a gracious loser.
— Don't blatantly pitch your private businesses to foreign diplomats and domestic political allies for illegal profit.
— Don't let your adult children (or children-in-law) presidential advisers pitch their private businesses for illegal profit in the course of government duties. Better yet don't nepotistically appoint them to high-level White House advisory positions for which they hopelessly are unqualified.
— Don't collude with a foreign adversary while minutely calibrating that collusion so that it's *just shy* of criminal.
— Don't separate frightened foreign-born children from their parents by locking them in cages indefinitely — without proper diet, hygiene, and health care — because their parents are desperate or might have used poor emigration judgment.
— Don't double your Palm Beach private club initiation fees from $200,000 to $400,000 five days after taking office.
— Don't order an ethnically targeted travel ban seven days after taking office without telling any of your Cabinet or other government agencies. It might cause worldwide havoc.
— Don't eliminate numerous health and safety regulations and programs that save the lives of children and other living things.
— Don't disparage national retail brands because they decided to discontinue your daughter's line of fashions.
— Don't consistently disparage U.S. allies and obsequiously cozy up to world dictators.
— Don't eliminate ethics courses, terminate ethics department heads, and fire inspectors general who uncover wrongdoing by your political allies or bad news about you.
— Don't accuse your predecessor, with zero evidence, of nonexistent illegal acts and various phony scandals.

— Don't ignore a pandemic that is projected to kill 100,000 to 240,000 Americans — or far more depending upon your incompetence and corruption — because you need the economy to improve to be reelected to avoid multiple indictments.

— Don't lie to the country that you're taking a dangerous drug as a prophylactic against the aforementioned pandemic virus just to "prove" yourself right about promoting that unproved drug — a drug contra-recommended by your own FDA, CDC, and pandemic task force doctors.

— Don't obstruct justice (over 10 times that we know of).

— Don't systematically end all your predecessor's (or predecessor's wife's) indisputably good programs simply because you're consumed by hateful jealousy because you can never — and I mean *never* — be the person he is.

— Don't urge your supporters to inflict physical violence on journalists or other living things that report information you don't like.

— Don't say to a high-ranking Russian official visiting the Oval Office, "I just fired the head of the FBI. He was crazy, a real nut job. ... I faced great pressure because of Russia. That's taken off."

— Don't say in response to a pandemic, "Testing is overrated ... if we don't do as much testing, we have less cases ... it's common sense." Additionally in response, don't say, "I take no responsibility," and "I wouldn't have done anything differently."

There are so many more. Play the home game, fun for the entire family. See how many Trumpian *don'ts* you and your friends can add to each list.

———

In pandemic news this week, a statistic (and life) slapped me upside the head. The United States makes up 4.3% of the world's population, but it accounts for 28.4% of the world's COVID-19 death toll.

What else do you need to know to question President Trump's pandemic response?∎

05/27/20 — Trump Owns all Future Churchgoer Pandemic Deaths

COVID-19 Deaths

2/06/2020 — U.S.: 1 | World: 620
3/05/2020 — U.S.: 12 | World: 3,293
4/02/2020 — U.S.: 5,137 | World: 48,284
5/07/2020 — U.S.: 73,431 | World: 264,189
5/27/2020 — U.S.: 100,000 | World: 354,584

(COVID-19 Dashboard by the Center for Systems Science and Engineering at Johns Hopkins University)

Presidential Decree

"I call upon governors to allow our churches and places of worship to open right now. If there's any questions, they're going to have to call me, but they are not going to be successful in that call. … The people are demanding to go to church, and synagogue, go to their mosque. Many millions of Americans embrace worship as an essential part of life. … The governors need to do the right thing and allow these very important essential places of faith to open right now — for this weekend. If they don't do it, I will override the governors. In America, we need more prayer, not less."

(Trump, Donald, R-Fla., U.S. president; national address; White House; 5/22/2020.)

It's official: The same week the U.S. passed a grimmest of milestones — 100,000 pandemic deaths — President Trump ordered churches and other houses of worship opened for business as of Memorial Day weekend. (Clearly he did this to shore up his evangelical base.) The order doesn't consider how any given state's pandemic curve is trending. It doesn't consider if a church happens to reside in a county hot spot. It doesn't consider if the meat packing plant down the road was one of the many in the country recently shut down due to an explosion of COVID-19 infections and deaths — then forced to reopen by the president because his meat producer CEO friends convinced him America needs its meat at any cost.

To their credit, many faith leaders and governors are keeping their houses of worship closed to save lives despite Donald's order. They know the Lord also lives on the internet and in one's home and heart during pandemic emergencies.

Trump Owns Future Churchgoer Deaths

The country is not safe enough for churches to reopen across the land. This means that every new coronavirus death suffered by a churchgoer will be tied directly to Trump. There's no way around this. Maybe he thinks a certain number of deaths among the faithful is the "price of liberty." Maybe he thinks that number will be 100 or 1,000. I mean, any of these numbers would be — in Donald's words — only "a small percentage" of total pandemic deaths. Or maybe it will be 100,000 more or 200,000 more in a second wave — caused by President Trump's perverse pandemic response. Either way he'll be responsible directly for them all.

The president said that if governors defy his order he "will override the governors." Of course he does not have that power. Even his press secretary, an expert equivocator whom he left dangling in the wind to answer reporters' questions after his statement, grossly fumbled this equivocation about "hypothetical questions" of presidential power.

In his statement, Trump noted he has called upon the CDC to issue reopening guidelines for churches and that state and local officials should reopen "safely." He's given himself an out. If 100,000 churchgoers die over the next few months, he can blame governors for not reopening houses of worship "safely."

Churches should not be reopened. Churches pack together many bodies into enclosed spaces — creating exactly the best conditions for virus spread exceeded only by nursing homes, prisons, and meat plants. It was reported this week that 20 states are experiencing *increases* in pandemic infections and deaths, up from 13 states last week. I see a trend. Only a handful of states have met the White House's own guideline prerequisites for reopening: including recording a *two-week daily decrease* in numbers. Yet at the president's urging, all 50 states are at some stage of reopening for the first time since Washington state started shutting down early in the year.

Much of the Real Power Resides in Presidential Influence

The president does not have the power to override governors. But he does have the mighty power of influence, especially over his supporters and passive news consumers. When the president plays down the intensity of the pandemic and importance of safety guidelines, he influences people toward sickness and death. When he refuses to model safe behavior like wearing a mask and maintaining social distancing, he influences people toward sickness and death. When he says he can override governors, he can't, but his followers believe he can — thus they are influenced toward sickness and death in the name of supporting their cult leader.

Why does President Trump do this? Does he want more people to die unnecessarily? I don't believe the president *wants* more people to die, but he is willing to *allow* and *accept* more death to shore up the economy to win reelection. I know. As I write this, it's still hard to believe this is true of an American president. But the facts are not in dispute. These are part of the *corruption* and *amorality* components of Trump leadership.

Power of Incompetency

Here's the great irony. If Donald would have done the right thing in the beginning: led by (good) example; shuttered or tightened government facilities and businesses where possible and issued guidelines for governors to do the same; established and supported national social distancing guidelines; let the CDC do its job; fully implemented the Defense Production Act of 1950 to produce ventilators and PPE; established a national response for testing, tracing, and isolation; instituted a national supply chain so states would not be competing with HHS, FEMA, and other states for supplies — if the president would have done these things, he'd have half the total death count, a recovering economy, and the admiration of a grateful nation.

In other words if he had done what President *Obama* would have done, President Trump would have strengthened his reelection chances anyway. This represents the *incompetence* component of Trump leadership.

Presidential Response to a Grim Milestone

By the way: How did the two presidential candidates, the Democratic challenger and the Republican incumbent, mark this most solemn of dark milestones, the 100,000th COVID-19 death of an American?

Senator Joe Biden

> "My fellow Americans, there are moments in our history so grim, so heart-rending, that they're forever fixed in each of our hearts, as shared grief. Today is one of those moments: 100,000 lives have now been lost to this virus, here in the United States alone. Each one leaving behind a family that will never again be whole.

"I think I know how you're feeling. You feel like you're being sucked into a black hole in the middle of your chest. It's suffocating. Your heart is broken, and there's nothing but a feeling of emptiness. For most of you, you weren't able to be there when you lost your beloved family member, or best friend. For most of you, you weren't able to be there when they died, alone. …

"To all of you who are hurting so badly, I'm so sorry for your loss. I know there's nothing that I or anyone else can say or do to dull the sharpness of the pain you feel right now. But I can promise you from experience, the day will come when the memory of your loved one will bring a smile to your lips before it brings a tear to your eyes. My prayer for all of you is that day will come sooner rather than later. But I promise you it will come. And when it does, you know you can make it.

"God bless each and every one of you and the blessed memory of the one you lost. This nation grieves with you. Take some solace from the fact that we all grieve with you."

> (Biden, Joe, D-Del., 2020 U.S. presidential candidate, former U.S. senator; national address; 5/27/2020.)

President Donald J. Trump

"'[Donald Trump] is arguably the greatest president in our history.' Thank you @LouDobbs!"

> (Trump, Donald, R-Fla., U.S. president; Twitter post; 5/27/2020.) *(President Trump made no mention of the 100,000-death marker today, but he did retweet this pronouncement from Fox News' Lou Dobbs about an hour after the marker was hit)*■

05/27/2020 — Black Lives Matter Protests Erupt

05/25/2020 — George Floyd Is Murdered During Routine, Minor-Offense Encounter by Minneapolis Police Officer on Duty

06/01/2020 — President Trump Orders Federal Forces to Clear Legal, Peaceful D.C. Protesters for Photo Op, Using Rubber Bullets, Tear Gas, Flash-Bang Shells

06/04/20 — "Blessed Are the Peacemakers," Bunker Boy Trump Can Go to Hell

COVID-19 Deaths

2/06/2020 — U.S.: 1 | World: 620
3/05/2020 — U.S.: 12 | World: 3,293
4/02/2020 — U.S.: 5,137 | World: 48,284
5/07/2020 — U.S.: 73,431 | World: 264,189
6/04/2020 — U.S.: 107,175 | World: 386,464

(COVID-19 Dashboard by the Center for Systems Science and Engineering at Johns Hopkins University; approximately 8 a.m. each day)

Can President Trump do *nothing* right? Is there really no bottom to his incompetent, unscrupulous responses to the three major crises facing our country today: the worst (still raging) pandemic since 1918; the first U.S. depression since the 1930s; and civil unrest not seen since the 1960s?

Of course the president didn't start any of these. But there is no thinking person who doesn't believe Donald has exacerbated each of these crises exponentially. Between Inauguration Day and early this year it has been postulated often that Trump has done no real damage yet because he has had no significant crisis to respond to.

I disagree with the premise: Trump *has* caused major damage to American democracy and the country's psyche by creating his own crises and clearly violating the Constitution. But I wholly agree that now that major external crises have landed at his feet, the additional damage his responses have caused is enormous and increasing galactically.

George Floyd

On Memorial Day, Minneapolis resident George Floyd, a Black man, was summarily executed by a city police officer while three police officer co-workers stood by and watched. During what should have been a calm, low-key arrest for suspicion of passing a counterfeit $20 bill at a convenience store, Mr. Floyd, unarmed, was handcuffed and taken to the ground. Though he did not resist, an officer held a knee to his neck for almost nine (9) minutes.

During the first seven (7) minutes or so — while he still was conscious — George Floyd pleaded repeatedly, "I can't breathe!" Twice before he lost consciousness he called out for his deceased mother. During the last two (2) minutes or so, Mr. Floyd was "nonresponsive." In fact one of the three standing-by officers felt for a pulse when the nonresponsiveness manifested and announced he felt none. The knee remained on George's neck during those last two (2) minutes until other units arrived. George Floyd was pronounced dead at Hennepin County Medical Center.

Donald Trump — Has No Clue

Since March we've had a raging coronavirus pandemic and an accompanying economic depression. People are out of work. People have been sheltering in place to avoid virus spread. Racial tensions, already high and insufficiently addressed before the Trump era, have increased dramatically under this — let's just cut the euphemisms — *racist* president.

Now one more (caught-on-video) racist offense by police — the senseless, wanton murder of an unarmed, handcuffed, nonresistant African American man — has sparked massive protests, among all ethnicities, spanning 10 days and 100 American cities.

Granted, there have been multiple layers of violence with looters looting and thugs thugging. Trump blames this all on the loosely organized *antifa*, the anti-fascist ("What's wrong with being anti-fascist?" — *apologies to Spinal Tap*) hodgepodge of like-minded activists he's been using as a boogeyman for several years. But the FBI has found no evidence of antifa involvement in the violence and looting accompanying some protests. Many cooler heads suspect some of it is white supremacist groups posing as protesters, attempting to assign false blame and do their standard incite-racial-tensions thing.

In any event, how did the United States president attempt to dissipate the tension, cool passions, lower the temperature, and bring the country together?

"When the Tweeting Starts, the Stupid Starts. Thank You"

"When the looting starts, the shooting starts. Thank you."

"[White House protesters could] have been greeted with the most vicious dogs, and most ominous weapons, I have ever seen."

"Tonight, I understand, is MAGA NIGHT AT THE WHITE HOUSE???"

"We have our military ready, willing and able if [governors] ever want to call our military. We can have troops on the ground very quickly."

"[The protests are being spread by] antifa and the violent left."

"If a city or a state refuses to take the actions that are necessary … then I will deploy the United States military and quickly solve the problem for them."

<blockquote>
"I am dispatching thousands and thousands of heavily armed soldiers, military personnel and law enforcement officers to stop the rioting, looting, vandalism."

"I want you governors to dominate the streets. … Too many of you are weak and jerks."

(Trump, Donald, R-Fla., U.S. president; assorted tweets, statements; May 26-30, 2020.)
</blockquote>

As one pundit put it, rather than reaching out, Trump has been thumping his chest. Then last Friday he was spirited to a safe room — a "bunker" — below the White House for about an hour, after protesters gathered along 1600 Pennsylvania Avenue and nearby Lafayette Square. Then for a few days he became "Bunker Boy," the narrative being Trump is weak and scared of a few protesters — while his Democratic presidential opponent, Joe Biden, joined protesters in solidarity.

On Monday President Trump emerged to make his first public statements about the protests. Over the past few days, White House aides had debated the wisdom of a Trump address and decided against it fearing he would make the situation worse. Donald changed course and read scripted "American Carnage" remarks in the Rose Garden that evening. His aides were right.

"Then the Chaos Began"

<blockquote>
"Then the chaos began. Members of the National Guard knelt briefly to put on gas masks, before suddenly charging eastward down H Street, pushing protesters down toward 17th Street. Authorities shoved protesters down with their shields, fired rubber bullets directly at them, released tear gas and set off flash-bang shells in the middle of the crowd. Protesters began running, many still with their hands up,
</blockquote>

shouting, 'Don't shoot.' Others were vomiting, coughing, and crying.

"As Trump began to speak, some protesters took a knee several blocks from the White House, again yelling, 'Hands up! Don't shoot!' But they were never able to stay kneeling for more than a couple of minutes, because authorities kept pushing them forward, as a thick, yellow cloud of smoke hung over the crowd."

(Parker, Ashley & Dawsey, Josh & Tan, Rebecca; "Inside the Push to Tear-Gas Protesters Ahead of a Trump Photo Op"; *The Washington Post*; 6/1/2020.)

Then Trump strolled down forcibly-cleared-by-federal-troops-on-horseback-of-100%-peaceful-protesters H Street, past Lafayette Square, to the steps of iconic St. John's Episcopal Church. He stood uncomfortably for several minutes, ultimately framed by a half-dozen or so top lieutenants. He offered no comments or prayers. He held an upside-down Bible over his head to consummate his would-be-cartoonish-if-not-so-damaging-to-the-country photo op.

"When Trump had returned safely to the White House less than an hour later, the verdict seemed clear: The president had staged an elaborate photo op, using a Bible awkwardly held aloft as a prop and a historic church that has long welcomed presidents and their families as a backdrop. In the process, protesters had been tear-gassed and attacked, and Trump had taken a raging conflagration and doused it with accelerant.

"'We long ago lost sight of normal, but this was a singularly immoral act,' said Brendan Buck, a longtime former Hill aide who is now a Republican operative. 'The president used force against American citizens, not to protect property, but to soothe his own insecurities. We will all move on to the next outrage, but this was a true abuse of power and should not be forgotten.'"

(Ibid.; Parker, Dawsey, & Tan; 6/1/2020.)

The Right Reverend Mariann Budde, bishop of the Episcopal Diocese of Washington, responded for the nation:

"I am outraged. I am the bishop of the Episcopal Diocese of Washington and was not given even a courtesy call, that they would be clearing [the area] with tear gas so they could use one of our churches as a prop. … Everything [President Trump] has said and done is to inflame violence. We need moral leadership, and he's done everything to divide us."

(Budde, Mariann, Right Reverend, Episcopal bishop of Washington, D.C.; telephone interview with *The Washington Post;* 6/1/2020.)

James Mattis

On Wednesday night former U.S. Secretary of Defense James Mattis, President Trump's first Defense Department head, had finally had enough of the president's corruption and incompetence. Mattis left the administration at the end of 2018 in protest of Trump's plan to withdraw all U.S. troops from Syria. He also said in his resignation letter that he cannot agree with an administration that aligns with dictators and disrespects our allies.

But otherwise Mr. Mattis has remained unwilling to criticize a sitting president and former superior. Many political leaders including prominent anti-Trump Republicans and conservatives have been calling on him to break his silence (it's been reported widely that privately he thinks little of the president or his leadership). Secretary Mattis is loved and respected universally throughout the military as a retired charismatic four-star Marine Corp general who has served under Democratic and Republican presidents. Last night the dam finally broke:

> "I have watched this week's unfolding events, angry and appalled. The words 'Equal Justice Under Law' are carved in the pediment of the United States Supreme Court. This is precisely what protesters are rightly demanding. It is a wholesome and unifying demand — one that all of us should be able to get behind. …

> "When I joined the military, some 50 years ago, I swore an oath to support and defend the Constitution. Never did I dream that troops taking that same oath would be ordered under any circumstance to violate the constitutional rights of their fellow citizens — much less to provide a bizarre photo op for the elected commander in chief, with military leadership standing alongside. …

> "Donald Trump is the first president in my lifetime who does not try to unite the American people — does not even pretend to try. Instead he tries to divide us. We are witnessing the consequences of three years of this deliberate effort. We are witnessing the consequences of three years without mature leadership. We can unite without him, drawing on the strengths inherent in our civil society. This will not be easy, as the past few days have shown, but we owe it to our fellow citizens; to past generations that bled to defend our promise; and to our children.

> "We can come through this trying time stronger, and with a renewed sense of purpose and respect for one another. … We know that we are better than the abuse of executive authority that we witnessed in Lafayette Square. We must reject and hold accountable those in office who would make

a mockery of our Constitution. Only by … returning to the original path of our founding ideals will we again be a country admired and respected at home and abroad."

> (Mattis, James, former [Trump] secretary of defense, retired four-star Marine Corp general; letter to *The Atlantic;* as cited in Goldberg, Jeffrey; "James Mattis Denounces President Trump, Describes Him as a Threat to the Constitution"; *The Atlantic;* 6/3/2020.)

Barack Obama

In other news, last night former President Barack Obama addressed the My Brother's Keeper Alliance (part of The Obama Foundation) and the nation with a plea of understanding and unity. In his address he reminded the American people what a president looks like.■

06/05/2020 — Democratic Presidential Nomination: Joe Biden Clinches

06/11/20 — Why Wide Acceptance of "Black Lives Matter" Now? Trump, of Course

COVID-19 Deaths

2/06/2020 — U.S.: 1 | World: 620
3/05/2020 — U.S.: 12 | World: 3,293
4/02/2020 — U.S.: 5,137 | World: 48,284
5/07/2020 — U.S.: 73,431 | World: 264,189
6/04/2020 — U.S.: 107,175 | World: 386,464
6/11/2020 — U.S.: 112,924 | World: 417,133

(COVID-19 Dashboard by the Center for Systems Science and Engineering at Johns Hopkins University; approximately 8 a.m. each day)

Today's Quote

"White-male-centric xenophobia is the beating heart of Trumpism."

This is a quote from my good friend and ideological brother, American philosopher Bob O. I've been sitting on it for a few months, waiting for an applicable opportunity to tie it into current events. As the coronavirus pandemic began consuming news cycles in late January, the focus turned toward President Trump's other faults: primarily the corruption, incompetence, and amorality inherent in allowing some 50,000 unnecessary U.S. deaths. He's responded to the crisis by callously not responding to it, attempting to play it down, attempting to convince the country it has been wished away.

What has this accomplished? The exact opposite of what he wanted. Besides the deadly humanitarian effects, his (lack of) response has crippled the stock market, ballooned the unemployment rate, and threatened the president's one long-shot chance at reelection: his claim to have shepherded a booming U.S. economy — the greatest economy in Earth's 6,000-year history (shout out to his evangelicals). Never mind that Trump's (formerly) great economy was built squarely on the positively trending economic achievements of his predecessor, President Barack Obama, and all Donald had to do was not screw it up.

Memorial Day

Then came Memorial Day. Then came George Floyd, a 46-year old African American Minnesota resident accused of using a counterfeit $20 bill to buy a pack of cigarettes. Mr. Floyd, unarmed and unthreatening, was handcuffed by police and taken to the pavement of the Minneapolis street outside the small market he had just been in. A few bystanders began video recording the incident with their smartphones. Though the suspect did not resist, Officer Derek Chauvin held a knee to his neck for eight minutes and 46 seconds. Three other city cops stood by to help hold Floyd down and keep concerned bystanders at bay.

During the first six minutes — while he was still conscious — George Floyd pleaded at least 16 times, "I can't breathe!" Several times he injected a respectful, "sir," as in, "Sir, I can't breathe!" Before he lost consciousness he begged, "Don't kill me!" and twice called out for his deceased mother.

During the last two to three minutes, Mr. Floyd was limp. In fact one of the standing-by officers felt for a pulse when the suspect became unconscious and announced he felt none. No officer offered medical assistance. Derek Chauvin's knee remained on George's neck during those final minutes. An ambulance arrived. The officer maintained his position for almost another minute. A medic instructed Chauvin to free the suspect's throat, which occurred at the 8-minute, 46-second mark. George Floyd later was declared dead at Minneapolis' Hennepin County Medical Center.

Protests

The protests began within 48 hours. Record-setting. Across 100 American cities. Comprising all ethnicities. Including even the nicest of Caucasian families.

In the days after George Floyd's murder, Trump was beside himself, consumed with ineptitude and fear. Massive but largely peaceful protests were overwhelming the streets and park outside the White House. That Friday he had been humiliated with the label "Bunker Boy" for being whisked by the Secret Service to a safe compartment below ground for an hour while his arch enemy and presidential opponent, Joe Biden (D-Del.), visited the streets in fellowship with protesters.

Donald had to show toughness. So he ordered the 100%-nonviolent, legal protesters to be cleared by federal officers on horseback firing rubber bullets, releasing tear gas, and setting off flash-bang shells amid the crowd.

He did it. He cleared the bastards. Then Trump strolled down H Street, past now-protester-free Lafayette Square, to the steps of St. John's Episcopal Church. He made no public comments. He held a Bible over his head and ultimately was flanked by several of his top aides and leaders to pose for a photo op.

> [FUN FACT:] Gen. Mark Milley, current Joint Chiefs of Staff chair, later publicly apologized for appearing at Trump's Bible photo op, saying he "never should have been there."

Since the president's egregious use of military force on peacefully protesting citizens of his own country, and his threats to escalate those attacks, Mr. Trump has been excoriated by a dozen current or retired three- and four-star generals including James Mattis, Michael

Mullen, John Kelly, Douglas Lute, Martin Dempsey, Colin Powell, David Petraeus, and William McRaven. This list includes four former Joint Chiefs of Staff chairs and various Cabinet secretaries.

Retired four-star Marine Corp Gen. John R. Allen, former commander of the NATO International Security Assistance Force and U.S. Forces – Afghanistan, said Trump's use of federal force against peaceful citizens "may well signal the beginning of the end of the American experiment."

The Question

But one question has loomed since George Floyd's death: Why are *these* protests setting national records for number of sites, participation size, duration, and broad ethnic makeup?

Since the incident Memorial Day, May 25, protests have continued to spread across 100-plus large cities and many smaller — some formerly identified by racial intolerance — communities. They've continued growing with record turnouts for the 17th consecutive day. And they are attended by the widest cross-section of racially diverse participants ever seen in civil rights demonstrations. Cap these milestones with several poll results showing widespread support for the protests. The respected CNN/SSRS data reporting poll this week cites a whopping 84% of Americans believe the George Floyd, Black Lives Matter protests are justified.

What Has Changed?

What has changed? First, the multiple-video evidence of George Floyd's murder-by-cop is airtight, indisputable, and has been internet-propagated at the peak of the smartphone age.

Second, Donald Trump has been president for three and a half years and even many Caucasian families have had it up to here *(index finger at nostril level)* with his blatant racism, not to mention, as I've said, his other faults.

The apathetic, casual-news-consuming middle has been moved. To quote another of my favorite American philosophers, *SNL*'s Pete Davidson, and his rhetorical question to one of the "Weekend Update" hosts about being affected by the righteous protests: "Colin, you know how wrong about politics you have to be for, like, *me* to notice!?"

Well the passive center finally has been moved to notice Trump's galactic "wrongness about politics," his despicability concerning racial bigotry, and more. Even the damn lily-white-owner-representing NFL commissioner, Roger Goodell, has apologized publicly for the NFL's opposition to San Francisco Forty-Niners quarterback Colin Kaepernick respectfully protesting police brutality. Four seasons ago Kaepernick began taking a knee during the National Anthem before games.

> [FUN FACT:] Kaepernick's Forty-Niners contract was up after the 2016-2017 season, and he has been blackballed from the league since then.

This Has Changed

This shift among the passive center has supercharged the massive dissent against drastically statistically high police mistreatment of African Americans, primarily Black men. Get this: The protests are justified, say 84% of Americans. You can't find 84% of Americans who know what the First Amendment is all about. You can't find 84% of Americans who all like ice cream.

That's what is different from the civil rights protests of the 1960s and other movements leading up to Trump's presidency. The intensity of the George Floyd, Black Lives Matter cause has merged with the until-now-quiet disapproval of Donald Trump racism, turpitude, and chronic mendacity.

"White-male-centric xenophobia is the beating heart of Trumpism." And here, the xenophobia includes the Trump white-male-centric base's contention that African American (and other *ethnic*) citizens shouldn't be here in the first place and they should all "go back where they came from."

Even the politest of WASP's in largely segregated suburbs no longer can stomach video evidence of a pattern of violent and murderous police behavior toward Black men. Even the most genteel white people no longer recoil at the slogan "Black Lives Matter" and can explain the folly of responding with "All Lives Matter" or even worse, "White Lives Matter."

Even the nicest of Caucasian families now are willing to disapprove publicly of the worst criminal, self-dealing, anti-constitutional behavior of an American president in Earth's history — all 6,000 years.■

06/18/20 — GOP Senators: Nothing to See Here, Business as Usual

COVID-19 Deaths

2/06/2020 — U.S.: 1 | World: 620
3/05/2020 — U.S.: 12 | World: 3,293
4/02/2020 — U.S.: 5,137 | World: 48,284
5/07/2020 — U.S.: 73,431 | World: 264,189
6/04/2020 — U.S.: 107,175 | World: 386,464
6/18/2020 — U.S.: 117,717 | World: 449,397

(COVID-19 Dashboard by the Center for Systems Science and Engineering at Johns Hopkins University; approximately 8 a.m. each day)

This Week

Under President Trump, America's house on the otherwise decent world-community block continues to deteriorate. It desperately needs a paint job. The roof is sagging. The yard is overgrown with weeds. Several junk cars crowd the driveway. The head of household is a degenerate con man. And drunken family fights regularly overflow into the street on summer nights.

Even Jed Clampett says they've brought the neighborhood down.

Pandemic

Donald Trump still is perverse. In continuing attempts to downplay the pandemic, he said June 15, "If we stop [coronavirus] testing right now, we'd have very few cases, actually." In a mocking response, some smart*ss somewhere said, "And if we stop pregnancy testing right now, this family wouldn't have so many damn kids." Nine states are recording record-high daily new cases including Oklahoma, site of Trump's upcoming Saturday rally (his first since "reopening" the country and restarting his campaign).

Also June 15 the president instructed his vice president, Mike Pence, to exhort governors on a conference call to lie to citizens that the current surge in cases is due largely to increased testing. Virtually all credible experts dispute that. Why the disingenuous, prevaricacious attempts to play down pandemic danger? To reopen the country, kick-start the economy, and get reelected. Meanwhile people are dying needlessly due to inept and reprobate White House leadership.

Police Reform

In a transparently empty attempt to show he's responding to the nationwide, record-setting protests against police brutality (including murder) toward Black and brown citizens, President Trump held a roundtable discussion on policing and race in Dallas June 11. But he forgot on purpose to include three top law enforcement professionals in the county — who are African American: the district attorney, Dallas police chief, and county sheriff.

Meanwhile the Atlanta cop who shot and killed Rayshard Brooks in a Wendy's — the crime being falling asleep in his car while waiting in the drive-thru line — was seen on video kicking the Black suspect after shooting him dead. The officer has been charged with felony murder.

Trump wants to study law enforcement's use of chokeholds.

John Bolton's New Book

Also this week, copies of former Trump national security adviser John Bolton's tell-all book describing his 17-month White House tenure have been leaked to reporters despite DOJ attempts to block it even at this late stage. Among the neutron bomb revelations threatening to blow the lid off this presidency: 1) Donald adopted "obstruction of justice as a way of life"; 2) Secretary of State Mike Pompeo noted to Bolton of the president: "He's so full of sh*t"; 3) Donald didn't know Britain was a nuclear power; 4) Donald had to ask Bolton, "Is Finland part of Russia?"; 5) to seek a better trade deal, Donald approved of China supreme leader Xi Jinping's plan to build concentration camps for its Uighur Muslim minority; 6) Donald "pleaded" with Xi for reelection help in the form of trade concessions; and 7) most shocking of all, Donald lacked the respect of numerous people around him, and many ostensibly hardcore loyalists mocked him in private.

Business as Usual

So this week's presidential response to multiple crises is business as usual.

And to quote *SNL*'s Keenan Thompson appearing in a skit on a *Face the Nation*-type news pundit panel — with fellow panel members insisting that with the Bolton revelations, "This time is different" (compared to, e.g., when Trump said he "grabs women by the p***y," when Trump asked Putin for help with reelection, and when Trump extorted Ukraine for help with reelection) — "Ain't nothin' gonna happen. Ain't nothin' gonna change."

So what's the upshot? Republican senators boil it down for you: "I missed that tweet. No comment." ∎

06/25/20 — My Top Liberal Responses to MAGA Male Bovine Excreta

COVID-19 Deaths

2/06/2020 — U.S.: 1 | World: 620
3/05/2020 — U.S.: 12 | World: 3,293
4/02/2020 — U.S.: 5,137 | World: 48,284
5/07/2020 — U.S.: 73,431 | World: 264,189
6/04/2020 — U.S.: 107,175 | World: 386,464
6/25/2020 — U.S.: 121,979 | World: 483,207

(COVID-19 Dashboard by the Center for Systems Science and Engineering at Johns Hopkins University; approximately 8 a.m. each day)

This Week

This week has seen another hodgepodge of President Trump's disregard for human life — even MAGA-supporting life. He will do anything, say anything, to be reelected, to avoid indictment and possible prison.

For the second time this week, the president has held one of only two mass indoor gatherings in the U.S., by any organization, since the pandemic hit in February. He's ignored all his own medical experts' advice about mask-wearing and social distancing — and mass indoor gatherings. He insisted on pushing forward with these epidemiologist-described "superspreader" events in Tulsa and Phoenix, two hottest of the current COVID-19 hot spots in the country.

[FUN FACT NO. 1:] Trump for President 2020, Inc., insisted on signed waivers from rally attendees so they couldn't sue him for getting sick or dying.

[FUN FACT NO. 2:] Eight members of the Trump campaign's Tulsa advance team and security staff have tested positive for the virus. Dozens of Secret Service officers were ordered to self-quarantine after the event.

Oklahoma and Arizona are setting records for daily new cases, hospitalizations, ventilator use, and deaths. This is not a second wave. This is the first wave finally hitting secondary states due to toxic leadership from the White House. But President Trump wants to paint an alternate reality: "The pandemic almost is over, it was overblown by my enemies to bring me down, and even if I am paranoid, they're still out to get me."

Also this week, Attorney General William Barr was exposed at a congressional hearing yesterday by two DOJ attorneys who detailed how Barr has interfered in several Justice Department cases to "go easy" on the president and his political chums.

How Did We Get Here?

President Donald Trump has exacerbated exponentially the three concurrent historic crises of our time: 1) he's allowed tens of thousands of needless pandemic deaths with no end in sight; 2) he's ignored, then patronized, then inflamed the largest civil rights movement since the 1960s; and 3) he's pushed the nation further into Great Depression-era economic numbers. Also, as stated, he's conspired with AG Barr to have the DOJ look away from the crimes of Trump and his cohorts.

How did we get here? Enabling by complicit Republican representatives and senators. Do *not* forget that. If even a few of them along the way had not been obsessed with their own reelection and future social standing — and had had the backbone

and moral compass to stand up to the venal confidence artist —
Trumpian destruction of governing norms, rule of law, and all
things decent could have been aborted or at least impeded.

So it's not enough to oppose the president. Democrats,
enlightened Republicans, and newly awakened formerly apathetic
low-information voters must oppose all GOP legislators, national
and local, to excise the cancer within America that is Donald J.
Trump.

Therefore I'm treating readers to some of my top liberal
responses to Trump GOP bullsh*t.

Some of My Top Liberal Responses to MAGA Male Bovine Excreta

Impress your friends. Shut down Uncle Ed and his MAGA hat
when one of these topics comes up at the next family barbecue.

Black Lives Matter

If your first response to this social justice truism is, "All Lives
Matter," yes, it's true: You don't get it. The content of this response
is a given; however, "Black Lives Matter" supporters simply argue
that the African American component of "All" is a second-class
component to many.

If your first response is, "White Lives Matter," yes it's true:
Not only do you not get it, you've been exposed as colossally,
selfishly, hopelessly incapable of empathy — or worse.

These are the reasons I bought a Colin Kaepernick jersey: 1) I
support his original, respectful protests — which had *nothing* to do
with *dis*respecting America — against the grossly statistically high
number of Black (and brown) men killed by police and vigilantes
with no accountability; 2) I oppose the attempts by President
Trump to shut down legitimate NFL and other protests and make
racism acceptable; and 3) I oppose the blackballing of Kaepernick
from the league.

Wait: I *vehemently* support … , and *vehemently* oppose … .

The time for enlightenment is long overdue. As one of the *South Park* fourth grader boys said while apologizing to Token (the only Black student in school) after a racial slight, "I'm sorry, Token. As a white kid, I now get that I don't get it."

No Credibility

Let's make this clear: As soon as you use "TDS" ("Trump Derangement Syndrome"), "deep state," or "antifa" as an argument supporting Trumpism, you've exposed yourself as having zero credibility. You're simply repeating the focus-group-tested buzzwords of your cult leader. From that point on you're a known non-critical thinker not worthy of any further time spent on intelligent discourse. Using these terms in support of Trump is what we call a *tell*.

Fake News

Mr. and Ms. MAGA Supporter, let's stop and analyze your Trumpian slams against media organizations like *The Washington Post* and *The New York Times*, two of *the* most credible, accurate news sources in the country. Note that you never had any problems with them while they were focused on Hillary Clinton's non-crimes nonstop. Only when, out of journalistic integrity, they were required to report truths about Donald that he didn't like — quoting his statements verbatim, describing his actions accurately — did any MAGA hats begin to complain. The *Post's* and *Times'* news reporting divisions are accurate and beyond reproach. They correct their honest mistakes per the highest journalistic standards. Even their well-known liberal writers on the editorial side are balanced by commensurate hard-right columnists. There are no greater Trump lickspittles than the *Post's* Hugh Hewitt and Marc Thiessen, whom it features often.

Anyone that knee-jerk discounts these newspapers is a liar, delirious, or both. To repeat mindlessly what your leader has told you to is nothing more than cult members spewing the messiah's dogmatic, dangerous vitriol.

Military Support

How much longer can Trump's pro-military supporters hang on in the face of blistering decorated multi-star MAGA condemnation?

Let me reprise my earlier remarks about — as Donald would (publicly) say — "our great generals":

> Since the president's egregious use of military force on peacefully protesting citizens of his own country June 1, 2020, and his threats to escalate those attacks, Mr. Trump has been excoriated by a dozen-plus current or retired three- and four-star generals including John R. Allen, Martin Dempsey, Joseph Dunford, Michael Hayden, John Kelly, Douglas Lute, James Mattis, Barry McCaffrey, Stanley McChrystal, H. R. McMaster, William McRaven, Mark Milley, Michael Mullen, David Petraeus, and Colin Powell. This list includes several former Joint Chiefs of Staff chairs and various Cabinet secretaries. …

> Gen. Mark Milley, current Joint Chiefs of Staff chair, later apologized for appearing at Trump's June 1 Bible photo op [— to prepare for which, peaceful protesters were tear-gassed, shoved down with shields, bombarded with flash-bang shells, and fired upon with rubber bullets —] saying he "never should have been there." …

> Retired four-star Marine Corp Gen. John R. Allen, former commander of the NATO International Security Assistance Force and U.S. Forces – Afghanistan, said Trump's use of

federal force against peaceful citizens "may well signal the beginning of the end of the American experiment."

And don't get me started on Trump mocking Gold Star families, negating Sen. John McCain's (R-Ariz.) heroic war service, and belittling his generals after a briefing early in his presidency: "[M]y f***ing generals are a bunch of p***ies."

More? Donald snubbed the November 2018 multination veterans ceremonies at Aisne-Marne American Cemetery and Memorial while in Paris to commemorate the 100th anniversary of the end of World War I. (President Trump was the only world leader in France that Saturday to decline attendance.) *The Atlantic* reported him saying to senior staff members, "Why should I go to that cemetery? It's filled with losers." Trump also reportedly called revered U.S. Marines who died in the Battle of Belleau Wood "suckers."

The following Monday he declined to travel the two miles from the White House to Arlington National Cemetery on Veterans Day, a presidential tradition unbroken for over a half-century to honor deceased soldiers.

Once again, Donald Trump's first Defense secretary, the venerated Gen. Jim Mattis (from his letter to *The Atlantic* reported June 3, 2020):

> "Donald Trump is the first president in my lifetime who does not try to unite the American people — does not even pretend to try. Instead he tries to divide us. We are witnessing the consequences of three years of this deliberate effort. We are witnessing the consequences of three years without mature leadership."

Yeah, our president just oozes reciprocal respect for the military community.

Congratulations! It's official. *[insert full name]* has won the award for most asinine, simpleminded, fatuous comments on *[insert social media platform]*. The category was "Stupidest Collection of Posts From a Solo Artist or Duo." His boneheaded vacuity over the past year has been unsurpassed. When presented with the 2020 statuette, the "Postie," *[insert first name]* thanked his former cellmates and psych ward buds without whom he could not have achieved this honor. His closest friend offered this assessment: "I knew him in his younger days and he was always headed for a**hole-ian ignominy." His mother said simply, "His father and I failed. I'm so sorry." Our congratulations to *[insert first name]*.

———————

Copy and paste these as needed. You could add my name at the end. But this is more of a guideline than a rule *(— thanks to Peter Venkman, aka Bill Murray, "Ghostbusters")*.■

07/02/20 — Dog-Bites-Man News; No – Many Dogs Bite Many Men

COVID-19 Deaths

2/06/2020 — U.S.: 1 | World: 620
3/05/2020 — U.S.: 12 | World: 3,293
4/02/2020 — U.S.: 5,137 | World: 48,284
5/07/2020 — U.S.: 73,431 | World: 264,189
6/04/2020 — U.S.: 107,175 | World: 386,464
7/02/2020 — U.S.: 128,062 | World: 516,726

> (COVID-19 Dashboard by the Center for Systems Science and Engineering at Johns Hopkins University; approximately 8 a.m. each day)

This week brings a familiar collection of Trumpian dog-bites-man news, that is, more of the same bad news. But it's *much* more of the same. It's many dogs biting many men.

Pandemic

Red state governors across southern and western United States finally have felt the fire that was lit under their derrieres and now has migrated to their hair. The first wave of the pandemic is cresting across states that thought they had been spared. And with each smashed record (presidential failure) of new cases, hospitalizations, and deaths, President Trump has grown quieter. He allows almost no task force news conferences anymore and rarely mentions COVID-19.

> "Staggered by the resurgent novel coronavirus, cities and states are reinstituting restrictions on bars, pools, and large

gatherings days ahead of July 4 celebrations as the top U.S. infectious-disease expert warned Tuesday that the pandemic is out of control in some places and soon could reach 100,000 cases a day. Nationally, new infections have topped 40,000 in four of the past five days during an accelerating outbreak that exceeds the worst days of April.

"The number of people hospitalized with COVID-19, the disease the virus causes, is surging in seven states. … In Texas, Arizona, Nevada, South Carolina, West Virginia, Georgia, and California, seven-day averages are up at least 25% from last week. Anthony S. Fauci said during a Senate hearing Tuesday … 'Clearly, we are not in total control right now.' Fauci said half of all new cases are being recorded in just four states. Three of them — Arizona, Texas, and Florida — are led by Republican governors who moved quickly, after being urged by President Trump, to reopen their economies but have since begun closing bars and beaches."

(Gearan, Anne & Wilson, Scott & Gowen, Annie;
"As Shaken Cities and States Pull Back From
Reopening, Fauci Sounds Alarm on Surging Virus";
The Washington Post; 6/30/2020.)

[FYI:] The U.S. hit another milestone July 1 for COVID-19: 50,000 new cases in one day for the first time. New cases have increased 82% over the past two weeks. Forty-five states have more new cases this week than last week.

Your president, in response to the pandemic news of yesterday, said this:

> "I think we're going to be very good with the coronavirus. I think that at some point that's going to sort of just disappear, I hope. ... I do [believe it will] disappear."

> (Trump, Donald, R-Fla., U.S. president; interview; *Fox News;* 7/1/2020.)

And your president, in response to his until-now belittling of mask-wearers:

> "I'm all for masks. I think [voluntary] masks are good ... [if people] feel good about it. ... Actually I had a mask on and I said I liked the way I looked. I thought it was OK. It was a dark black mask and I thought it looked OK. It looked like the Lone Ranger, but I have no problem with that."

> (Ibid.; Trump; 7/1/2020.)

Protests

President Trump is doing his best to unite the nation and quell continuously rising (with each new Black male death at the hands of police) Black Lives Matter protest tensions.

Just kidding.

Last Sunday he retweeted to his jillion followers a video of a supporter yelling, "White Power!" — twice — then retreated to his Florida golf course. His aides immediately freaked out and tried to get authorization to delete the tweet, but the president was in radio blackout, on the links, his phone out of reach. After three hours aides finally reached Donald who succumbed to their exhortations to tweet-delete his vile post. Though somehow the world still found out about it.

And Mr. Trump has vowed to veto the annual ($740 billion) military spending bill — necessary to keep jeeps rolling, troops armed, and paper pushed — if senators, including Republican Senate supporters, retain their amendment to change the names of military bases named after Confederate luminaries.

These actions by the president come in the face of even the formerly most Confederate-symbol-friendly states moving to extinguish the glorification of slavery-supporting imagery.

> "Mississippi Gov. Tate Reeves (R) signed a bill Tuesday abandoning the state's flag and stripping the Confederate battle flag symbol from it, capping a remarkable turnaround on a banner that had flown over the state for more than a century. With Reeves' move, Mississippi will take down one of the country's most prominent Confederate tributes, withdrawing the only state flag that still bears such an emblem. The new flag's design will be determined later, but lawmakers have barred it from including the most recognizable icon of the Confederacy, which many people associate with racism, slavery, and oppression. … Reeves' signature came two days after Mississippi lawmakers, facing a nationwide campaign for racial justice, passed the measure removing the state's flag and calling for a replacement."

> (Berman, Mark & Guarino, Ben; "Mississippi Governor Signs Bill Changing State's Flag, Abandoning Confederate Symbol"; *The Washington Post*; 6/30/2020.)

Russia

The big Russia news expanding since last Thursday is that Putin authorized bounties to the Taliban for killing American (and coalition) troops in Afghanistan during 2018-19. And. President Trump knew about it in 2019. And. The president has had several calls with Vladimir Putin since then and has said nothing to him about it. And. President Trump has continued to suck up to Putin by 1) ignoring Vlad's purloining of a Massachusetts-size portion of Ukraine, 2) pushing for Russia's readmittance to the G8 world body of power nations, 3) removing U.S. troops from Germany, and 4) trashing NATO.

> [FUN FACT:] Russia was booted from the G8 in response to its illegal annexation (theft by military force) of the Crimean Peninsula from Ukraine in 2014.

This is another great example of how even Trump's most egregious behaviors — e.g., figuratively bowing to the Russian leader at their 2018 Helsinki summit news conference by accepting Putin's denials of U.S. election interference over all U.S. intelligence sources — get buried in the mountain of Donald's inept, corrupt behaviors. The late Sen. John McCain (R-Ariz.) called the Helsinki back-down at the time, "one of the most disgraceful performances by an American president in memory." (Of course our memories have been augmented since.) But then the next Trumpian outrage occurs, the country moves on, and the electorate forgets about Trump's until-that-time worst act of presidential incompetence and corruption.

But now Russia is back. And the question is renewed: What does Vladimir Putin have on Donald Trump?

> "White House officials were first informed in early 2019 of intelligence reports that Russia was offering bounties to Taliban-linked militants to kill U.S. and coalition military personnel in Afghanistan. … Intelligence analysts believe that the bounties probably resulted in the deaths of three Marines killed in April 2019. …
>
> "This week, White House officials have said that intelligence about the Russian bounty program … was not sufficiently

substantiated to be brought to Trump's attention. …
[However,] numerous intelligence and former government
officials have said that such reports would normally have
reached the highest levels of government, including the
president. … But several people familiar with the matter
noted that information is sometimes withheld from Trump,
who often reacts badly to reports that he thinks might
undermine what he considers his good relationship with
Russian President Vladimir Putin."

(DeYoung, Harris, Nakashima, & Demirjian;
"Intelligence Reports on Russian Bounty Operation
First Reached White House in Early 2019"; *The
Washington Post*; 6/30/2020.)

It's now been reported that this intelligence was, at a minimum,
included in the Presidential Daily Briefings.

Trump knew and did nothing about it? Trump didn't know
because he doesn't read the Presidential Daily Briefings? Trump's
top advisers didn't tell him because it would upset him? Every
possible explanation is galactically bad.

The question is renewed: What does Vladimir Putin have on
Donald Trump?∎

07/09/20 — Depraved

COVID-19 Deaths

2/06/2020 — U.S.: 1 | World: 620
3/05/2020 — U.S.: 12 | World: 3,293
4/02/2020 — U.S.: 5,137 | World: 48,284
5/07/2020 — U.S.: 73,431 | World: 264,189
6/04/2020 — U.S.: 107,175 | World: 386,464
7/02/2020 — U.S.: 128,062 | World: 516,726
7/09/2020 — U.S.: 132,309 | World: 550,135

(COVID-19 Dashboard by the Center for Systems Science and Engineering at Johns Hopkins University; approximately 8 a.m. each day)

Never forget. Vote.

This is a list of depraved horrors perpetrated by Donald Trump against America since he's been in the White House, any one of which would have imploded another presidency:

— *Associates Convicted of Crimes:* Donald has at least six close political associates in, in and out of, or awaiting prison: Michael Cohen, former personal attorney-fixer; Michael Flynn, former national security adviser; Rick Gates, 2016 campaign deputy chair; Paul Manafort, 2016 campaign chair; George Papadopoulos, 2016 campaign adviser; Roger Stone, 2016 campaign adviser, lifelong ally

— *Border Troops:* Donald frivolously sent military soldiers to southern border in political stunt, defying "his" generals, to stop benign migrant "caravan"

— *FBI Building:* Donald canceled plan to move FBI building out of Washington, D.C., after several years and millions of dollars invested in planning; vacant building would have created potential competition for Trump's D.C. hotel

— *George Floyd Protests:* Donald used federal unmarked personnel to violently disperse peaceful protesters; he intentionally inflamed national racial tensions over weeks of turmoil

— *Hurricane Maria:* Donald withheld and bungled aid to, and repeatedly disparaged, Puerto Rico

— *Impeachment:* Donald extorted Ukraine for election help; he ended the careers of many honest impeachment witnesses

— *Individual-1:* Donald was implicated as an unindicted co-conspirator in the campaign finance crime for which his attorney-fixer Michael Cohen was convicted; prosecutors agreed the crime did not benefit Cohen but was ordered by Trump who also laundered the illegal hush-money payments through Trump Org.

— *Judge Mary Trump:* Donald's older sister, Mary, resigned her lifelong federal judgeship appointment to head off Trump family tax probe that was part of an ethics review

— *Migrant Children:* Donald separated thousands of migrant minors, including babies, toddlers, and other young children, from their families for months, locking them up in squalor; many hundreds have been separated permanently through poor record keeping — ICE, DHS, and HHS can't find the parents

— *Mueller Report:* Donald obstructed justice at least 10 times, committed perjury, dangled pardons to prospective witnesses and threatened others, and colluded with Russia: he asked for and happily accepted foreign election help; he continues to pander to Putin

— *Pandemic:* Donald has caused tens of thousands of needless deaths by playing down coronavirus to restart economy early solely for reelection; he's refused to nationalize guidelines, testing, supply production, and supply chain; he's pressuring all schools to reopen without limitations at the height of a pandemic, threatening funding if they don't, while watering down CDC school reopening guidelines

— *Rule of Law:* Donald has ordered AG Barr to quash numerous Trump-related criminal investigations

— *Russia Troop Bounties:* Donald has refused to confront Putin after receiving solid-intelligence briefings in 2019 stating Russia paid Taliban bounties in 2018-19 for U.S. and coalition troop deaths in Afghanistan; he continues to pander to Putin

— *Sexual Assault:* Donald currently is facing over 20 lawsuits stemming from credible accusations of sexual assault or misconduct

— *Sharpie-Gate:* Donald (or his staff) altered, with childlike Sharpie markings, a national weather center map of Hurricane Dorian to include Alabama, a state never in danger; he did this to avoid admitting a simple mistake he'd made in days previous; he then pressured NOAA (National Oceanic and Atmospheric Administration) to back up his mistake retroactively; Commerce Dept. inspector general later reprimanded NOAA for this false (corrective) reporting

— *Trump Foundation:* Courts ordered Donald's foundation to pay $2 million in fines/restitution, and that this Trump "charitable" entity be shut down permanently due to widespread fraud and campaign finance violations; his adult children and board members, Don Jr., Ivanka, and Eric, earned a lifetime court order never to be involved in charities again

— *Trump Inaugural Committee:* Federal prosecutors have been investigating the committee since 2018 for soliciting illegal foreign contributions, using straw donors, money laundering, financial mismanagement, and misappropriation of funds (it only spent a small fraction of the money raised on inaugural activities); at least two men have been indicted

— *Trump University:* Courts ordered Donald to pay $25 million in settlements to "students" who had been victimized by fraudulent marketing claims and worthless "degrees," and that the "university" be shut down permanently

— *100's of Other Miscellaneous Scandals and Malfeasance* (Helsinki, *Access Hollywood*, 20,000-plus documented lies, telling intel secrets to Russians in Oval Office, insulting Gold Star families, mocking physically challenged reporters, pushing to disqualify a judge with Mexican heritage solely because of that heritage, and many more)

If you want four more years of Donald Trump, vote for him. If not, don't. But note that a "protest" vote for anyone not named Joe Biden is a vote for Trump. Staying home in "protest" on Election Day is a vote for Trump. ∎

07/16/20 — Pandemic Deaths Due to Trump Malfeasance: 68,709 – so Far

COVID-19 Deaths

2/06/2020 — U.S.: 1 | World: 620
3/05/2020 — U.S.: 12 | World: 3,293
4/02/2020 — U.S.: 5,137 | World: 48,284
5/07/2020 — U.S.: 73,431 | World: 264,189
6/04/2020 — U.S.: 107,175 | World: 386,464
7/02/2020 — U.S.: 128,062 | World: 516,726
7/16/2020 — U.S.: 137,419 | World: 584,922

> • Conservatively estimated Trump malfeasance deaths: 68,709

> > (Glanz, James & Robertson, Campbell; "Lockdown Delays Cost at Least 36,000 Lives, Data Show"; *The New York Times;* 5/20/2020.)
> > (as conservatively extrapolated from COVID-19 Dashboard by the Center for Systems Science and Engineering at Johns Hopkins University; 7/16/2020.)

Frankly Speaking

Frankly (an overused term usually misapplied as an intensifier for emphasis, as I just did), the time to talk about the president's lethal pandemic policies is long past.

Donald Trump's corrupt coronavirus response is responsible for the unnecessary deaths of Americans. Tens of thousands of fatalities. I'm calculating my new weekly to-date estimates as a conservative 50% of prevailing U.S. total pandemic deaths.

Since February I've been documenting the number of COVID-19 fatalities in our country and the world. Every Thursday morning at approximately 8 a.m. I access the website of the Center for Systems Science and Engineering at Johns Hopkins University and note the devastating numbers.

This morning the U.S. aggregate is 137,419.

It's now clear, crystal, that Mr. Trump has had a direct hand in a conservatively estimated 68,709 — half — of those.

> "If the United States had begun imposing social distancing measures one week earlier than it did in March [15], about 36,000 [approximately 50%] fewer people would have died in the coronavirus outbreak, according to new estimates from Columbia University disease modelers. And if the country had begun locking down cities and limiting social contact on March 1, two weeks earlier than most people started staying home, the vast majority of the nation's deaths — about 83% — would have been avoided, the researchers estimated. Under that scenario, about 54,000 fewer people would have died by early May. …
>
> "'It's a big, big difference. That small moment in time, catching it in that growth phase, is incredibly critical in reducing the number of deaths,' said Jeffrey Shaman, an epidemiologist at Columbia and the leader of the research team."
>
> (Glanz, James & Robertson, Campbell; "Lockdown Delays Cost at Least 36,000 Lives, Data Show"; *The New York Times;* 5/20/2020.)

Lack of Leadership

If Mr. Trump had shown even flawed, limited leadership *one week earlier* (than March 15), 50% of U.S. fatalities could have been averted (as of May). *Two weeks earlier:* 83%. Now combine this with his *continued* lack of leadership.

Remember that Trump received early dire warnings from epidemiological experts around the country and many corners of his own government including the CDC and top aides such as Peter Navarro, director of the Office of Trade and Manufacturing Policy. Donald's own damn ultraconservative trade director was sounding the alarm to him in December and January but Trump didn't want to hear it. To act on or even acknowledge the danger would hurt his economy. He ignored warnings while having the advantage of a preview from seeing the pandemic play out in China and Europe, having been warned that its assault on the U.S. was inevitable, that it would occur within weeks or months.

Trump did nothing before March 15 except put some limited, porous restrictions on travel to and from China (and a few European countries, notably, incomprehensibly, *not* countries that contained Trump properties) — well after 38 other countries and U.S. airlines already had begun implementing their own China travel bans.

Finally, Trump Acted — Sort Of

Finally March 15 the White House issued guidelines for shelter-at-home recommendations, social distancing, and mask-wearing. But Trump's corrupt fatal flaw — which persists to this day — is that he left it all up to the states. The lack of leadership is manifest in many things but especially in his refusal to role-model and lead on the White House's own safe-behavior recommendations. He wishy-wash-ily has given conflicting messages from the beginning: "You can follow the guidelines if you want to, but real MAGA heroes know I'm winking to them that I think the whole thing is a hoax."

Donald's worst fears have come true: The economy has tanked. Rather than learn from his mistakes, he continues to play down the pandemic to restart the economy and the stock market solely to save his political life. He has not wavered on this, a key indication that, in this instance, it's not primarily Trumpian *incompetence* (though there is a mountain of that), it's *corruption* and *amorality* driving his decisions. Donald has and will sacrifice human life to be reelected to avoid indictment, possible prison time, and maybe worse for him, humiliation.

Trump has refused to support the components necessary to fight the pandemic effectively, i.e., to nationalize clear and consistent guidelines, virus testing, supply production, and the supply chain. As hot spots and hot states surge with infections, hospitals still are suffering drastic shortages of essential personal protective equipment and lifesaving ventilators, not to mention beds. Huge testing kit shortages are legendary. Where tests are available, the long wait time for results hobbles contact tracing, a key component of virus containment.

The president has left an anemic patchwork response to the individual states — to compete with each other, FEMA, and other countries for desperately needed resources. This also decentralizes guidance, handing the fate of many states off to Republican, virus-downplaying, Trump-favor-currying governors. The patchwork approach serves two functions: 1) he can blame the states when things go south; and 2) it allows him to continue downplaying and ignoring the plague, hoping (and saying) it will "just disappear" — all to restart the economy to win reelection.

For all these reasons, putting Trump's share of responsibility for U.S. COVID-19 deaths at 50% of the total at any given time is a conservative estimate.

(Mixed) Message Is Clear

Meanwhile nearly half the country — Trump's supporters — believe in his efforts to hoax away COVID-19. Following his lead, they scoff at the pandemic, ignore health guidelines, and continue their colossal virus spread as a result of political manipulation. Even people in the independent middle are left to wonder: "Could a United States president really be so callous as to sacrifice lives through deception just for reelection purposes?" Many conclude the answer is "no," choosing to ignore warnings and safety guidelines because they're inconvenient.

The first wave of the pandemic is resurging bigger than ever, now into red states such as Florida, Texas, Arizona, South Carolina, and others. The president must be correcting course and finally realizing a consistent message is good for the country, good for the economy, good for saving lives, Right?

No.

No Lessons Learned

In the past month President Trump has held three superspreader gatherings for campaign purposes (at which many attendees have contracted the virus including a dozen presidential staffers). He retweeted game show host Chuck Woolery (who has no other discernible credentials) to support his contention that the virus is a hoax and "doctors are lying to us." Trump continues to discount, discourage, and defund testing, which almost all experts agree is the primary method, in conjunction with contact tracing, of controlling the virus' spread.

The president and the White House have mounted a full-blown opposition research campaign to discredit his own top U.S. government epidemiologist, Dr. Anthony Fauci (who still enjoys three times the credibility compared to Trump in polls), who thankfully has been disputing President Trump's pandemic lies and misinformation left and right. Why doesn't he just fire Fauci? That would look far worse for Donald than his campaign of dis-accreditation. So the president continues abetting the mass confusion, a powerful perverse tool, with plausible deniability.

Now President Trump is pressuring all American school districts to reopen in the fall five days per week with no masks or social distancing, contradicting virtually all credible medical and scientific recommendations. He's threatening public funding if they don't open — claiming school closures are a ploy to make him look bad rather than a measure to save children's lives — and he's watering down CDC student guidelines. He sees schools reopening as integral to parents going back to work. And that's all he sees.

Obstruction of justice. Trashing the rule of law. Consistent obsequious deference to Putin. Pardoning felonious friends for their silence. Buddying up to dictators. Alienating allies. Paying hush money to pornographic actors. Transparent racism. And now, unnecessary pandemic death. There is no bottom — until he's gone.

That's why there is a historically unprecedented number of luminaries from the president's own party who are supporting the opposition candidate in November to stop the frightening, horrendous damage Trump has done to our government and institutions. That's why there is a Lincoln Project, assembled long before the pandemic, comprising innumerable distinguished Republican, conservative thinkers and former legislators, spending millions of dollars on effective ads to abort the Trumpian destruction of America.■

07/23/20 — Pigs-Fly Theorem

COVID-19 Deaths

2/06/2020 — U.S.: 1 | World: 620
3/05/2020 — U.S.: 12 | World: 3,293
4/02/2020 — U.S.: 5,137 | World: 48,284
5/07/2020 — U.S.: 73,431 | World: 264,189
6/04/2020 — U.S.: 107,175 | World: 386,464
7/02/2020 — U.S.: 128,062 | World: 516,726
7/23/2020 — U.S.: 143,193 | World: 624,131

• Conservatively estimated Trump malfeasance deaths: 71,596

(Ibid.; Glanz & Robertson; 5/20/2020.)
(as conservatively extrapolated from COVID-19 Dashboard by the Center for Systems Science and Engineering at Johns Hopkins University; 7/23/2020.)

Biggest Story

The biggest story of the Trump presidency continues to be that he is responsible for a conservatively estimated half — equaling 71,596 to date — of all U.S. coronavirus pandemic deaths.

This is on top of, after, all his other presidential depravities, any one of which would have sunk another administration:

1) Multiple *associates convicted of felonies*
2) Sending *troops to southern border stunt*
3) Massive *emoluments clauses violations*

4) Family, personal *tax fraud*

5) Cancellation of new *FBI building* to protect Trump D.C. hotel profits

6) Exacerbation of *George Floyd protest* tensions with blatant racism

7) Withholding, bungling of aid to Puerto Rico after *Hurricane Maria*

8) Acceptance at *Helsinki* of Putin's election interference denial over all U.S. intel

9) Impeachment for *extorting Ukraine* to get dirt on Joe Biden

10) *Individual-1:* unindicted co-conspirator ordering hush money, money laundering

11) *Firing of multiple inspectors general* to stop malfeasance probes of Trump, allies

12) *Sister's resignation from federal judgeship* to avoid family tax fraud probe

13) *Separation of thousands of migrant children* from families

14) *Election help from Russia, obstruction of justice* x10, *dangling of pardons, witness intimidation*

15) *Ordering AG Barr to quash* numerous Trump-related investigations

16) Refusal to confront Putin on *bounties paid for killed U.S. troops*

17) 20-plus *sexual assault,* sexual misconduct lawsuits pending

18) *Ordering of NOAA to falsify hurricane data* retroactively to cover his mistake

19) *Trump ("charitable") Foundation* court order to pay $2M in restitution and dissolve

20) *Trump Inaugural Committee* probe for multiple financial fraud offenses

21) *Trump University* court order to pay $25M in fraud settlements and dissolve

22) *And others: Access Hollywood,* 20,000-plus documented lies, telling of intel secrets to Russians in Oval Office, attacks on Gold Star families, mocking of physically challenged

reporters, push to disqualify a judge with Mexican heritage solely because of that heritage, attacks on NATO, dissing of allies, support for dictators, and many more.

Pigs-Fly Theorem

But even considering *all* this, President Trump conceivably still could win reelection by making an about-face and immediately starting to do everything right in dealing with the pandemic.

I call this the "pigs-fly" theorem.

As *The Washington Post* columnist Greg Sargent pointed out, however, in his July 17 piece, making this about-face would involve Donald admitting he made a mistake, simply by the act of changing course. And he is constitutionally incapable of doing or saying *anything* that would be construed as a mistake admission.

Mr. Sargent determined this in the course of perusing Donald's niece Mary Trump's new book, *Too Much and Never Enough: How My Family Created the World's Most Dangerous Man*, and hearing a book tour interview. Mary has a Ph.D. in psychology and was an integral part of the extended family (daughter of Donald's older brother, Freddy) until the late 1990s when she and her brother became involved in an inheritance lawsuit with Donald and his siblings, her aunts and uncles. In her book she combines Trump clan stories with professional psychological analysis.

Skeletons in the White House

Mary knows where the family skeletons are, what they said about each other before becoming skeletons, and what each skeleton's DSM-5 psychiatric diagnosis is.

> "Let's call them President Trump's twin pathologies: The absolute refusal to admit to any sort of fallibility no matter what, and the unshakable faith in lying as an instrument of power that can be wielded with impunity. ... Mary Trump

explain[s] how each of these functions for her uncle with unsettling clarity."

(Sargent, Greg; "In a New Interview, Mary Trump Lays Bare Our National Nightmare: Her Uncle"; *The Washington Post;* 7/17/2020.)

———————

Mr. Trump held his first pandemic task force briefing — without the task force — in three months. When asked about Ghislaine Maxwell (recently indicted child-sex ring madam for Jeffrey Epstein, and an old Trump friend), Donald "wished her well" three times *(wink, wink translation: "Keep quiet and I'll take care of you.")*.

My copy should be here any day. She's a Ph.D. And Donald's niece. In psychology.∎

07/30/20 — Needless Virus Deaths, Separated Children. Why Are White Evangelicals Unmoved?!

COVID-19 Deaths

2/06/2020 — U.S.: 1 | World: 620
3/05/2020 — U.S.: 12 | World: 3,293
4/02/2020 — U.S.: 5,137 | World: 48,284
5/07/2020 — U.S.: 73,431 | World: 264,189
6/04/2020 — U.S.: 107,175 | World: 386,464
7/02/2020 — U.S.: 128,062 | World: 516,726
7/30/2020 — U.S.: 150,716 | World: 667,693

> • Conservatively estimated Trump malfeasance deaths: 75,358

> (Ibid.; Glanz & Robertson; 5/20/2020.)
> (as conservatively extrapolated from COVID-19 Dashboard by the Center for Systems Science and Engineering at Johns Hopkins University; 7/30/2020.)

Poll of White Evangelicals

According to the *Christian Broadcasting Network*'s reporting of a (*CBN*-respected) Pew Research Center poll this month, President Trump's approval rating among Caucasian evangelicals has dropped to 72%. But 82% say they're at least leaning toward reelecting the president in November. This is virtually the same number (81%) that supported Donald in 2016.

Among white evangelicals 10% are admitting to disapproval of Mr. Trump but likely still voting for him. Most of the 72% who "approve" aren't admitting any disapproval and are supporting him blindly.

For what reason?

I recently was disheartened by a comment from a friend, a white evangelical Christian who I thought, hoped, was one of the 18-19% wanting Trump out of office. She put an arrow through my heart with this (her first political) social media post:

> "Trump may not always say the right things but he is getting more done than all of the other politicians combined, and he doesn't even take a paycheck. He has my vote!"

This is like saying,

> "Jim Jones may not always use the right flavor of Kool-Aid, but he's sent more souls to heaven at one time than all of the other pastors combined, and he provides the Kool-Aid free. He has my vote!"

I know. Jim Jones used Flavor Aid not Kool-Aid.

Of course the no-paycheck line easily is explained away: Trump uses this as a misleading bragging point because he takes in 100 times his White House salary through illegal foreign and domestic emoluments clauses violations.

This respected friend's blindness to reality weighed on me for days. I responded respectfully with my list of 20-plus Trump depravities foisted upon America. But nothing got through. She ended our thread on the friendly falsely equivalent, "Let's agree to disagree."

Why Are so Many Caucasian Christians Unmoved?

White evangelicals, I beg you to consider these facts with an open mind.

Unnecessary Pandemic Deaths

These numbers are conservatively extrapolated from Columbia University research and Johns Hopkins University's COVID-19 Dashboard: Donald has allowed a conservatively estimated 3,762 unnecessary pandemic deaths this week alone and 75,358 to date.

How? Why?

By consistently, still, playing down the coronavirus and spreading dangerous disinformation to restart the economy early solely for reelection to avoid almost certain indictment. He's refused to nationalize health guidelines, testing, treatment supply production, and the supply chain. He's demanding all school districts reopen without limitations at the height of a pandemic, without any guidance, threatening their funding if they don't. He's risking the lives of millions of children across the country for political gain.

Child Separation

Donald has separated thousands of migrant minors including babies, toddlers, and other young children from their families for months, locking them up in overcrowded prison conditions, causing lifelong-lasting trauma. Hundreds of these children have been separated permanently through government incompetence, the failure to track their locations. And this barbaric policy continues.

The adults who brought them might have broken laws. But the children are innocent human beings put through the horror of losing their parents in a strange land, not knowing if they'll ever see them again, so the president could "set an example."

This one item on the list, by itself, should have convinced all Christians that President Trump is unfit to lead as a president and a human being.

Hurricane Maria, Puerto Rico

Donald intentionally slowed down and withheld aid to the victims of Hurricane Maria in Puerto Rico because of criticism from one city's desperately-pleading-for-help mayor, distaste for Puerto Ricans, and the mistaken belief that those citizens are something less than American citizens. There's no estimating how many lives were lost due to lack of water, electricity, food, and medicine because of the president's bias against this U.S. territory.

Cutting Regulations

Donald loves to boast that he's built the economy by eliminating regulations. The fact is it already was doing great even under President Obama's protections before President Trump took over. Most of the regulations Trump has eliminated were there to protect our children and other citizens from 1) illness, accident, and death; 2) destruction of the environment; 3) weakening of the family; 4) predatory lending; and 5) fraudulent, malfeasant banking practices that enabled the 2008 financial crash.

Again, we'll never know how many child and adult lives were lost due to environmental poisons, unchecked climate change, preventable accidents, workplace dangers, hunger, product defects, unfair bankruptcies, or lack of common sense gun safety guidelines.

Many of Your Own Have Seen the Light

White evangelical Christians, 18-19% of your brethren see through the smoke and mirrors and know that Mr. Trump is unfit intellectually and morally to be president. That's not a majority but it's not nothing. About 1 in 5 of your fellow believers knows the truth. Seek him out. Ask her why she knows.

For the record, 39% of all other white Protestants and 43% of white Catholics also have seen the anti-Trumpian light.

As I've said earlier:

> There's a historically unprecedented number of luminaries from the president's own party who are supporting the opposition candidate in November to stop the frightening horrendous damage President Trump is doing to our country. The Lincoln Project, assembled long before the pandemic, comprises innumerable distinguished Republican and conservative thinkers who are raising money to abort the Trumpian destruction of America.

Virtually all these Republicans (and the 18-19%) are pro-life, anti-Roe-v.-Wade Christians who want more conservative federal and Supreme Court justices. But they also all know that none of these things matter if we allow Donald Trump to continue tearing down the institutions and moral foundation of our country's government. ■

08/06/20 — U.S.: 4.3% of World Population, 22% of World Pandemic Death

COVID-19 Deaths

2/06/2020 — U.S.: 1 | World: 620
3/05/2020 — U.S.: 12 | World: 3,293
4/02/2020 — U.S.: 5,137 | World: 48,284
5/07/2020 — U.S.: 73,431 | World: 264,189
6/04/2020 — U.S.: 107,175 | World: 386,464
7/02/2020 — U.S.: 128,062 | World: 516,726
8/06/2020 — U.S.: 158,268 | World: 708,278

• Conservatively estimated Trump malfeasance deaths: 79,134

• U.S.: 4.3% of Earth's population, 22% of its pandemic deaths

(Ibid.; Glanz & Robertson; 5/20/2020.)
(as conservatively extrapolated from COVID-19 Dashboard by the Center for Systems Science and Engineering at Johns Hopkins University; 8/6/2020.)

This Week

The biggest story of the Trump presidency continues to be his responsibility for a conservatively estimated half — equaling 79,134 to date — of all U.S. coronavirus deaths. Note that the U.S. accounts for 4.3% of Earth's population but 22% of the world's total COVID-19 deaths. This is all you need to know to refute Donald's lies about how well he's handled the pandemic and how under control he has it.

The deaths come on top of the other presidential headlines just this past week.

In spite of tens of thousands of needless deaths and consistent attacks on our Constitution, institutions, rule of law, and governmental norms, Mr. Trump's Republican enablers in Congress — even the ones who secretly loathe him and most of what he stands for — remain cravenly unmoved.

> "Yes, and how many times can a man turn his head
> And pretend that he just doesn't see?
>
> "The answer, my friend, is blowin' in the wind
> The answer is blowin' in the wind"
>
> (Dylan, Bob; "Blowin' in the Wind"; *The Freewheelin' Bob Dylan* [LP record album]; 1963.)

My good friend Bob O. reminded me of the significance of this verse in the iconic 1963 Dylan song to the willful ignorance of GOP legislators today. He pointed out that in the Old Testament, Book of Ezekiel he thinks, there is mention of having ears but not hearing, eyes but not seeing. And the lesson still is being learned some 2,600 years hence.

More Headlines

Last Thursday President Trump tweet-floated the idea of delaying the Nov. 3 election until sometime after when people felt safe voting in person — because absentee voting is a hoax, or a scam, or a fraud, or something. This idea was shot down immediately by prominent conservative media outlets and lawmakers. But it accomplished two things important to the president: 1) the resulting national discussion and outrage contributed to his un-American doubt-sowing in the U.S. electoral system; and 2) it took the focus off 150,000-plus COVID-19 deaths, for which Mr. Trump still has no effective plan to address.

Last Friday it was reported that the president's son-in-law, Jared Kushner, was appointed to oversee the U.S. coronavirus crisis in the early days of its manifestation. Jared had commissioned a national testing plan, then aborted it after observing that only Democratic states were being affected. Mr. Kushner decided it would be better politically to leave the testing response solely to the states (a plan his father-in-law enthusiastically approved), to allow the administration to blame blue-state (Democratic) governors for the pandemic later on.

Last Friday it also was reported that President Trump's U.S. ambassador to Brazil asked that government for a "favor" to help reelect our president. Ambassador Todd Chapman informed Brazilian officials that a favorable ethanol tariff decision would help reelect Trump by strengthening his support in Iowa, a crucial swing state.

On Monday Manhattan District Attorney Cyrus Vance said in court filings that his office's current probe of Mr. Trump's finances goes far beyond hush-money payments to two of Donald's paramours. The filing stated Trump's offenses involve "possibly extensive and protracted criminal conduct at the Trump Organization ... possible bank and insurance fraud."

It's been determined that President Trump's recently installed head of the U.S. Postal Service has made significant policy changes to slow down drastically mail delivery across the country. What's notable is the president has been denouncing absentee voting consistently, predicting ballot delays (and nonexistent fraud), and now has implemented policies through his appointee that will ensure the mail-ballot delays he's predicted. The Trump administration also is suing Nevada for implementing mail-in voting.

President Trump has ordered the ongoing census count to be halted one month early. He originally *extended* the cut-off date by one month due to office closures and a greatly impeded process caused by the pandemic. Mr. Trump, however, since has determined an earlier count stop will benefit him politically because the harder-to-find-and-count population likely would *not* be MAGA supporters.

> "Yes, and how many times can a man turn his head,
> And pretend that he just doesn't see?

> "The answer, my friend, is blowin' in the wind,
> The answer is blowin' in the wind" ∎

08/13/20 — Trump Attacks Biden VP Pick, Kamala Harris; He Would've Attacked Virgin Mary

COVID-19 Deaths

2/06/2020 — U.S.: 1 | World: 620
3/05/2020 — U.S.: 12 | World: 3,293
4/02/2020 — U.S.: 5,137 | World: 48,284
5/07/2020 — U.S.: 73,431 | World: 264,189
6/04/2020 — U.S.: 107,175 | World: 386,464
7/02/2020 — U.S.: 128,062 | World: 516,726
8/06/2020 — U.S.: 158,268 | World: 708,278
8/13/2020 — U.S.: 166,038 | World: 749,965

• Conservatively estimated Trump malfeasance deaths: 83,019
• U.S.: 4.3% of Earth's population, 22% of its pandemic deaths

(Ibid.; Glanz & Robertson; 5/20/2020.)
(as conservatively extrapolated from COVID-19 Dashboard by the Center for Systems Science and Engineering at Johns Hopkins University; 8/13/2020.)

Joe Biden's VP Pick

On Tuesday Democratic presidential candidate Joe Biden announced his choice for vice presidential running mate: Sen. Kamala Harris (D-Calif.). Donald Trump and his campaign immediately accused her of being too soft on crime as a left-wing radical and simultaneously too tough on crime as California's attorney general.

Citing an additional disqualification for office, many Republican Party notables say she's "too ambitious."

The president pontificated shortly *before* the (anticipated) announcement: "Some people would say men are insulted" by Biden choosing a woman vice president. But he added that Kamala Harris would "be a fine choice."

After Biden's VP announcement, Donald called her "a phony … Phony Kamala Harris." He said she was "nasty … she was probably nastier than even Pocahontas" (Trump's ad hominem for Sen. Elizabeth Warren, D-Mass.). He went on to characterize her as "the meanest, the most horrible, most disrespectful of anybody in the U.S. Senate" and the "most liberal." Mr. Trump then proceeded to mischaracterize grossly Sen. Harris' policy positions.

A Trump-supporting "friend" opined that latte liberals like me might think she's great but Donald will "tear apart Kamala Harris."

Joe Biden's VP Pick Doesn't Matter to Trump

Let's be clear: I did go through a brief latte phase. But my choice of coffee drink has been a working-class red eye — black, hot — for many years.

Let's also be clear: Donald Trump would attempt to destroy Biden's VP pick no matter whom she might have been, with mendacity, slander, mischaracterization, sexism, racism, ad hominem attacks, and more mendacity. Did I mention mendacity?

I responded to my "friend" that President Trump would tear apart the *Virgin Mary* if she were Biden's pick. I can hear Donald now:

> "She had a kid without having *sex*!?! Give — me — a — break! She's lying. She's a phony. Phony Virgin Mary. Men are insulted by this claim. She's nasty, probably nastier than even Pocahontas, who got pregnant out of wedlock. Yeah,

Pocahontas eventually married Johnny Rolfe, the guy who knocked her up, but the kid's birthday was weeks short of nine months after the wedding date.

"*Virgin* Mary?!? Yeah, right. You know she cheated on Joseph to get pregnant because he swears he never moved on her. We can believe *him* — let's just put it this way: Joseph was not that great with the ladies, OK? And that hair. Those clothes. But that's another story. Virgin Mary is the meanest, the most horrible, most disrespectful of anybody coming out of Nazareth, and the most liberal! Where do you think her son Jesus picked up his radical left-wing socialist ideas!?!

"And she's way too ambitious. It's unseemly. Some people are saying, many people say she lobbied hard to be the Blessed Mother, beating out the other Marys — Magdalene, Clopas — who were much more qualified for the job."

Speaking of Trump Mendacity

President Trump has been accusing former President Obama and former Vice President Biden of treason and spying in tweets, news conferences, and interviews.

"BIG NEWS! The Political Crime of the Century is unfolding. ObamaBiden illegally spied on the Trump Campaign, both before and after the election. Treason!"

(Trump, Donald, R-Fla., U.S. president; Twitter post; 8/5/2020.)

This has been debunked, disputed, disconfirmed, discredited, disproved, denied, disaffirmed, disallowed, disavowed, disclaimed, and every other synonym for *proved wrong* starting with the letter "d."

We need to have White House reporters standing up at Trump news conferences and saying, "I'm sorry, sir, that's a false statement." One by one they would have their press credentials revoked. Wouldn't it be great eventually to see a near-empty White House briefing room with only *Fox* and *OAN* sycophants lobbing softball questions? ∎

08/20/20 — "No Collusion" Claim Blown out of Water by GOP Senate Report

COVID-19 Deaths

2/06/2020 — U.S.: 1 | World: 620
8/20/2020 — U.S.: 173,193 | World: 788,030

> • Conservatively estimated Trump malfeasance deaths: 86,597
> • U.S.: 4.3% of Earth's population, 22% of its pandemic deaths

>> (Ibid.; Glanz & Robertson; 5/20/2020.)
>> (as conservatively extrapolated from COVID-19 Dashboard by the Center for Systems Science and Engineering at Johns Hopkins University; 8/20/2020.)

GOP Senate Russia Report

> "[There was] a breathtaking level of contacts between Trump officials and Russian government operatives that is a very real counterintelligence threat to our elections."

>> (Warner, Mark, D-Va., U.S. Senate Intelligence Committee ranking Democrat; accompanying statement to GOP-controlled Senate Intel. Cmte. Russia report; 8/18/2020.)

"collusion: secret agreement or cooperation especially for an illegal or deceitful purpose"

("collusion"; *Merriam-Webster.com;* retrieved 8/20/2020.)

The Senate Intelligence Committee Tuesday released the long-awaited last installment of its near-1,000-pages-total report on Russian involvement in corrupting the 2016 presidential election. The committee is chaired by Sen. Marco Rubio (R-Fla.) and majority-controlled by (Trump) Republicans.

The report blows Trump World's fallacious mantra of "no collusion" out of the water, into the upper atmosphere, where it ricochets back down, straight through the MAGA heartland. In a Republican nutshell, the GOP Senate's final word says the Trump 2016 campaign solicited, welcomed, accepted, used, benefited from, and vigorously covered up illegal Russian help to win the election. Donald and his team tiptoed as close as humanly possible up to the line of American indictable illegality without crossing it — as far as we know. But the report confirmed there were myriad essential reasons and sufficient evidence for the FBI to investigate the 2016 Trump campaign for traitorous breaches of national security.

Trump Republicans said that.

Sen. Rubio and other majority members on the panel attempted to soften the news-cycle blow to the president by misrepresenting (i.e., lying about) what their own report says in the apparent hope that the public won't read it or won't believe verbatim quotations in the "lame-stream media."

If any other commander in chief were in office — or if the electorate currently were not shell-shocked, exhausted, and completely numb to Donald's numerous lies and outrages — the president would be resigning the day after this report's release. It goes beyond the Mueller Report (which itself would've forced any other president's resignation) with damning revelations of presidential perjury and high-level campaign contacts with a Russian agent to whom confidential high-value polling information was passed multiple times.

Report Speaks for Itself

I'll tell you what: Let the Aug. 18, 2020, "Report of the Select Committee on Intelligence, United States Senate, on Russian Active Measures, Campaigns, and Interference in the 2016 U.S. Election, Volume 5: Counterintelligence Threats and Vulnerabilities" speak for itself.

Roger Stone

> "The Trump campaign sought to maximize the impact of those [GRU, WikiLeaks] leaks to aid Trump's electoral prospects. Staff on the Trump campaign sought advance notice about WikiLeaks releases, created messaging strategies to promote and share the materials in anticipation [of] and following their release, and encouraged further leaks.

> "Trump and senior campaign officials sought to obtain advance information about WikiLeaks' planned releases through Roger Stone. At their direction, Stone took action to gain inside knowledge for the campaign and shared his purported knowledge directly with Trump and senior campaign officials on multiple occasions.

> "Despite Trump's [lack of] recollection, the committee assesses that Trump did, in fact, speak with [Roger] Stone about WikiLeaks and with members of his campaign about Stone's access to WikiLeaks on multiple occasions. ... [Stone] obtained information indicating [Clinton campaign chief] John Podesta would be a target of an upcoming release, prior to WikiLeaks releasing Podesta's emails on

Oct. 7. Stone then communicated this information to Trump and other senior campaign officials.

> "The committee found evidence … [that] WikiLeaks was knowingly collaborating with Russian government officials. … WikiLeaks actively sought, and played, a key role in the Russian influence campaign and very likely knew it was assisting a Russian intelligence influence effort."

> ("Report of the Select Committee on Intelligence, United States Senate, on Russian Active Measures, Campaigns, and Interference in the 2016 U.S. Election, Volume 5: Counterintelligence Threats and Vulnerabilities"; 8/18/2020.)

Candidate Trump repeatedly expressed his support for WikiLeaks at rallies and news conferences during his campaign: "WikiLeaks — I love WikiLeaks!" "This WikiLeaks is like a treasure trove." "WikiLeaks, it sounds like, is going to be dropping some more." "Boy, I love reading those WikiLeaks."

The report states that immediately after the infamous *Access Hollywood* hot-mic outtake video (in which Donald said of women he's attracted to that he can just "grab 'em by the p***y") was released to the press, Roger Stone told WikiLeaks through an intermediary to "drop the Podesta emails immediately." They were "dropped" 30 minutes after the video's media release.

The dump of thousands of private emails was damaging to the Clinton campaign and distracted the day's news away from Trump's caught-on-tape disgusting misogyny. Note that there were no wrongdoings or misdeeds exposed in these emails, only private sausage-making discussions and content that no campaign, no business, no family ever would want released to the public.

Paul Manafort

Trump campaign Chair Paul Manafort's passing of confidential material to a Russian agent was a "grave counterintelligence threat." Manafort's partner and Russian contact, Konstantin Kilimnik, was part of "a cadre of individuals ostensibly operating outside of the Russian government but who nonetheless implement Kremlin-directed influence operations. ... Kilimnik is a Russian intelligence officer ... who may have been connected to the GRU's hack and leak operation targeting the 2016 U.S. election," the existence of which is beyond dispute. (Ibid.; U.S. Senate report; 8/18/2020.)

Phony Ukraine Pro-Clinton Election Interference Story

President Trump has attempted to divert the (true) Russian pro-Trump election interference story to a (false) Ukrainian pro-Clinton election interference story. This has been debunked by all credible U.S. (and other) intel sources then and now. It's been long known that this narrative originated with Russian agents including Konstantin Kilimnik and had been perpetuated by Trump campaign Chair Paul Manafort. Russian President Vladimir Putin even told a version of the whopper to Trump. Many Trump Republicans have continued pushing this propaganda long after being warned by the intelligence community that they were doing Russia's bidding.

> "The committee has determined that this theory espoused by Kilimnik and Manafort ... that the Ukrainians were responsible [for U.S. election interference], not the Russians ... has no factual basis."

> (Ibid.; U.S. Senate report; 8/18/2020.)

Without presenting evidence that Vladimir Putin definitely has kompromat on Donald Trump, the report devoted a lot of ink to Russia's kompromat-harvesting methods and activities, and hinted at the possible existence of such blackmail-able material.

> "The committee found that the Ritz Carlton in Moscow [where Trump is reported to have hired two prostitutes] is a high counterintelligence risk environment. The committee assesses that the hotel likely has at least one permanent Russian intelligence officer on staff, government surveillance of guests' rooms [including hundreds of security cameras], and the regular presence of a large number of prostitutes, likely with at least the tacit approval of Russian authorities."

> (Ibid.; U.S. Senate report; 8/18/2020.)

Additionally the report states Trump likely had several relationships with Russian women starting in the 1990s.

Presidential Denials of Russian Influence

> "The Trump campaign publicly undermined the attribution of the hack-and-leak campaign to Russia [the truth of which is beyond dispute] and was indifferent to whether it and WikiLeaks were furthering a Russian election interference effort."

> (Ibid.; U.S. Senate report; 8/18/2020.)

In other words, "Hoax! Hoax! Witch-Hunt Hoax!"

Consensus

The Republican-led committee along with its Democrats all signed off on this spine-chilling conclusion:

> "What happened to the United States in 2016 should be an alarm bell for the nation. … Russia is actively interfering again in the 2020 U.S. election to assist Donald Trump, and some of the president's associates are amplifying those efforts. … The Russian intelligence services' assault on the integrity of the … U.S. electoral process, and Trump and his associates' participation in and enabling of this Russian activity, represents one of the single most grave counterintelligence threats to American national security in the modern era."

> (Ibid.; U.S. Senate report; 8/18/2020.)

Trump Republicans said that.

Collusion

> "We can say, without any hesitation, that the committee found absolutely no evidence that then-candidate Donald Trump or his campaign colluded with the Russian government to meddle in the 2016 election."

> (six Republican members including Sen. Marco
> Rubio, R-Fla., U.S. Senate Intelligence Committee
> chair; accompanying statement to the GOP-
> controlled Senate Intel. Cmte. Russia report;
> 8/18/2020.)

"We can say, without any hesitation, that the committee found absolutely no evidence that its Republican members know the definition of the word *collusion*."

> (one political observer including Tom Ersin, *GraniteWord.com;* accompanying statement to the GOP-controlled Senate Intel. Cmte. Russia report; 8/18/2020.)

"[The report] unambiguously shows that members of the Trump Campaign cooperated with Russian efforts to get Trump elected. This is what collusion looks like."

> (five Democratic members including vice presidential nominee Sen. Kamala Harris, D-Calif., U.S. Senate Intelligence Committee; accompanying statement to the GOP-controlled Senate Intel. Cmte. Russia report; 8/18/2020.)

President Trump called the Republican-led Senate Intelligence Committee report "a hoax." Really.■

08/27/20 — Trump Doctrine: "Every Day It's Something Else. Who Cares?"

COVID-19 Deaths

2/06/2020 — U.S.: 1 | World: 620
8/27/2020 — U.S.: 179,743 | World: 826,380

> • Conservatively estimated Trump malfeasance deaths: 89,872
> • U.S.: 4.3% of Earth's population, 22% of its pandemic deaths

> (Ibid.; Glanz & Robertson; 5/20/2020.)
> (as conservatively extrapolated from COVID-19 Dashboard by the Center for Systems Science and Engineering at Johns Hopkins University; 8/27/2020.)

Trump Doctrine

> "All he wants to do is appeal to his base. ... He has no principles. None. ... You can't trust him. ... And his base, I mean my God, if you were a religious person, you want to help people. Not do this. ... His g*ddamned tweeting and lying, oh my God. I'm talking too freely, but you know. The change of stories. The lack of preparation. The lying. Holy sh*t. ... He doesn't read. ... It's the phoniness of it all. It's the phoniness and this cruelty. Donald is cruel. ... He was a brat. I did his homework for him. I drove him around New York City to try to get him into college. He went to Fordham [for two years] and then he got into University of Pennsylvania because he had somebody take the exams.

SATs or whatever. ... That's what I believe. I even remember the name ... Joe Shapiro."

(Barry, Maryanne Trump, former federal judge, president's sister; statements made while being surreptitiously recorded 2018-19; released by *The Washington Post*; 8/22/2020.)

"Every day it's something else. Who cares?"

(Trump, Donald, R-Fla., U.S. president; statement issued in response to release of surreptitiously recorded 2018-19 tapes of Maryanne Trump Barry, former federal judge, president's sister; 8/23/2020.)

In a series of unguarded conversations recorded over the past two years and released this week, President Trump's older sister, former federal Judge Maryanne Trump Barry, exposed him to the world for what he is: a cruel, ignorant grifter. It's apparently the first time any family member's discouraging words about the president have become public (with the obvious exception of his Ph.D. psychologist niece and recorder of the sister tapes, Mary Trump).

These taped truths from a highly accomplished sibling would end any other politician's career. Donald's defense? "Every day it's something else. Who cares?"

He's counting on this.

And it's been effective.

He counts on voters to be numb, in shock, to lose track of his multitudinous offenses and depravities. When Donald's never-ending crimes, scandals, and outrageous utterances are exposed on a daily basis he retains his power, his political vitality through long-term desensitization of the electorate to his transgressions. There are just too many to keep track of, too many to analyze, too many to prosecute. "And besides, nobody can be *that* bad."

He's counting on his mantra, "Who cares?" He's counting on enough of the country not to care.

"Every Day It's Something Else. Who Cares?"

Separated 5,400 migrant children from their families to "set an example"

Withheld aid to Puerto Rico after Hurricane Maria's devastation saying the U.S. territory and its (American) citizens "needed to do more to help themselves"

Has had record number of top aids indicted and convicted for fraud, perjury, campaign crimes

Attacked Gold Star families

Attacked Sen. John McCain's (R-Ariz.) war-hero service

Sent military troops to southern border for immigration stunt, defying "his" generals

"Every day it's something else. Who cares?"

Is taking in hundreds of millions of dollars in illegal emoluments clauses violations

Canceled plan to build new FBI headquarters to protect Trump D.C. hotel profits

Masterminded massive family tax fraud to increase his inheritance

Called white supremacists and neo-Nazis "very fine people"

Mocked physically challenged journalists

"Every day it's something else. Who cares?"

Deployed federal agents to use brutality and tear gas on peaceful, legal protesters to clear the way for a Bible photo op

Capitulated to Russian president, publicly accepting (at the Trump-Putin summit press conference in Helsinki) Putin's denials of election interference over Trump's own U.S. intel agencies' unanimous findings

Caught red-handed extorting Ukraine for dirt on his presidential rival, causing Ukrainian deaths while withholding desperately needed (congressionally authorized) military assistance for that country's defense against Russian aggression

Fired numerous inspectors general for initiating investigations related to him

Solicited, welcomed, accepted, used, benefited from, and covered up Russian help to win election

"Every day it's something else. Who cares?"

Continues to attack NATO and U.S. allies

Causing tens of thousands of unnecessary pandemic deaths through corruption, incompetence

Ordered Attorney General Barr to favor, help him by impeding or stopping harmful (to Trump) investigations

Has never confronted Putin about suspected Russian bounties paid for dead U.S. troops in Afghanistan

Currently facing 20-plus lawsuits over credible accusations of sexual assault or misconduct

Committed substantial perjury during Russia investigation

"Every day it's something else. Who cares?"

Ordered NOAA to falsify hurricane information retroactively to "prove" himself right after refusing to admit a small honest mistake anyone could have made

Continues to favor, compliment dictators

Trump ("charitable") Foundation ordered to pay $2 million and shut down permanently due to fraud

Trump adult children (Trump Foundation board members) court-ordered for life never again to be associated with a charity

Trump Inaugural Committee is under investigation for multiple frauds

Trump University ordered to pay $25 million and shut down permanently due to fraud

Said in an unguarded moment, of women he's attracted to, that he can just "grab 'em by the p***y"

Fired FBI director in attempt to stop Russia investigation

Told intel secrets to high-level Russian officials in Oval Office, prompting U.S. intel agencies to call home top undercover operatives in Russia out of concern Trump could inadvertently expose them

Bragged to Russian officials about eliminating "nutjob" FBI director and "Russia stress"

Ordered USPS to slow down mail service to suppress mail-in ballots (which many experts believe will break for Joe Biden) in November

Committed obstruction of justice at least 10 times in attempting to impede Russia investigation, including dangling pardons for silence and intimidating (publicly and privately) other potential witnesses

Has refused consistently to criticize America's archenemy Russia, continuing to fawn over Putin while dissing allies

Refused sanctions to hold business ally Saudi Arabia and its leader responsible for brutal murder of Saudi citizen-critic and *The Washington Post* correspondent

Ordered CDC to weaken COVID-19 testing guidelines to minimize case number reports

Continues to spread unfounded lie that mail-in ballots lead to fraud, to suppress the vote and help his reelection

Repeatedly claims that the only way he loses November election is if it's rigged

Has told 20,000-plus documented lies in his capacity as president

"Every day it's something else. Who cares?"

———————

This presidential rat is being cornered. He knows he's losing and he's willing to do anything — anything — to try and win, to avoid near-certain indictment after leaving office. The existing damage caused by the Trump presidency is about to increase exponentially as the November election looms. There is no bottom. It will get worse.

And then there will be the period between his election loss and Joe Biden's inauguration.■

09/03/20 — Trump Supporters: Here Are the True Deal-Breakers

COVID-19 Deaths

2/06/2020 — U.S.: 1 | World: 620
3/05/2020 — U.S.: 12 | World: 3,293
4/02/2020 — U.S.: 5,137 | World: 48,284
5/07/2020 — U.S.: 73,431 | World: 264,189
6/04/2020 — U.S.: 107,175 | World: 386,464
7/02/2020 — U.S.: 128,062 | World: 516,726
8/06/2020 — U.S.: 158,268 | World: 708,278
9/03/2020 — U.S.: 185,752 | World: 863,577

> • Conservatively estimated Trump malfeasance deaths:
> 92,876
> • U.S.: 4.3% of Earth's population, 22% of its pandemic
> deaths

> (Ibid.; Glanz & Robertson; 5/20/2020.)
> (as conservatively extrapolated from COVID-19
> Dashboard by the Center for Systems Science and
> Engineering at Johns Hopkins University;
> 9/3/2020.)

Fact

> [FACT:] Virtually all racists and white supremacists support
> Donald Trump over Joe Biden. And Mr. Trump refuses to
> disavow support from well-known white supremacist leaders
> and organizations.

I'm not using this fact to assert that *President Trump* is a racist and white supremacist. Draw your own conclusion.

But I'll now address the remaining bulk of "Make America Great Again" supporters who deny any racist, white supremacy sympathies, overt or covert. I speak of Donald's "pro-life" apostles and apologists whose single-issue support manifests in their desire for more conservative judges and repeal of Roe v. Wade at the expense of everything else.

> [FACT:] The abortion-rights-versus-abortion-prohibition issue comprises people of high moral standing and integrity residing in both factions.

Many sincere people of faith oppose abortion on the grounds that all life is sacred. And many other sincere people of faith believe that after careful consideration, within certain reasonable guidelines, and after consulting her doctor and searching her conscience, a woman's right to control her own body is just that: her right. Both camps can find biblical references or absence of references to support their argument. This philosophical debate has raged since medical science (and backroom butchers) developed the abortive procedure and made an issue of the right to choose.

Therefore I have difficulty understanding how the issue of abortion prohibition, pro or con, can be a presidential deal-breaker. There are many fine people, on both sides. On both sides.

A deal-breaker would be the indiscriminate allowance of nearly 100,000 post-born American pandemic deaths.

A deal-breaker would be the policy-driven emotional torture and physical mistreatment of thousands of innocent migrant children.

A deal-breaker would be the systematic attempts to weaken American democracy through blatant corruption, strong autocratic tendencies, and Orwellian disregard for truth.

A deal-breaker would be the belief that there are very fine people among neo-Nazis.

MAGA supporters, please step up and identify yourselves as being on the Trumpian side of these issues. Please tell me about the "very fine people — on both sides."

Friends and Family

I don't hate Trump supporters, some of whom are dear friends and family members. I don't think they're stupid. How can many of them be stupid and still earn college degrees and respectable or even high incomes? I am, however, desperately trying to figure them out. They have some kind of blind spot, are under some kind of mass hypnotic hold from which they can't break free.

They need an intervention, a deprogramming. And I'm just the guy to help them because I care about Trump supporters — unlike those other weak-on-crime, anti-law-and-order, throw-money-at-the-problem radical Biden socialists.

Trump Supporters: Here Are the True Deal-Breakers

Child Separation to "Set an Example"

How is this *not* a deal-breaker for Trump supporters?

In 2017-2018, Donald separated some 5,400 migrant minors — including babies, toddlers, and other young children — from their parents or other family-member guardians for months, locking them up in squalor, 6-year-olds wailing for their mothers and fathers, causing lifelong-lasting psychic damage. The non-profit Physicians for Human Rights has determined that this trauma constitutes torture.

Hundreds of these children have been separated permanently through government incompetence — immigration authorities failed to track their or their families' whereabouts. And Mr. Trump continued to push this brutal, inhumane policy while illegal immigration was at its lowest levels in decades. He only stopped it after widespread national moral outrage from even his supporters.

The adults who brought their kids might have broken laws, though many were legal asylum seekers. (Either way, the vast majority simply were desperate to save their families.) But the children are innocent human beings, lambs of God, put through the horror — the torture — of losing their parents in a strange country, not knowing if they would ever see them again, so the president could "set an example."

Allowing Needless Pandemic Deaths to Support Reelection

How is this not a deal-breaker for Trump supporters?

Donald has caused many tens of thousands of needless deaths by consistently, still, playing down the coronavirus and spreading dangerous disinformation to restart the economy early solely for reelection to avoid otherwise near-certain indictment. My conservative estimate of lives lost due to Trump corruption and incompetence is half of the current 186,000 U.S. pandemic deaths. The United States — with the greatest health care research expertise in the world — accounts for 4.3% of Earth's population but 22% of world COVID-19 deaths. You do the math.

In recent weeks President Trump has claimed COVID-19 prevention guidelines (masks, social distancing, limiting gatherings) are a Democratic plot to abolish church attendance. He's now pushing a dangerous, fraudulent "herd immunity" policy, i.e., tacitly encouraging healthy people to contract the disease. And he's ordered the CDC to recommend less testing.

From the beginning he's refused to nationalize health guidelines, testing, treatment supply production, and the supply chain. He's demanding school districts reopen without limitations at the peak of a pandemic, without any guidance. And he's threatening to pull funds if they don't. He's risking the lives of millions of children across the country for personal, political gain. He's crushed CDC and FDA independence and bastardized their public guidelines.

The president did institute a porous (40,000 nationals still were allowed to enter the U.S.) Chinese travel ban in late January. Contrary to his claims of bold action, however, he simply was catching up to what much of the rest of the world and the U.S. airline industry already were doing. Since the ban, Trump has sabotaged virus containment efforts by squandering lead time provided by the European preview, issuing false assurances and solutions, ridiculing near-universal medical recommendations, suppressing data, and discrediting his own top infectious disease experts.

Believe It or Not

Mr. and Ms. Trump Supporter, I guess you can claim not to believe any of this, that's it's all "fake news." But that's simply classic denial from an addict, your blind spot. That's the cigarette junkie who lost half a lung claiming the butts "relax" him. That's the active alky justifying that she can't have a problem because she never drinks alone, only drinks beer, or still has her good job. That's the closet racist averring "*All* lives matter."

I understand being anti-abortion. I understand opposing Roe v. Wade. I *don't* understand tearing down government and its moral foundations so that Roe and other laws will be moot. I don't understand blowing up democracy until there's nothing left to fight for, nothing left to defend. I don't understand being "pro-life" while accepting the torture of children and needless American pandemic deaths — not to mention needless Puerto Rican (also American) and Ukrainian deaths caused by Trump incompetence and corruption.

By the way, I still would do everything in my power to defeat Mr. Trump even if he were a Democrat vehemently supporting a woman's right to choose, and Joe Biden were a Republican vehemently vowing to repeal Roe v. Wade. Abortion prohibition, pro or con, is not a deal-breaker when the rule of law, American democracy, and American morality are at stake.

[FUN FACT:] Donald's near-universal support from white
supremacists and white nationalists was *not* a deal-breaker
for his ostensibly nonracist supporters.

If psychological torture of children, needless loss of post-born life,
and burning down American democracy aren't deal-breakers for you
we're done talking. My mental health depends on it. But I'll miss
you.■

09/10/20 — The Best People

[TOPICS: new book out, "Rage" by Bob Woodward]

COVID-19 Deaths

2/06/2020 — U.S.: 1 | World: 620
9/10/2020 — U.S.: 190,885 | World: 904,364

> • Conservatively estimated Trump malfeasance deaths: 95,443
> • U.S.: 4.3% of Earth's population, 21% of its pandemic deaths
>
> > (Ibid.; Glanz & Robertson; 5/20/2020.)
> > (as conservatively extrapolated from COVID-19 Dashboard by the Center for Systems Science and Engineering at Johns Hopkins University; 9/10/2020.)

Rage

We already know Donald is corrupt to the core. An impeachment and a Mueller report proved that (notwithstanding GOP obstruction and obfuscation of both).

We already know Mr. Trump is a liar, with 20,000-and-counting whoppers documented since Inauguration Day.

We already know he's a traitorous cheat. Intelligence community whistleblower accounts of suppressing Russian 2020 election-interference analysis and white supremacist threat warnings corroborate that.

We already know he holds deep contempt for the military, having disparaged members who were injured, killed, and captured; soldiers who failed to evade the draft; and his "bunch of dopes and babies" generals.

We already know he's a serial sexual predator through his unguarded machismo on an *Access Hollywood* video outtake and 20-plus-and-counting sexual assault lawsuits.

Now with Bob Woodward's new book, *Rage*, the revered nonpartisan reporter and historian has confirmed indisputable, unparalleled presidential depravity: a willingness to allow Americans to die so he can secure reelection. It's on tape.

Make no mistake. President Trump played down, denied, and belittled the pandemic danger from its inception; knowingly lied to the country; knowingly caused tens of thousands of needless deaths to protect "his" economy — his sole lifeline to reelection — to avoid electoral defeat and near-certain indictment.

Astonishingly Bob's book also tells us that Trump revealed to Woodward the existence of a super-secret nuclear weapons system. When the author confirmed this with top military officials, they were shocked and appalled at the president's loose-lipped carelessness.

Rage reveals that Donald's Director of National Intelligence Dan Coats (March 2017 – August 2019), though he couldn't prove it, felt certain that Russian President Vladimir Putin had "something" on Trump, some form of kompromat that contained the only explanation for Donald's consistent, panderous acquiescence to Putin. Defense Secretary Gen. Jim Mattis told Coats in May 2019, "Maybe at some point we're going to have to stand up and speak out. There may be a time when we have to take collective action."

Let's Face It

Let's face it. I like Joe Biden well enough. And yeah, yeah, yeah, it's good if Biden gives us something to vote *for*, which he does. But the

2020 presidential election is about one thing: voting *against* — getting rid of — President Trump. Most of the electorate would vote for any candidate who isn't a convicted ax-murderer over Donald as long as they were motivated to vote. My dog, Bob Barker, would make a better commander in chief: I'd be his top adviser and would surround President Barker with the best people.

I mean really, the *best people*, not the corrupt element with whom Mr. Trump feels most comfortable. Not jailbirds and pardon-whores like Michael Flynn, former national security adviser (perjury, Russian election-help enabling); Rick Gates, 2016 campaign deputy chair (fraud); Paul Manafort, 2016 second campaign chair (fraud, Russian election-help enabling); George Papadopoulos, 2016 campaign adviser (perjury); Roger Stone, 2016 campaign adviser, lifelong ally (perjury, Russian election-help enabling); Michael Cohen, former personal attorney-fixer (fraud, campaign finance violation); Louis DeJoy, soon-to-be-indicted postmaster general (campaign finance violation); and Steve Bannon, 2016 third campaign director, top adviser ("build-the-wall" fraud).

Remember the "businessman" argument, that Donald was so successful in business that he was sure to run America the same way, always winning?

> "Well, this is embarrassing. Seems President Trump has run his reelection campaign into financial distress, a status that will not surprise those familiar with the Trump Taj Mahal, the Trump Castle, the Trump Plaza Atlantic City, the Trump Plaza New York, Trump Hotels and Casino Resorts, Trump Entertainment Resorts, the Trump Tower Tampa, the Trump Shuttle, Trump: The Game, Trump magazine, Trump Mortgage, Trump Steaks, Trump mattresses, Trump pillows, Trump perfume, Trump shirts, Trump underwear, Trump shoes, Trump eyeglasses, Trump University, Trump Vodka, the Trump Foundation, and the U.S. Treasury."

(Milbank, Dana; "How You Can Help Save the
Trump Campaign From Financial Ruin"; *The
Washington Post*; 9/8/2020.)

There's a reason why you haven't (or have) heard of these former
Trump businesses. And it's not due to a great businessman
surrounding himself with the best people.∎

09/17/20 — Progressive Babies (Cut off Nose, Spite Face)

COVID-19 Deaths

2/06/2020 — U.S.: 1 | World: 620
9/17/2020 — U.S.: 196,831 | World: 941,363

> • Conservatively estimated Trump malfeasance deaths: 98,416
> • U.S.: 4.3% of Earth's population, 21% of its pandemic deaths

> > (Ibid.; Glanz & Robertson; 5/20/2020.)
> > (as conservatively extrapolated from COVID-19 Dashboard by the Center for Systems Science and Engineering at Johns Hopkins University; 9/17/2020.)

MAGA Cultism and Progressive Babies — Two Sides of the Same Self-Destructive Coin

It's bad enough I have to fight with Trump Republicans: brainwashed MAGA cult members for whom absolutely *nothing matters*. Here lately I've encountered a group of "true progressives," babies who want to boycott Joe Biden and blow it all up because their guy didn't win the Democratic nomination.

I'm not talking about sincere progressives who were lukewarm on Biden: He wasn't their first choice in the primary, but they're still voting for him because the country will implode under four more years of Trump. I feel for those people. They're my people. Biden wasn't my first choice, either. (Though us practical liberals will acknowledge Uncle Joe has made significant movement toward progressive policy positions.)

No, I'm talking about the people who are advocating a Joe Biden boycott by voting third party or not voting to somehow force a "real progressive" on Democrats someday.

I've heard some say they don't support "lesser-evil voting," that this has given us 40 years of "the same," whatever "the same" is. (In 2016 eschewing "the same" got them Donald J. Trump.) So instead they're going to use or withhold their vote to send a message to establishment Democrats by writing in a protest choice or sitting out the election.

This is like playing shortstop on the Little League baseball team your mom coaches, then she takes you out of the game for poor sportsmanship, then you go behind the opposing bench and start rooting loudly for the other team. (Full disclosure: My mom *did* take me out of the game. I *did* get mad, I *did* go behind the opposing bench, and I *did* start rooting loudly for the other team. But I was 11.)

If you don't understand that this election is different you're beyond hope. You're insincere and, worse, counterproductive to your ostensible goals.

"Neoliberals"

No, what progressive babies are engaged in is indirect *worst-evil* voting. If they can't have their first choice, the most leftist candidate in the lot, they'll not vote for second-best. They will in effect support a dangerous, corrupt, incompetent autocrat instead. That'll show the milquetoast neoliberals. Take that. If I can't have the one I love, then blow it all up. If my mom takes me out of the game, my team is dead to me.

This is classic perfect-is-the-enemy-of-the-good thinking. And it could destroy a great country.

Progressive babies love to describe us sincere realists with terms like *neoliberal,* a now watered-down meaningless pejorative that sounds cool to them (comparable to MAGA supporters using the term *RINO, Republican in Name Only*, to describe any non-Trump Republican). These babies wear their zero-tolerance attitude on their sleeves to say, "Look at me, I'm the only liberal with morals, with scruples, with integrity — it's my way or the (destroy-our-country) highway." They believe it's worth four more years of Trumpism, possibly destroying American democracy beyond repair, to convince us they're right.

By the way, *neo-* is defined as *new*, as in *new* liberal. I've been a progressive, a liberal since before these progressive babies learned what *neo-* — or *liberal* — means.

They're All the Same

Then there are the cretins who believe — or say they believe — that Biden essentially is the same as Trump: no policy, ethical, or competence differences to speak of. I don't know if some of these guys are all shock value or what. But the ones who do believe this and are willing to reelect Trump are out of their minds. It's like the spurned psychopath boyfriend *(progressive baby)* who wants to kill his ex *(Democratic Party)* because if he can't control her she should suffer and die. These Biden-equals-Trump miscreants are urging that since their guy didn't win the primary, burn the mutha down.

If you believe Donald Trump and Joe Biden are the same, I can't help you. If you can't understand that this election is different, there's no further value in conversing.

Bernie

Let me remind everyone: Bernie Sanders is not a Democrat. He's an Independent. What right do these babies have to try and force a non-Democrat down party members' throats? Be thankful they let him run in their primary, accept that he lost, and shut the hell up. Get your own damn party if you don't like the way Dems run theirs.

In the meantime as a progressive — and a Democrat — I'll support the most liberal party and candidate that can win.

I love Bernie. I've loved him for many years since long before he became a superstar, before most progressive babies ever heard of him. But he chooses *not* to be a Democrat. I love the progressive AOC, aka Alexandria Ocasio-Cortez. I love the balance she creates in the party. She chooses to *be* a Democrat. She chooses to work from within. She creates ideological tension with House Speaker Nancy Pelosi, a less rabid (but highly effective) Democrat. Fantastic. This is how the system is supposed to work.

As actor Steven Hill's character on *Law and Order*, District Attorney Adam Schiff, said after a tough government corruption case, "America: the worst system of governing on Earth — except for all the others." It has its faults. But you work with those. If you don't like the way the DNC runs strategy, work with the team from within for change, in good faith. Don't try to force Bernie into the end zone, then stamp your feet and take your ball home after the majority of the party decided he probably couldn't beat Trump. We couldn't take that chance.

What's a Progressive?

I'm a progressive, a critically thoughtful, realistic practical liberal. I support social democracy. I'm about as left as you can get without being a socialist or communist. (Note to democratic socialists: I'm not conflating the two.) But practically speaking I don't want my country to burn down. Progressive babies, the ones who don't now support Biden-Harris (a very strong ticket, i.e., capable of beating Trump), are pouty, recalcitrant, dangerous children who don't see any big picture and are willing to turn America into one of Billy Mumy's *Twilight Zone* jack-in-the-boxes.

You must support the most ideologically aligned candidate to you who has a chance to win at each juncture along the way. If your candidate loses the primary, then you support the next ideologically closest candidate who has a chance to win. Then you work for change from within.

There is *no other* realistic, effective way forward. After the most perverse U.S. president in history is removed, *then* you babies can resume blowing up the system to seek the perfect progressive candidate.

What this means for *reasonable* and *effective* progressives is that they can resume responsibly attempting to move the Democratic Party leftward from within.

I'm tired of you phony purists who refuse to consider even the thinking of Bernie Sanders, AOC, et al. who right now are staunch Biden-Harris supporters. There's currently one practical solution: Vote Biden. Anything else supports burning down the country so that there's nothing left for you or any other histrionic ideologues to fight for. I'm sick of your whining.

MAGA cult members, whining progressive babies, come together, see the light. (It could happen.)■

09/24/20 — "Death Cult": Fascism 101

COVID-19 Deaths

2/06/2020 — U.S.: 1 | World: 620
9/24/2020 — U.S.: 201,920 | World: 977,357

> • Conservatively estimated Trump malfeasance deaths: 100,960
> • U.S.: 4.3% of Earth's population, 21% of its pandemic deaths

> (Glanz, James & Robertson, Campbell; "Lockdown Delays Cost at Least 36,000 Lives, Data Show"; *The New York Times;* 5/20/2020.)
> (Gupta, Vin, MD, MPA, MSc, University of Washington Institute for Health Metrics and Evaluation professor, global health policy expert, formerly with WHO, CDC; "Dr. Vin Gupta: 'Evidence That 70% of Lives Could Have Been Saved'"; *MSNBC's Meet the Press Daily* with Chuck Todd; 9/18/2020.)
> (as conservatively extrapolated from COVID-19 Dashboard by the Center for Systems Science and Engineering at Johns Hopkins University; 9/24/2020.)

[EDITOR'S NOTE:] On *Meet the Press Daily* with Chuck Todd Sept. 18, 2020, it was disclosed (prompted by a FOIA request) that according to internal White House documents, several months ago the Trump administration scrapped a plan to send masks to every American household. The president actively was discouraging COVID-19 prevention guidelines at that time. Also on the show, global health policy expert Dr. Vin Gupta declared that 70% of pandemic deaths could have been avoided had Trump acted sooner, and 200,000 future lives could be saved if he acts now. Unfortunately the president still is downplaying the pandemic and resisting prevention efforts.

> (Gupta, Vin, MD, MPA, MSc, University of Washington Institute for Health Metrics and Evaluation professor, global health policy expert, formerly with WHO, CDC; "Dr. Vin Gupta: 'Evidence That 70% of Lives Could Have Been Saved'"; *MSNBC's Meet the Press Daily* with Chuck Todd; 9/18/2020.)

No More "Likes"

I used to say the MAGA following was *like* a cult. Now I say it clearly *is* a cult. Donald Trump is the leader with all the incredibly effective brainwashing skills of Charles Manson, Jim Jones, and the rest of the best. If The Donald announced at his next superspreader rally that he wanted his people to start killing reporters and anti-Trump protesters, there is no doubt in my mind that we would begin to see this happen, slowly at first, then in larger numbers as cult members gained confidence.

He already celebrates the *injuries* of journalists and anti-Trump protesters. *MSNBC* anchor Ali Velshi getting hit with a police rubber bullet (at an entirely peaceful protest in May) has become a rally applause line: "I remember this guy Velshi. He got hit … and he went down. … It was the most beautiful thing. … It's called law and order."

He already long ago promised, "I'll pay the legal fees" if rally attendees would "knock the crap out of [protesters]" — another raucous applause line.

Heck, he's essentially said to his supporters, "You know, several hundred of you from each of my rallies will get sick or die from covid, but thanks for ignoring the guidelines and laughing at the masks. You're my people, taking one for the team!" They willingly risk their lives for him.

He's got the best of Charles Manson (kill our enemies) *and* Jim Jones (kill ourselves).

Since author Bob Woodward's presidential interview tapes have come out in recent weeks — containing devastating, self-incriminating statements by Donald in his own voice — one thing is clear, crystal: MAGA cult members *do not care* what truth is. They *do not care* that their leader literally is killing tens of thousands of Americans with corrupt incompetence — including many of *them* — simply to be reelected and avoid indictment.

No, they have simple reasons to discard all respect for truth, empathy, and humanity: 1) they worship a leader who is as openly uncouth, racist, and corrupt as they wish they could be; and/or 2) they worship a leader who hates all the same people they do, i.e., civil rights advocates, women's rights proponents, of course Democrats, and anyone else who threatens white majority control; and/or 3) they worship the single issue of stopping abortion at the expense of all other humankind issues. It may be conscious, unconscious, or subconscious. But it's that simple.

I Said, "No More Likes"

I used to say Donald was *like* an aspiring autocrat, that he was exhibiting autocratic, dictatorial *tendencies*. I used to discount other pundits' characterizations that President Trump was a fascist or at least exhibiting fascist tendencies. I thought that was too harsh, over the top, hyperbolic.

Not anymore.

"fascism: a political philosophy, movement, or regime … that exalts nation and often race above the individual and that stands for a centralized autocratic government headed by a dictatorial leader, severe economic and social regimentation, and forcible suppression of opposition"

("fascism"; *Merriam-Webster.com;* retrieved 9/24/2020.)

John Heilemann, *NBC News* political analyst and co-author of *Game Change* (about the 2008 presidential election campaign) yesterday called Donald Trump's presidency, "Literally a death cult." I wish I had said that.

Steve Schmidt, Sen. John McCain's (R-Ariz.) 2008 presidential campaign director, this week called President Trump's corrupt, incompetent handling of the coronavirus pandemic, "The greatest malfeasance in the history of the United States." I wish I had said that.

Death Cult

President Trump — literally — has allowed many tens of thousands of Americans to die needlessly from COVID-19 for the sole purpose of supporting his reelection. Once again: *for the sole — sole — purpose of reelection.*

We already knew — and the Woodward tapes have confirmed beyond any doubt — that Trump knew last January the virus was coming, it was deadly, it was airborne, and that it could kill hundreds of thousands of Americans. But he made a determination to which he continues to hold that any mention of precautions, any role-modeling of prevention guidelines hurts the economy, thus hurts his reelection chances. He was determined not to talk precautions, and when others did, he would discount them, ridicule them.

From the beginning he's refused to nationalize health guidelines, testing, treatment supply production, and the supply chain: The Big 4 components that virtually all honest scientists agree were/are integral to fighting the pandemic. Trump is demanding all school districts reopen without limitations at the height of a pandemic, without any guidance, threatening their financial support if they don't. He continues to push for the elimination of health care for millions of Americans — at the height of a pandemic. He's emasculated the CDC and FDA, subverting their public guidelines and destroying their reputations here and around the world.

On Monday the U.S. passed the devastating milestone of 200,000 pandemic deaths with nary a condolence from the president for victims' families. In recent weeks President Trump has claimed COVID-19 prevention guidelines are a Democratic scheme to crush church attendance. He's called the pandemic story a "Democrat hoax." He's now promoting a dangerous "herd immunity" policy, i.e., tacitly allowing healthy people to contract the disease (which could produce 200 million cases, 2-3 million deaths). And he's saying at rallies that the virus affects almost exclusively the elderly, "virtually nobody below the age of 18."

Say Its Name

There is no clearer indication of an aspiring autocrat — fascist — attempting to consolidate power than his willingness to kill his own citizens to do it. The other signs have been there all along: breaking governmental norms and traditions; blatantly interfering with DOJ cases and deliberations; destroying the independence of Cabinet members and their departments; threatening political allies with career destruction for any dissention no matter how slight; corrupt nepotism and self-dealing; consistently buddying up to autocrats and favoring world dictators over allies.

And running the government like a crime boss. In what could be his most politically heinous act, days after escaping accountability for committing and covering up his crimes exposed in the Mueller report, President Trump said in a call to newly elected Ukrainian President Volodymyr Zelenskyy: "We have been very, very good to Ukraine. ... I would like you to do us a favor though." And thus

Donald personally furthered his traitorous, illegal extortion of Ukraine to get (false) dirt on a political rival (Joe Biden) in exchange for releasing $400 million in already congressionally authorized military aid.

There were nearly a dozen aides on the call and several of them were terrified at what they heard. One told the CIA, "The president had clearly committed a criminal act."

> "He was a president entirely unrestrained, free from the shackles of seasoned advisers who sought to teach him to put duty to country above self and to follow protocols. He had concluded he was above the law, after dodging accountability for flouting rules and withstanding the Mueller investigation. He had grown so confident of his own power, and cocksure that Republicans in Congress would never dare break with him, that he thought he could do almost anything."

> (Rucker, Philip & Leonnig, Carol; *A Very Stable Genius: Donald J. Trump's Testing of America;* 2020.)

Of course we know that when the Ukrainian extortion plot was exposed by several brave patriots in government, President Trump was impeached by Democrats in Congress. Ultimately he was sprung from accountability again by Senate Republicans — a prime benefit of owning them.

> "Trump was the kind of president [Alexander Hamilton in *The Federalist*] had in mind — a populist demagogue who would foment frenzy, pander to prejudices, feed off chaos, and secretly betray the American people in the accumulation of power."

> (Ibid.; Rucker & Leonnig; 2020.)

But killing? His own citizens? This simply leaves no doubt, no mistaking what's going on. Except by members of the cult — the death cult.

This Just In

> [REPORTER:] "People are rioting. Do you commit to making sure that there's a peaceful transferal of power [after the election]?"

> [PRESIDENT TRUMP:] "We're going to have to see what happens. ... Get rid of the ballots, and you'll have a very — we'll have a very peaceful — there won't be a transfer, frankly. There'll be a continuation. The ballots are out of control. ... I think this will end up in the Supreme Court. And I think it's very important that we have nine justices. ... This [mail-in ballot] scam that the Democrats are pulling — it's a scam — the scam will be before the United States Supreme Court. And I think having a 4-4 situation is not a good situation."

> (news conference; White House; 9/23/2020.)

> [TRANSLATION:] *The president will not commit to a peaceful transfer of power if he loses the election.*

This is an absolute first in American history. Trump is telling us that 1) he expects to lose the vote, 2) he will ram through a SCOTUS justice before the election because he plans to use the Supreme Court to overrule the popular vote and Electoral College to retain power, and 3) he plans not to leave the White House either way on Jan. 20, 2020, Inauguration Day.

Schiff's Prescience

"He has betrayed our national security and he will do so again. He has compromised our elections and he will do so again. You will not change him. You cannot constrain him. … He is who he is. Truth matters little to him. What is right matters even less, and decency matters not at all. …

"Can we be confident that he will not continue to try to cheat in [this] very election? Can we be confident that Americans and not foreign powers will get to decide? … The short, plain, sad, incontestable answer is no, you can't. You can't trust this president to do the right thing. Not for one minute, not for one election, not for the sake of our country. You just can't. He will not change and you know it."

> (Schiff, Adam, D-Calif., House Intelligence Committee chair, lead impeachment manager; closing impeachment trial arguments; Senate floor; 2/3/2020.)

Denouement

Here's the ultimate question:

"Do you believe in the peaceful transfer of power? Or do you believe that this is a country that is no longer a democracy?"

> (Nyhan, Brendan, Dartmouth College professor of government; *MSNBC's Morning Joe;* 9/24/2020.)

Some doubt these truths put forth by Adam Schiff. Some doubt the sun rises in the east. ∎

10/01/20 — POTUS Debate No. 1: "Oh Yeah, I Want 4 More Years of THAT"

COVID-19 Deaths

2/06/2020 — U.S.: 1 | World: 620
3/05/2020 — U.S.: 12 | World: 3,293
4/02/2020 — U.S.: 5,137 | World: 48,284
5/07/2020 — U.S.: 73,431 | World: 264,189
6/04/2020 — U.S.: 107,175 | World: 386,464
7/02/2020 — U.S.: 128,062 | World: 516,726
8/06/2020 — U.S.: 158,268 | World: 708,278
9/03/2020 — U.S.: 185,752 | World: 863,577
10/1/2020 — U.S.: 206,963 | World: 1,014,958

- Conservatively estimated Trump malfeasance deaths: 103,483
- U.S.: 4.3% of Earth's population, 21% of its pandemic deaths

> (Ibid.; Glanz & Robertson; 5/20/2020.)
> (Ibid.; Gupta, MD; 9/18/2020.)
> (as conservatively extrapolated from COVID-19 Dashboard by the Center for Systems Science and Engineering at Johns Hopkins University; 10/1/2020.)

Debate

There was a presidential debate Tuesday night. It was a once-in-a-lifetime rhetorical political event. I won't go into detail here because historians and pundits already are flooding the airwaves and will be writing books about it.

Let me just say, the word *logorrhea* underwent a 56,000% increase in lookups Sept. 29, 2020. Describing the president's debate performance Rachel Maddow said this:

> "A monstrous unintelligible display of logorrhea that has nothing to do with any idea of civic discourse."
>
> (Maddow, Rachel, Ph.D., news anchor; *MSNBC's Debate Analysis;* 9/29/2020.)

> "logorrhea: excessive and often incoherent talkativeness or wordiness"
>
> ("logorrhea"; *Merriam-Webster.com;* retrieved 10/1/2020.)

Linguistics enthusiasts might notice the suffix "-rhea," as in "diarrhea." My junior high school gym teacher would characterize it as: Trump had a bad case of "diarrhea of the mouth."

Logorrhea.

You could also call it "circumlocution, diffuseness, diffusion, garrulity, garrulousness, long-windedness, periphrasis, prolixity, redundancy, verbalism, verboseness, verbosity, windiness," or any of the other synonyms listed in *Merriam-Webster's* thesaurus.

Or bullsh*t. You could call it bullsh*t. From a quintessential a**hole.

— The vast majority of political experts have determined Donald's performance was the most egregious display of presidential (anti-)decorum in U.S. history on a debate stage or elsewhere. It brought monumental shame and embarrassment to America on the world stage.

— President Trump grotesquely abused the debate format, moderator, and his opponent. He refused to *debate* within the common understanding of the term, choosing not to follow agreed-upon rules and chronically interrupting Joe Biden and the moderator, *Fox News'* Chris Wallace. He talked over both and rarely addressed the topic at hand. He reiterated his greatest (fallacious) hits with the force of a vein-busting, hellfire-threatening preacher at a megachurch.

— His behavior was so disturbing that fact-checking this colossal fabulist took a backseat to a national discussion of how he's broken the presidential election process, the presidency, and America's world standing.

— Trump mocked Joe Biden again for wearing a mask and role-modeling pandemic guidelines, then mocked the way Biden *looked* in a mask.

— Trump exhorted his supporters to overwhelm polling places, ostensibly as "poll-watchers" for fairness but in reality to intimidate voters and suppress the minority vote. He again refused to say he would accept the election results, instead averring his clear intention to use the Supreme Court — including his pending illegitimate nominee — to disqualify millions of legal ballots, thereby ensuring his victory.

— When asked by the moderator if he would "here and now" denounce white supremacist groups such as the Proud Boys, Trump hesitated, stumbled, and finally said, "[They should] stand back and stand by ... but antifa!" He would not denounce white supremacy. And he clearly threatened violence upon the country to be perpetrated by his gun-toting white supremacist followers if he lost the election through legitimate means, i.e., the vote.

— The day after the debate, a Proud Boys leader wrote on the group's websites: "That's my president!" The organization immediately began using Trump's slogan, "Stand back and stand by," as a recruiting tool and merchandizing opportunity. At a day-after-the-debate news conference, given a chance to clarify his debate remarks, Donald again refused to condemn white supremacist groups and denied knowing who the Proud Boys are.

For more information on how the debate went down, see every newspaper and media site on Earth.

Presidential Advantage

President Trump has created for himself an advantage that almost no one else in politics can match (though he has spawned acolytes): his ability to abandon ethics and morality *completely*. This is not hyperbole. It's an exclusive advantage he maintains because almost all other human beings who aren't ax-murderers have some rhetorical bottom below which they will not sink.

Donald has no such limitations. Even Newt Gingrich says he's a liar. Even Mitt Romney says Trump is an inveterate and invertebrate flip-flopper. Even Ted Cruz says he's dishonest and ought to leave Ted's wife alone. Even Lindsey Graham has called The Donald "a race-baiting, xenophobic, religious bigot ... a nut ... a kook ... unfit for office." Even Triumph the Insult Comedy Dog says Trump uses too many school-yard insults and demeaning nicknames.

Cornered Rat

We all know about the dangers of a cornered rat. Currently this orange rodent (of the class: Manhattan Mammalia; order: Mar-a-Lago Rodentia) has had his taxes exposed to show he's a failed businessman who has paid $0 in federal taxes for 10 of the past 15 years, paid (exactly) $750.00 federal tax in 2016 and 2017, and incurred over $400 million in personal debt coming due within the next four years. He's been exposed — on tape — as having known in January that the coronavirus would be staggeringly deadly. But he chose to take grossly inadequate actions to protect the country because he feared too much acknowledgement, let alone life-saving precautions, would harm the economy and hurt his reelection chances.

He's disparaged numerous U.S. military leaders and heroes in despicable terms. He's been exposed as having characterized fighting men and women killed or injured in battle as "losers" and "suckers." He sought, encouraged, accepted, and used Russian influence and other help to beat a presidential rival and then obstructed justice to cover it up, as confirmed by a Republican-controlled Senate Intelligence Committee. He extorted Ukraine for dirt on a presidential rival as most of the GOP has conceded. He's under multiple criminal investigations that will turn into indictments once he's out of office, hence the cornered-rat efforts to remain in office.

And he's got the worst comb-over in celebrity cosmetic history. Who does he think he's kidding? It's insulting.

Debate Advice

The Biden presidential campaign has not sought my advice for debate prep. If they do I will tell Joe to rotate these responses every time Donald tries to make a mendacious, disgusting point:

"I don't kill Americans with pandemic inaction. $750."

"Veterans' cemeteries: Not suckers and losers. $750."

"I don't kill children by forcing them to school during a pandemic. $750."

"Failed businessman. $400 million in debt. Show us your taxes. $750."

"I'm not trying to take away health care for millions during a pandemic. $750."

"Do we really want another four years of this? Oh, by the way: $750."

Pandemic Note

Perhaps the most telling quote we have from Donald is this revealing aside:

"Maybe this virus is a good thing. I don't have to shake hands with those disgusting people [who attend my rallies]."

> (Trump, Donald, R-Fla., U.S. president; White
> House Coronavirus Task Force meeting; spring 2020;
> as cited by Troye, Olivia, R-Texas, former White
> House Coronavirus Task Force aide; Republican
> Voters Against Trump video; 9/18/2020.)

This was reported by former top aide to Vice President Mike Pence and White House Coronavirus Task Force member Olivia Troye. Ms. Troye is a lifelong Republican whose conscience forced her to resign the task force in July and go public with this information: President Trump has based every task force-related decision on ensuring his reelection rather than saving American lives.

The cult members are the last ones to know their leader despises them, looks down on them. Radio host and Trump friend Howard Stern famously tried to alert Trump supporters, MAGA cult members:

> "The oddity in all of this is the people Trump despises most, love him the most. The people who are voting for Trump for the most part ... he wouldn't even let them in [his] f***ing hotel. He'd be disgusted by them. [Trump supporters, g]o to Mar-a-Lago, see if there's any people who look like you. I'm talking to you in the audience. ... I don't hate Donald. I hate you for voting for him, for not having intelligence."

> (Stern, Howard; *SiriusXM's The Howard Stern Show*; 5/12/2020.)

C'mon, man. One of VP Pence's top aides, a lifelong Republican, says the president is killing Americans needlessly so he can be reelected. It's possible Olivia Troye could be one more GOP member who's had her leg grabbed by the submerged swamp monster and hauled in. Yeah, she could be a deep-stater willing to destroy her career to keep the Democrat child-sex ring operating.

But this is Howard Stern telling you. No swamp monster here. No deep-stater here.

"Stand back and stand by."

"That's my president." ∎

10/08/20 — Trump Infected – AND He Got the Virus

COVID-19 Deaths

02/06/2020 — U.S.: 1 | World: 620
10/08/2020 — U.S.: 211,844 | World: 1,056,768

> (COVID-19 Dashboard by the Center for Systems Science and Engineering at Johns Hopkins University; 10/8/2020.)

Pandemic

The United States, with the greatest health care research and medical expertise in the world, accounts for 4.2% of Earth's population but 21% of world COVID-19 deaths. You do the math.

The president literally is allowing Americans to die needlessly. His malfeasance has caused a conservatively estimated 105,922 deaths, 50% of the U.S. total.

> (Glanz, James & Robertson, Campbell; "Lockdown Delays Cost at Least 36,000 Lives, Data Show"; *The New York Times;* 5/20/2020.)
>
> (Gupta, Vin, MD, MPA, MSc, University of Washington Institute for Health Metrics and Evaluation professor, global health policy expert, formerly with WHO, CDC; "Dr. Vin Gupta: 'Evidence That 70% of Lives Could Have Been Saved'"; *MSNBC's Meet the Press Daily* with Chuck Todd; 9/18/2020.)
>
> (editors; "Dying in a Leadership Vacuum"; *The New England Journal of Medicine;* 10/8/2020.)

(as conservatively extrapolated from COVID-19 Dashboard by the Center for Systems Science and Engineering at Johns Hopkins University; 10/8/2020.)

MAGA Republicans, please don't bellyache about the source media. These experts from Columbia University, University of Washington, and Johns Hopkins University — who are beyond reproach — have appeared in disparate media outlets.

Donald is consistently, still, playing down the coronavirus and spreading dangerous disinformation to restart the economy early solely for reelection to avoid near-certain indictment.

Ultimately by completely ignoring precautions for political purposes, Trump (and nearly three dozen associates, senators, and White House aides) caught the virus. He endangered donors, members of Congress, and numerous staffers by exposing them — via a fundraiser, a debate, a Gold Star families meet-and-greet (which he blames for his infection), and routine business meetings and contacts — after he likely knew he was infected, which almost certainly occurred before or at the Sept. 26 superspreader White House reception for his Supreme Court nominee.

During his hospitalization, Oct. 2-5, a highly contagious commander in chief forced Secret Service agents to accompany him in an air-tight SUV on a photo op joyride for supporters, endangering myriad hospital and government staff for political theater. A veteran of the Service expressed outrage saying the president does not care about agents.

"Don't Be Afraid"

Even after Donald fell sick, he's still refused to emphasize or even mention recommended safety guidelines to the country, though conversely he made several rah-rah videos minimizing his illness while at Walter Reed Hospital. He tweeted, "Don't be afraid of Covid, Don't let it dominate your life," apparently forgetting about the deceased 210,000-plus and their loved ones — whose lives clearly have been dominated by "it." He ghoulishly continued the art of the downplay.

After three days of several experimental drug cocktails usually reserved for the sickest of COVID-19 patients, Mr. Trump left the hospital against medical advice, mystifying the medical establishment. He did a video/photo op outside the White House after stepping off *Marine One*, immediately shedding his mask. Though his doctors told him he still was contagious, he proceeded to endanger everyone in the presidential headquarters, a workplace for hundreds of staff. It was one of the most irresponsible, selfish actions of a U.S. chief executive in history.

Once inside, remaining maskless, he recorded another propaganda video, again shockingly-but-not-surprisingly praising his own crisis leadership and playing down the pandemic, telling us all: "Don't let it dominate you. Don't be afraid of it. You're gonna beat it. … Get out there."

210,000-plus.

News footage that evening showed the president on a White House balcony: Rather than projecting an image of strength, he was laboring for breath after ascending the South Portico steps. Before standing pompously for the cameras, over-extending a salute to the departing military helicopter, then entering the residence through large double doors, Donald ripped off his mask in a symbolic bras d'honneur to families of loved ones who have succumbed to coronavirus.

Remaining in character, President Trump has not offered any thoughts, prayers, or acknowledgement to those families during his illness.

From the Beginning

Early on Mr. Trump called the pandemic story a "Democrat hoax" while knowing it was real and deadly. He still dismisses COVID-19 prevention guidelines. He continues to mock Joe Biden and others for wearing masks. He's now tacitly pushing a dangerous "herd immunity" policy (the deadly, failed Sweden approach), i.e., allowing healthy people to contract the disease. And he's ordered the CDC to recommend less testing.

> [FUN FACT:] So-called herd immunity would require a 60-70% infection rate across the country before attaining efficacy, that is, having the virus die out sometime in 2022. By conservative estimates this would result in 3-6 million American lives lost.

Mr. Trump consistently has refused to role-model and encourage safety guidelines for the American people since the pandemic's genesis in this country. White House officials claim they can't control every aspect of human behavior and that they're "on the side of freedom." But the administration knows full-well that the potential (mostly MAGA) recalcitrants and apathetics, nearly half the country, would follow the president's lead. In fact they have: They've adopted his stance that safety guidelines are a political statement against their president, whom they therefore support by ignoring and fighting medical science.

From the beginning, Donald has put self above country. He willfully ignored all the warnings. That's corruption, amorality. Now we know had he put country above self he would have helped himself by saving the economy. That's incompetence.

Leadership Vacuum

Now consider the many billions of dollars in *additional* stimulus that will be required to fend off another Great Depression. Many months after the disease has taken hold in America, President Trump *still* hasn't taken the leadership responsibility necessary to control the pandemic's spread and accompanying economic carnage. To do so would be to admit a mistake.

And just for kicks the president and his Republican Senate enablers are working vigorously, tirelessly to kill the Affordable Care

Act, which effectively would eliminate health care insurance for tens of millions of Americans — at the height of a pandemic.

The coronavirus, economic bloodletting, and psychological harm from both will run rampant until Donald Trump is turned out of office.

> "Don't let it dominate you. Don't be afraid of it. You're gonna beat it. … Get out there."

But don't just take my word for it. On Wednesday *The New England Journal of Medicine* for the first time in its 208-year history weighed in on a presidential election, calling for the current administration to be removed from power. And this sentiment among its nearly three dozen editors is unanimous:

> "This crisis has produced a test of leadership. … Here in the United States, our leaders have failed that test. They have taken a crisis and turned it into a tragedy. The magnitude of this failure is astonishing. … [They've] failed at almost every step. We had ample warning. …

> "The federal government has largely abandoned disease control to the states. Governors have varied in their responses, not so much by party as by competence. But whatever their competence, governors do not have the tools that Washington controls. Instead of using those tools, the federal government has undermined them. …

> "[T]ruth is neither liberal nor conservative. When it comes to the response to the largest public health crisis of our time, our current political leaders have demonstrated that they are dangerously incompetent. We should not abet them and enable the deaths of thousands more Americans by allowing them to keep their jobs."

(editors; "Dying in a Leadership Vacuum"; *The New England Journal of Medicine;* 10/8/2020.)

210,000-plus families.

Breaking News

> "More than a dozen men were arrested on federal and state charges in connection with an alleged foiled plot to kidnap Michigan's Democratic governor, Gretchen Whitmer. …
>
> "The arrests grew out of an FBI-led inquiry that began in March and focused on militia groups' discussing the 'violent overthrow' of certain government and law enforcement officials. Each of the federally charged men faces up to life in prison if convicted on all charges, authorities said. …
>
> "[S]even are linked to the Wolverine Watchmen militia[, which] sought to 'instigate a civil war' and had 'engaged in planning and training for an operation to attack the Capitol building of Michigan and to kidnap government officials.' … [They believe] in the 'boogaloo' movement, a term that refers to an impending civil war. … [They're] an anti-government movement that advocates for a violent uprising targeting liberal political opponents and law enforcement."
>
> (Winter, Tom & Kosnar, Michael & Li, David K.; "13 Men Charged in Alleged Plot to Kidnap Michigan Gov. Gretchen Whitmer"; *NBCNews.com;* 10/8/2020.)

Reportedly the Wolverine Watchmen were inspired partly (largely?) after President Trump tweeted April 17, 2020: "LIBERATE MINNESOTA! … LIBERATE MICHIGAN! … LIBERATE

VIRGINIA, and save your great 2nd Amendment. It is under siege!"■

10/15/20 — Undecided: "Gee, I Guess I'll Vote for 4 More Years of Trump"

COVID-19 Deaths

02/06/2020 — U.S.: 1 | World: 620
10/15/2020 — U.S.: 216,904 | World: 1,092,968

> • Conservatively estimated Trump malfeasance deaths: 108,452
> • U.S.: 4.2% of Earth's population, 20% of its pandemic deaths

> (Ibid.; Glanz & Robertson; 5/20/2020.)
> (Ibid.; Gupta, MD; 9/18/2020.)
> (Ibid.; *The New England Journal of Medicine;* 10/8/2020.)
> (as conservatively extrapolated from COVID-19 Dashboard by the Center for Systems Science and Engineering at Johns Hopkins University; 10/15/2020.)

You know, I'm really undecided about this election. They say it's the most important election of our lifetime. But I'm just not sure. So I did some reading and some talking to a smart friend. Here's what I found out.

— *World abortion rates are rising under Trump* because his program to cut money for abortion services also cuts money for birth control, resulting in more unwanted pregnancies in "Tan-ZANE-ia," "NAM-bia," "NAMBLA," and other sub-Saharan African country names he mispronounces or fabricates. This means more abortions, legal and backroom. (I learned this after finding a copy of the scientific journal *The Lancet* stuck to my latest issue of *People* magazine.)

— *Trump's corrupt leadership has caused at least half our pandemic deaths.* The U.S. fatality rate is five times the world average. I found this online while searching for my lottery numbers, a great site called *GraniteWord.com*. The guy who writes that thing is smart. He laid it all out. All Donald had to do was stop worrying about the stock market. But he was afraid the economy would crash and he'd lose reelection. So he played down, belittled, and lied about the virus. Anyway some of the important people who say so are Dr. Irwin Redlener, MD (Columbia University National Center for Disaster Preparedness director); Dr. Vin Gupta, MD (University of Washington Institute for Health Metrics and Evaluation professor and global health policy expert, formerly with WHO, CDC); Columbia University disease modeling researchers; and as I mentioned last week, all 34 editors of the *New England Journal of Medicine.*

— *The military thinks he's destroying our country.* Also stuck to my *People* mag was an August issue of *Military Times* with a poll showing that active military service members support Joe Biden over Donald Trump by 41-37% — even though only 16% call themselves Democrats. And I heard Donald has received heavy three- and four-star MAGA condemnation from highly respected generals including Barry McCaffrey, Colin Powell, David Petraeus, Douglas Lute, H. R. McMaster, James Mattis, John Kelly, John Allen, Joseph Dunford, Mark Milley, Martin Dempsey, Michael Hayden, Michael Mullen, Stanley McChrystal, and William McRaven. Almost all of *them* are endorsing Joe Biden, which is for most of them the first presidential endorsement of their lives. (My smart friend told me this list includes four former Joint Chiefs of Staff chairs and various Cabinet secretaries.)

— Donald has taken thousands of crying children away from their parents to make a point. He's separated some 5,400 migrant minors including babies and toddlers from their families for months, locking them up in squalor, small children sobbing for their mothers and fathers, causing lifelong-lasting trauma. (My friend says the Physicians for Human Rights technically has classified this as *torture.*) I also heard hundreds have been separated permanently through government screw-ups — immigration authorities failed to keep track of where they sent many of these kids and their parents.

— Trump hires and hangs around with crooks. He has at least six close political associates in, released from, or awaiting prison: Michael Cohen, his former personal attorney-fixer; Michael Flynn, his former national security adviser; Rick Gates, 2016 campaign deputy chair; Paul Manafort, 2016 campaign chair; George Papadopoulos, 2016 campaign adviser; and Roger Stone, 2016 campaign adviser and near-lifelong ally. Steve Bannon, Donald's 2016 campaign CEO and top adviser, has been indicted on a build-the-border-wall crowdfunding fraud. And several former Trump Cabinet members are under ethics investigations, i.e., they lie, cheat, and steal.

— Donald's illegally making real money off being president. He fools his followers by bragging about not taking the $400,000 annual presidential paycheck. But I read that by using and abusing the presidency through emoluments clauses violations (these are in the Constitution) he reaps 100 times that amount. He does this mostly through solicitation and acceptance of domestic and foreign money into his businesses. In the past few weeks his now-not-so-secret tax records have shown that the big spenders at his properties get the big government favors — way crookedly, not just typical mutual back-scratching.

— Speaking of federal taxes, he doesn't pay any. His now-not-so-secret tax returns show he paid $0 in federal taxes for 10 out of the past 15 years. In 2016 and 2017 he paid $750, to the penny, because paying

$0 after he became president would look way too bad if it ever came out.

— *He believes Putin over his own government.* And he's consistently sucked up to Vlad for four years. My smart friend told me that Trump kowtowed to Russian President Vladimir Putin on the world stage at the Helsinki summit news conference with the two leaders. In front of God and everyone, President Trump disbelieved and discounted his own intelligence experts' unanimous conclusions that Russia brazenly interfered with our 2016 election. The Donald disgracefully, pitifully accepted Putin's lame denial of, "Don't look at me, I didn't do it." On top of that, Trump has been afraid to confront Putin after our CIA found out the Russian leader was paying big-money bounties for American deaths in Afghanistan. Can you believe that crap?!?

— *Donald is an unindicted co-conspirator — a criminal, free only because he's president.* He was tagged as "Individual-1" in the Mueller report court documents pertaining to the campaign finance crime that got his personal lawyer-fixer Michael Cohen convicted and jailed. Prosecutors agreed the crime did not even benefit Cohen but was ordered by Trump who likely laundered the criminal hush-money payments through Trump Org. as illegal tax deductions. Now my friend is no lawyer but this sounds pret-ty, pret-ty hinky to him.

— *He's got 20-plus women suing him for sexual assault.* Can they all be anti-Trump conspirators, identified by QAnon, working hard to keep the Democrat child-sex ring going?

— *He extorted highly vulnerable Ukraine for phony dirt on Joe Biden.* He called and said, "The U.S. has been very good to your country," and he wanted the Ukrainian leader to "do me a favor though" before Trump would release $400 million in military aid. (Congress authorized this money for Ukraine to protect itself against Russia's illegal military invasions). Then he released the phone transcript, which proved it. Then he got impeached for it. Then he got acquitted by extorting Senate Republicans, i.e., "Vote against me on impeachment and I'll tweet you out of office." Trump said, "Jump," and GOP senators asked, "How many pounds, sir?"

— *He cheated the government and relatives out of hundreds of millions of dollars when his father died.* His older sister, federal Judge Mary Trump, had to resign her judgeship to stop an ethics investigation that would have blown the lid off Donald's crimes mid-presidency. I read in *Us Weekly* that she said on secret tapes that he was an "a**hole" and "can never be trusted" and "has no principles." She was a damn federal judge! Judges don't lie!

— *Trump University and the Trump ("charitable") Foundation had to pay millions in fraud claims.* And get this: As part of the settlements, the courts ordered both scams be closed down — forever. And Ivanka, Don Jr., and Eric Trump were banned from any involvement in a charity — forever.

— *Donald won't commit to leaving office peacefully if he loses the election.* And him and Senate Republicans are ramming through a Supreme Court nominee against their own not-in-an-election-year rule — just weeks before the 2020 election — so she'll be there to vote Trump's way when his army of lawyers contests mail-in ballots, to steal the election.

— *Donald and his sleazy Senate Majority Leader Mitch McConnell are stealing a Supreme Court Justice appointment.* Did I mention Senate Republicans are ramming through a SCOTUS nominee, Amy Coney Barrett, against their own not-in-an-election-year rule — just weeks before the 2020 election? My friend reminded me that McConnell refused to consider President Obama's March 2016 nominee, Merrick Garland, upon the death of Justice Antonin Scalia (eight months before the next election). Mitch and other leading GOP senators defended this unprecedented (non)move by devising a new "rule": High court nominees should not be considered in the last year of a presidential term:

> "I want you to use my words against me. If there's a Republican president [elected] in 2016 and a [SCOTUS] vacancy occurs in the last year of the first term, you can say Lindsey Graham said, 'Let's let the next president, whoever it might be, make that nomination.' And you could use my words against me and you'd be absolutely right. We're setting a precedent here today. … That's going to be the new rule."
>
> (Graham, Lindsey, R-S.C., U.S. senator; Senate Judiciary Committee hearing; 3/10/2016.)

Sen. Graham then re-confirms his commitment in 2018:

> *[SEN. LINDSEY GRAHAM (R-S.C.):]* "Now, I'll tell you this. This may make you feel better, but I really don't care. If an opening comes in the last year of President Trump's term and the primary process has started, we'll wait 'till the next election."
>
> *[JEFFREY GOLDBERG (THE ATLANTIC):]* "You're on the record."
>
> *[SEN. LINDSEY GRAHAM (R-S.C.):]* "Yeah. … Hold the tape."
>
> (*The Atlantic* Festival; 10/8/2018.)

Sen. Graham then clarifies his words in 2020 when liberal Supreme Court Justice Ruth Bader Ginsburg dies seven weeks before the presidential election: "The rules have changed." (Precedent? What precedent? What new rule? Tough luck, suckers.)

Just for kicks my smart friend pointed out some Fun Facts about Donald J. Trump: 1) he was recorded by *Access Hollywood* saying he likes to "grab women by the p***y" because "if you're a celebrity you can get away with it"; 2) he told CIA secrets to Russian visitors in the Oval Office just to show off; 3) he mocked a physically challenged reporter at a rally; 4) he said of another, paralyzed journalist: "And then I get [criticized] by a guy that can't buy a pair of pants"; 5) he's told over 20,000 documented lies while president; and 6) he once ridiculed Sen. Rand Paul (R-Ky.) for having bad hair.

Wait. Trump says someone else has bad hair!?!

I don't know — I'm still so undecided. The "bad hair" dis on Rand Paul really was uncalled for. But this country needs someone to shake up Washington.

Gee, I guess I'll have to vote for four more years of Trump. ■

10/22/20 — If You're Under 88, It IS "The Most Important Election of …" Yada, Yada

COVID-19 Deaths

02/06/2020 — U.S.: 1 | World: 620
10/22/2020 — U.S.: 222,220 | World: 1,132,321

> • Conservatively estimated Trump malfeasance deaths: 111,110
> • U.S.: 4.2% of Earth's population, 20% of its pandemic deaths

> > (Glanz, James & Robertson, Campbell; "Lockdown Delays Cost at Least 36,000 Lives, Data Show"; *The New York Times;* 5/20/2020.)
> > (Gupta, Vin, MD, MPA, MSc, University of Washington Institute for Health Metrics and Evaluation professor, global health policy expert, formerly with WHO, CDC; "Dr. Vin Gupta: 'Evidence That 70% of Lives Could Have Been Saved'"; *MSNBC's Meet the Press Daily* with Chuck Todd; 9/18/2020.)
> > (editors; "Dying in a Leadership Vacuum"; *The New England Journal of Medicine;* 10/8/2020.)
> > (Redlener, Irwin, MD & Sachs, Jeffrey D., Ph.D. & Hansen, Sean, MPA & Hupert, Nathaniel, MD, MPH; "130,000-210,000 Avoidable COVID-19 Deaths – and Counting – in the U.S."; *National Center for Disease Preparedness, Earth Institute, Columbia University;* 10/21/2020.)

(as conservatively extrapolated from COVID-19 Dashboard by the Center for Systems Science and Engineering at Johns Hopkins University; 10/22/2020.)

"This report looks at the staggering and disproportionate nature of COVID-19 fatalities in the United States, which now ranks first in the world in the total number of fatalities, to estimate how many deaths were 'avoidable.' With more than 217,000 lives lost, and a proportional mortality rate twice that of neighboring Canada and more than 50 times that of Japan — a country with a much older population than the U.S. — the United States has turned a global crisis into a devastating tragedy.

"Through comparative analysis and applying proportional mortality rates, we estimate that at least 130,000 deaths and perhaps as many as 210,000 could have been avoided with earlier policy interventions and more robust federal coordination and leadership. Even with the dramatic recent appearance of new COVID-19 waves globally, the abject failures of U.S. government policies and crisis messaging persist."

(Redlener, Irwin, MD & Sachs, Jeffrey D., Ph.D. & Hansen, Sean, MPA & Hupert, Nathaniel, MD, MPH; "130,000-210,000 Avoidable COVID-19 Deaths – and Counting – in the U.S."; *National Center for Disease Preparedness, Earth Institute, Columbia University;* 10/21/2020.)

"Most Important Election of …" Yada, Yada

Many people have been decrying the overuse of the declarative noun-phrase "most important election of our lifetime." They think it's like *word inflation:* it doesn't mean (or buy) what it used to. *The Atlantic* called for its permanent retirement in 2012.

Can I just say they're all dead wrong this year? If you're under 88 years old — born after America was desperate for FDR to pull her out of the Great Depression, then later depending on President Roosevelt to steer her through the heating up and boiling over of World War II — then this *is* the most important election of your lifetime.

We can retire the phrase after the existence of the-United-States-as-we-know-it is no longer threatened.

Some independents, apathetics, and even "progressive babies" (Disclaimer: I'm a progressive, albeit one who doesn't want our country to burn down) still like to profess there's no difference between the candidates, Joe Biden and Donald Trump. They grouse that "nothing ever changes" or "all politicians are on the take." They plan not to bother voting. Or they will cast a protest vote (because they detest "lesser-evil" voting) for some alternative candidate, a third-party vote that might produce a coveted progressive party and president someday. Down the road. In a few decades. Maybe.

Apples to NO Apples

These guys say that Biden-compared-to-Trump is just another (bad)-apple-to-(bad)-apple comparison, the juxtaposition of two pieces of the same distasteful fruit (these guys don't like apples) from the same politician bushel basket.

But this isn't apples-to-apples. It's not even apples-to-oranges. It's apples to *no* apples *(— thanks to Dr. Lipi Roy, infectious disease expert).* It's having a recognizable America after 2020 or not. If

Trump is reelected, the country likely will be damaged beyond repair.

Historically Unprecedented

Don't just take my word for it. Listen to the declarations of nearly two dozen top-top generals, several formerly in Donald's administration. Listen to the pronouncements of 230-plus former members of President George W. Bush's (R-Texas) administration; 70-plus former national security officials of various Republican administrations; 500 former Cabinet secretaries, generals, admirals, senior NCOs, ambassadors, and senior civilian national security leaders of both parties; 100 former Sen. John McCain (R-Ariz.) staffers; 30 former Sen. Mitt Romney (R-Utah) aides; 400 video statements by Republican and former Trump voters.

Hundreds — if not *thousands*, a historically unprecedented number — of icons and notables from the president's own party are supporting the opposition candidate in November to stop the damage President Trump is doing to America. It doesn't matter if some on the list are Never Trumpers from 2016. It doesn't matter if some are GOP moderates (unaffectionately known as *RINOs: Republicans in Name Only*). It doesn't matter that plenty are solid-right staunch conservatives. It doesn't matter if some are dead. What matters is that they're all from the president's own party and they all desperately want him out of office. Unprecedented.

The vast majority of these Republicans are pro-life Christians who want more conservative judges. They all dislike socialism. Almost all of them hold traditional conservative policy values — which I generally disagree with but still respect. But they also all know that none of these things matter if we allow an aspiring autocrat to tear down the institutions and moral foundation of our country's government until there's nothing left to fight for.

Just This Week

The following are four terrifying Trumpian developments, any single one of which would have exploded GOP legislators' heads in the pre-Trump era. Today's Republican senators, representatives, and other Trump apologists, however, simply turn their heads and pretend they "just doesn't see" *(— thanks to Bob Dylan)*. Meanwhile the rest of us (thinking, caring people) continue drowning in a never-ending tsunami of legitimate outrage.

Meet Russian Agent Giuliani

Rudy Giuliani, a top Trump lawyer, has been a witting or unwitting Russian asset feeding pro-Putin, anti-Biden propaganda to the president as acknowledged by the intelligence community. Trump was warned of this but ignored the warnings because he loved the (false) information.

> "The intelligence agencies warned the White House late last year that Russian intelligence officers were using President Trump's personal lawyer Rudolph W. Giuliani as a conduit for disinformation aimed at undermining Joseph R. Biden Jr.'s presidential run. ... Mr. Trump shrugged it off. ...
>
> "Mr. Trump and Mr. Giuliani have promoted unsubstantiated claims about Mr. Biden that have aligned with Russian disinformation efforts. ... [A] meeting [occurred] on Dec. 5 between Mr. Giuliani and Andriy Derkach, a Ukrainian member of Parliament who takes pro-Kremlin positions. The Treasury Department recently labeled him 'an active Russian agent for over a decade.'"
>
> (Barnes, Julian E. & Schmitt, Eric & Haberman, Maggie; "Trump Said to Be Warned That Giuliani

Was Conveying Russian Disinformation"; *The New York Times*; 10/15/2020.)

White House Says Masks Don't Work

Dr. Scott Atlas (*not* an infectious disease expert), a new Trump Coronavirus Task Force member who has consolidated control, told the country that masks don't work. This thrilled the president and horrified all legitimate medical and scientific health experts in America who already are fearing major surges even *with* precautions in place.

> "Twitter removed a tweet from top White House coronavirus adviser Dr. Scott Atlas for questioning the effectiveness of masks in combatting COVID-19. Atlas' tweet read 'Masks work? NO' and preceded several others that questioned the use of face coverings in preventing the spread of the coronavirus. In a statement to The Hill, Twitter said the doctor's tweet 'was in violation of our COVID-19 Misleading Information Policy' that 'prohibits sharing false or misleading content related to COVID-19 which could lead to harm.'"
>
> (O'Reilly, Andrew; "Twitter Removes Top White House Coronavirus Adviser Tweet Claiming Masks Don't Work"; *FoxNews.com*; 10/19/2020.)

Trump Calls on AG Barr to "Lock Him (Joe Biden) Up"

Trump is calling on Attorney General William Barr to investigate (and potentially indict) — before the election — his presidential opponent, Joe Biden, based on propaganda fed to him by witting or unwitting Russian asset Rudy Giuliani, Trump's lawyer.

"President Donald Trump on Tuesday called on Attorney General William Barr to immediately launch an investigation into unverified claims about Democrat Joe Biden and his son Hunter, effectively demanding that the Justice Department muddy his political opponent and abandon its historic resistance to getting involved in elections. … Trump for the first time explicitly called on Barr to investigate the Bidens and even pointed to the nearing Nov. 3 election as reason that Barr should not delay taking action. 'We've got to get the attorney general to act,' Trump said in an interview on 'Fox & Friends.' 'He's got to act, and he's got to act fast.' … Julian Zelizer, a presidential historian at Princeton University, suggested that Trump's pressure campaign on Barr has moved into uncharted territory for presidential politics."

> (Madhani, Aamer & Long, Colleen; "Trump Ups Pressure on Barr to Probe Bidens as Election Nears"; *The Associated Press;* 10/21/2020.)

545 Migrant Children Feared Permanently Separated From Parents

Some 545 separated migrant children (of the 5,400 separated for months in 2017-2018) are in danger of never seeing their parents again because the Trump border patrol lost track of those (probably deported with no record) parents.

"Lawyers appointed by a federal judge to identify migrant families who were separated by the Trump administration say that they have yet to track down the parents of 545 children. … The Trump administration instituted a 'zero-tolerance' policy in 2018 that separated migrant children and parents at the southern U.S. border[, then] later confirmed that it had actually begun separating families in 2017. … [M]any of the more than 1,000 parents separated from their children under the [2017] pilot program had already been deported before a federal judge in California ordered that they be found.

"'It is critical to find out as much as possible about who was responsible for this horrific practice while not losing sight of the fact that hundreds of families have still not been found and remain separated,' said Lee Gelernt, deputy director of the ACLU Immigrants' Rights Project."

> (Ainsley, Julia & Soboroff, Jacob; "Lawyers Say They Can't Find the Parents of 545 Migrant Children Separated by Trump Administration"; *NBCNews.com;* 10/20/2020.)

Joe Biden compared to Donald Trump? This isn't apples-to-apples. It's apples to *no* apples. It's having a recognizable America or not.■

10/27/2020 — President Trump's Third Supreme Court Nominee Confirmed; Conservative Majority Now at 6-3

09/18/2020 — Supreme Court Justice (Liberal) Ruth Bader Ginsburg Dies at 87

10/27/2020 — Republican Senate Confirms Trump Nominee Amy Coney Barrett, 7 Days Before Presidential Election *(breaking its own 2016 Obama-nominee-denying rule of no confirmations in last year of a presidential term)*

10/29/20 — Critical Thinking: "Pro-Life" Vote Must Include Consideration for the Post-Born

COVID-19 Deaths

02/06/2020 — U.S.: 1 | World: 620
10/29/2020 — U.S.: 227,703 | World: 1,175,684

> • Conservatively estimated Trump malfeasance deaths: 113,852
> • U.S.: 4.2% of Earth's population, 20% of its pandemic deaths

> (Ibid.; Glanz & Robertson; 5/20/2020.)
> (Ibid.; Gupta, MD; 9/18/2020.)
> (Ibid.; *The New England Journal of Medicine;* 10/8/2020.)
> (Ibid.; Redlener, MD & Sachs, Ph.D. & Hansen, MPA & Hupert, MD, MPH; 10/21/2020.)
> (as conservatively extrapolated from COVID-19 Dashboard by the Center for Systems Science and Engineering at Johns Hopkins University; 10/29/2020.)

[FACT NO. 1:] The United States under President Trump has experienced 227,703 COVID-19 deaths, at least half of which almost certainly are due to the president's corruption and incompetence. (And don't give me any guff about this 227,703 number being inflated, i.e., based on a count that includes many victims who also had asthma, heart disease, or a hangnail. When the planes hit the Twin Towers, those

also-properly counted victims of the 9/11 attacks — 2,996
— didn't die of any preexisting heart disease.)

[FACT NO. 2:] The U.S. has separated 5,400 innocent
migrant children from their families, caging them in
subhuman conditions away from parents or other guardians
for months in a strange land.

[FACT NO. 3:] President Trump caused an undetermined
number of deaths by delaying aid (for petty political reasons)
to Puerto Rico in the aftermath of Hurricane Maria. Mr.
Trump caused an undetermined number of Ukrainian deaths
while extorting that country — for personal, illegal political
gain — by withholding funds authorized to fight the Russian
invasion of Ukraine.

Trump supporters still holding on either are grossly, willfully
disinformed or selfishly amoral.

Disinformed or amoral.

Astonishingly 40% or so of Americans still believe a President
Donald Trump is good for the country. This is why I continue my
call for basic critical thinking instruction to be mandated in the
public K-12 curriculum. It is for lack of essential reasoning and
information-processing skills that 40% or so of Americans can deny
(or excuse) Mr. Trump's corruption, incompetence, and amorality
— his blatant disregard for human life — to support political
expediency.

My good friend and spiritual consultant, Keith B., has taught
high school history and social studies his entire career. When I
mentioned critical thinking studies to him he said, "Oh, that would
involve the *humanities*." I knew the word included works from a
certain category of academic disciplines (Homer's *Iliad*, other Greek
blogs) but admittedly was a little vague on the term. I've come to
learn that humanities include the study of language, literature,

history, philosophy, religion, politics, and the like. The idea is that studying topics like these inherently teaches thinking and reasoning.

I sometimes hear young people (and their parents) complain, "Why do I have to take history classes in high school or read *To Kill a Mockingbird*? — or know about the *Iliad*? These aren't going to help me be a hair dresser or a mechanic!" Maybe not. But they'll help you to be a better citizen, a better human being. You just might learn to critically think your way out of voting for another Donald Trump.

Young People

I cut the young some slack. I have to. Several 20-somethings for whom I care a great deal are voting for Trump. Though I care about them, nevertheless they still fall into one of my two categories: *grossly, willfully disinformed*. Most of the fault lies in the natural tendency of young people to adhere to the beliefs of their parents — for whom I cut *no* slack.

These nephews, nieces, and other young people close to me are influenced heavily by social media videos that reinforce the Trump-Republican views supported by Mom and Dad. One is adamant that police, as a statistical nationwide group, treat Black lives no differently than white lives despite mountains of evidence to the contrary. Another perpetuates preposterous pandemic conspiracy theory videos and unwittingly promotes QAnon opposition to life-saving vaccinations being developed.

One is convinced — with no room for doubt — that Democratic presidential candidate Joe Biden is mentally unfit and suffers from dementia. He "proved" this by showing me several obviously manipulated online videos.

Never mind that Mr. Biden consistently speaks thoughtfully and intelligently in unmodified media footage and has been sharp as a tack in interviews and debates.

Another of my young people is convinced that antifa is a violent terrorist group whose sole purpose is to burn and bash property and injure (perhaps even kill) peaceful citizens. I asked her how she knows this. She said, "I've just seen too many videos."

Never mind that the FBI repeatedly has said antifa is an anti-fascist *ideology* — not an organized (or terrorist) group. It opposes racism, Nazis, and white supremacists (as the U.S. government and military did in WWII-Europe, notwithstanding their imperfect opposition at home). And yes, isolated incidents of violence have occurred — among "very fine people, on both sides" — within right-left clashes.

Never mind that the FBI repeatedly has emphasized the greatest internal American terrorism threat is the vast network of white supremacist organizations, so-called militias, and other far-right extremist groups. But young people don't come across many anti-white-supremacy videos online. One can only speculate why not and why they've never heard the FBI's determinations.

Seasoned adult MAGA supporters — those who haven't realized their mistake by now — probably are beyond hope. Let's all encourage them not to vote anymore. (I'm half-kidding.) But young-adult Trump voters still have a life ahead of them to become enlightened, albeit after the 2020 election. My young adults have plenty of time to see the light, acknowledge their error, and maybe thank me some day.

> "Two things I want my nieces and nephews to remember about their uncle long after I'm gone: He loved us with the fierceness of a summer storm, and he did all that he could to help stop Donald Trump" (— *thanks to inspiration from journalist Connie Schultz*).

Critical Thinking

Critical thinking must be taught as part of primary and secondary education. It's at least as important as the third "R" (of the notorious 3 R's) and a necessity for properly understanding all other non-"R" required courses. It is for lack of critical thinking that nearly half of Americans believe that 1) Donald Trump has done a good job and cares about them, 2) Joe Biden is a dementia-ridden criminal, 3) antifa is coming to burn our suburbs, 4) white supremacists are benign, and 5) social media videos are accurate information sources.

So-Called Meme

This week I'm introducing only my second so-called meme (graphic with text superimposed) in the history of this country. It could be the greatest, maybe *the* greatest meme ever made. A lot of people are saying that. Everyone is talking about it. Anyway my meme (and my health plan) is very big (*yuge*) and very, very beautiful.

It's a map of the U.S. with this text overlaid: "4.2% of Earth's population; 20% of world COVID-19 deaths: *You do the (MAGA 'pro-life') math*."

Many may remember my first meme, which went spiral: a photo of former President Richard Nixon standing at a lectern giving the thumbs-up sign, with the caption, "Cool, I'm out of last place." Yes, that one was colossally incisive and clever as my seven Facebook *likes* proved.

But my second graphic-with-text-superimposed is galactically serious. It's about lives devastated and lost.

For single-issue voters, a "pro-life" vote must include consideration for the *post*-born, for *their* lives and deaths, no matter their heritage or citizenship status.

Consider these attacks on life:

> — 227,703 U.S. pandemic deaths, half due to corruption and incompetence

> — 5,400 migrant children caged away from their parents for months in a strange land

— Untold Puerto Rican (U.S.-citizen) fatalities through bigoted withholding, delay of disaster aid

— Attacks on peaceful Black Lives Matter protesters and their factually righteous cause

— Untold U.S. fatalities from climate change denial and environmental protection rollbacks

— Attacks on Latino congresswomen, judges, "rapists, [and] some, I assume, are good people"

— Attacks on Muslim congresswomen, immigrants, and "sh*thole country" residents

And consider this factoid: Abortions have increased in many parts of the world under President Trump's denial of reproductive health aid, which suppresses birth control (the so-called Mexico City Policy).

It seems reality (and decency) *does* have a liberal bias. ∎

11/03/2020 — Election Day: Joe Biden Beats Incumbent President Donald Trump

— **Joe Biden Wins Presidency** *(popular vote: 51.3%-46.9%, 81.2M-74.2M; Electoral College: 306-232) (not confirmed until 11/7/2020)*
— **House Democrats Lose Seats, Retain (Narrow) Control**
— **Senate Democrats Gain Seats, Attain (Narrow) Control** *(not confirmed until 1/5/2021)*

11/05/20 — Election Day Last Tuesday, Still Counting, It's Close

COVID-19 Deaths

02/06/2020 — U.S.: 1 | World: 620
03/05/2020 — U.S.: 12 | World: 3,293
04/02/2020 — U.S.: 5,137 | World: 48,284
05/07/2020 — U.S.: 73,431 | World: 264,189
06/04/2020 — U.S.: 107,175 | World: 386,464
07/02/2020 — U.S.: 128,062 | World: 516,726
08/06/2020 — U.S.: 158,268 | World: 708,278
09/03/2020 — U.S.: 185,752 | World: 863,577
10/01/2020 — U.S.: 206,963 | World: 1,014,958
11/05/2020 — U.S.: 234,756 *(est.)* | World: 1,231,003 *(est.)*

• Conservatively estimated Trump malfeasance deaths: 117,378
• U.S.: 4.2% of Earth's population, 19% of its pandemic deaths

(Ibid.; Glanz & Robertson; 5/20/2020.)
(Ibid.; Gupta, MD; 9/18/2020.)
(Ibid.; *The New England Journal of Medicine;* 10/8/2020.)
(Ibid.; Redlener, MD & Sachs, Ph.D. & Hansen, MPA & Hupert, MD, MPH; 10/21/2020.)
(as conservatively extrapolated from COVID-19 Dashboard by the Center for Systems Science and Engineering at Johns Hopkins University; 11/5/2020.)

Presidential Election

Election Day has dragged into election week. A half-dozen or so battleground states still are counting their mail-in ballots because those Republican state legislatures refused to consider requests to allow the counting to begin a day or three before Nov. 3. That is, they wanted the results to drag out, deferring to President Trump who has telegraphed for many months his intention to challenge mail-in votes.

The speculation was that early returns (reflecting in-person votes cast on election Tuesday) would favor the president, which they did. This was because he's been attempting to invalidate the mail-in process rhetorically since the pandemic began, and his supporters have listened.

Democratic voters, however, respected the power of the pandemic and the legitimacy of mail-in voting. So they mostly mailed it in. Therefore the bulk of Democratic votes were counted and posted later — much later — as mentioned, due to GOP state laws against "pre-canvassing," i.e., beginning to count the ocean of mail-in votes sometime before Election Day.

Trump's strategy was to see himself ahead on election night, Nov. 3, then get the courts to invalidate — stop the counting of — mail-in votes while he still was ahead. Then he would declare himself the winner.

That's not happening.■

11/12/20 — Truism No. 1: "You May Hear Statements Detrimental to Our Republic"

COVID-19 Deaths

02/06/2020 — U.S.: 1 | World: 620
11/12/2020 — U.S.: 241,808 | World: 1,286,322

> • Conservatively estimated Trump malfeasance deaths: 120,904
> • U.S.: 4.2% of Earth's population, 19% of its pandemic deaths

> > (Ibid.; Glanz & Robertson; 5/20/2020.)
> > (Ibid.; Gupta, MD; 9/18/2020.)
> > (Ibid.; *The New England Journal of Medicine;* 10/8/2020.)
> > (Ibid.; Redlener, MD & Sachs, Ph.D. & Hansen, MPA & Hupert, MD, MPH; 10/21/2020.)
> > (as conservatively extrapolated from COVID-19 Dashboard by the Center for Systems Science and Engineering at Johns Hopkins University; 11/12/2020.)

2020 Election Truisms

> *2) Joe Biden is the duly elected legitimate president-elect.* He will be inaugurated Jan. 20, 2021.

> *3) Donald Trump successfully has created another (big) lie that won't die:* "The stolen election." Trump and GOP enablers are

endangering national security, weakening the republic, and emboldening world autocrats.

4) *The polls were wrong — again:* Legions of voters still were embarrassed to admit their MAGA support even to pollsters.

5) *"Press is the enemy of the people" worked — almost.* It made the election closer than warranted.

6) *Voluminous, shameless lying — even when all your supporters KNEW you were lying — worked — almost.* Having zero integrity is a *yuge* advantage. Virtue, honesty, and decency ultimately won, but 40% or so of the country doesn't accept it.

7) *Bernie Sanders would have been obliterated.* I love Bernie. But the effective socialist-takeover disinformation campaign to which he opened the door hurt down-ballot Democrats. As I said all along, we could not risk another four MAGA years with anything less than our strongest presidential candidate. Even Donald knew that was Joe.

8) *The U.S. is divided severely.* A little over half its citizens believe in truth, reason, and character. A little less than half believe any lies that support their personal grievances. Instituting standardized critical thinking instruction in the American K-12 educational curriculum remains essential.

9) *Even a loser Trump maintains tremendous power over Republicans* through control of his base supporters. GOP incumbents and candidates will fear his tweet-attacks for years to come.

There Was an Election on Tuesday

The election occurred Nov. 3, 2020, Tuesday. There was a so-called red mirage Tuesday night and Wednesday day as Trump-leaning in-person votes were counted first, creating a temporary MAGA scoreboard lead. Then Biden-friendly mail-in ballot results came in slowly but consistently over the succeeding 48 hours. On Thursday night Joe Biden became president-elect by almost all legitimate assessments.

President Trump, sensing his imminent loss, went on national television to comment on the state of the race. Based on recent tweets, previous statements, and Donald's inherent personality traits, one pundit remarked to viewers while prefacing Mr. Trump's remarks: "You may hear statements detrimental to our republic." The president did not disappoint. He claimed widespread cheating where there was none. He weakened a country. He was a temper-tantrum-throwing 74-year-old 2 year old.

"If you look at the legal votes, I win very easily. They're trying very obviously to commit fraud [in Philadelphia and Detroit]. … We were winning in all the key locations, by a lot, actually, and then our numbers started miraculously getting whittled away, in secret. … I've said very strongly that mail-in ballots are going to end up being a disaster. … It's really destroyed our system. It's a corrupt system. … It's getting worse and worse every day. … [I expect] a lot of litigation. … We can't be disgraced by having something like this happen. There's been a lot of shenanigans, and we can't stand for that in our country. … The voting apparatus of those [contested] states are run in all cases by Democrats."

(Trump, Donald, R-Fla., U.S. president; national address; White House Brady Briefing Room; 11/5/2020.)

[EDITORS NOTE:] Mr. Trump was wrong on all counts.

[FUN FACT:] In the midst of the president's most dangerous dissembling since his inauguration — that the election was being stolen from him through (nonexistent, unsubstantiated) extensive Democratic fraud — the three major networks, *ABC*, *NBC*, and *CBS*, cut away from Mr. Trump's speech just several minutes into it.

Saturday the Election Was Called Officially

I stand with comedian Dave Chappelle and President-elect Joe Biden: It's not a time to gloat. Almost half the country is disappointed and in pain. It is a time to practice good sportsmanship, to be gracious, humble winners.

But it's also time to face reality, to accept the results — as we always have when they've gone the other way — and do the best we can to prepare for the next administration, for the good of the country. Only four Republican senators (Mitt Romney, Lisa Murkowski, Susan Collins, and Ben Sasse) have congratulated Biden on his win, effectively accepting the election results. The rest of them *still* are choosing selfish political expediency, fearing a Trumpian tweet, over national security and protecting our republic. Unfortunately this is a really bad sign.

C'mon, people. Even *Fox News* has accepted that 1) Trump lost, 2) Trump's lawsuits are without merit, and 3) Trump's lying, traitorous fraud accusations — leveled even at Republican-run states and GOP vote-counting secretaries of state — are undemocratic and show clear disdain for the American people and the United States Constitution.

Fox News wryly ridiculed the president's accusations of election fraud last Thursday night:

"Trump, meanwhile, accused Democrats of trying to 'steal' the election in remarks he made from the White House.

'Our goal is to defend the integrity of the election; we will not allow the corruption to steal such an important election or any election for that matter,' Trump said, though the only specific accusation of voter fraud his campaign has presented — one woman in Nevada — was disputed by the voter registrar in the county where the campaign made the allegation."

(Olson, Tyler; "Where the Race Stands: Biden Erases Trump Lead in Georgia and Pennsylvania, Nears 270 Electoral Votes"; *FoxNews.com*; 11/6/2020.)

Dog-Bites-Man News

President Trump is the ultimate sore loser everyone expected. Donald never "grew into" the presidency like so many had hoped he would. And he certainly won't grow into the maturity and patriotism required for an orderly, nationally secure, democratic transition of administrations. He will be eased out of his other-worldly reverie and denial only as his aides, family members, and GOP enablers can figure out a way to massage his ego and help him mentally turn acceptance into selfish benefit.

I empathize with Trump voters. I'm sorry for you, that your guy lost. But I have zero patience or empathy for GOP lawmakers whose self-serving mendacity continues to impede the work of government, endanger national security, and prolong the pain of suffering Trump supporters. Those poor bastards deserve better.∎

11/19/20 — Trumpism Causes Heavy Hearts

COVID-19 Deaths

02/06/2020 — U.S.: 1 | World: 620
11/19/2020 — U.S.: 250,548 | World: 1,351,381

> • Conservatively estimated Trump malfeasance deaths: 125,274
> • U.S.: 4.2% of Earth's population, 19% of its pandemic deaths

> (Ibid.; Glanz & Robertson; 5/20/2020.)
> (Ibid.; Gupta, MD; 9/18/2020.)
> (Ibid.; *The New England Journal of Medicine;* 10/8/2020.)
> (Ibid.; Redlener, MD & Sachs, Ph.D. & Hansen, MPA & Hupert, MD, MPH; 10/21/2020.)
> (as conservatively extrapolated from COVID-19 Dashboard by the Center for Systems Science and Engineering at Johns Hopkins University; 11/19/2020.)

Outside of my spouse, the number of family members with whom it's safe to talk politics has just dropped to zero. I'm sad about this.

Like Sons to Me

I've mentioned my 20-something nephews who are like sons to me. The relationship, however, has been disrupted periodically throughout their lives. Someday I will write about this. For now I'll just say I wish I had had more time with them, more of an influence on them.

I've written recently about how my nephews and nieces depend almost solely on social media for their news, their informational source upon which to base — not only personal opinions but — their factual interpretation of goings-on in the world around them. Initially it was the altered videos of Joe Biden that "prove" he has dementia. Then it was the overwhelming number of propaganda videos "proving" that antifa is a left-wing terrorist organization bent on burning down the suburbs.

Rounding out their world perspective is the disinformation spread by white evangelical pastors, often filtered through simplistic, tacitly bigoted parental lenses. (This is not meant to cast aspersions on all white evangelicals, about 18-19% of whom realize that rooting out a racist, venal president who's endeavoring to destroy democracy trumps the single issue of abortion restriction, which has people of great integrity on both sides.)

Now one of my young men believes the coronavirus pandemic is a hoax, at least a partial one. Now one of my young men believes the "better" man — the bane-of-humanity incumbent president — probably was cheated out of reelection victory.

And I'm left to contemplate my nephews' apparent insensitivity to humankind.

Heavy Heart

It is with a heavy heart that now when I'm with them I must eliminate a category of conversation that is 1) highly interesting and meaningful to me, and 2) important to their future well-being and educational development. What's an uncle/father figure for if not to educate and positively influence his nephews who are like sons to him? I eliminate these topics — politics, pandemics, and Trumpism — not simply because we disagree. I would love to engage them in vigorous debate while teaching the components of reasoning, critical thinking, and ethical rhetorical persuasion in the process.

No, I eliminate these topics because they choose or have learned not to seek facts but instead blindly latch onto disinformation that feeds their — and by extension, their parents' — specious grievances. My attempting to engage with fallacy consistently leads to hurt feelings on both sides. It leads to 20-something emotional outbursts, useless tension, and strengthened stubbornness that serves no purpose.

Nevertheless I feel helpless, unable to intervene on their malignant emotional and intellectual growth.

Problem, Solution

Of course this same problem exists with all my living extended family. (My parents, parents-in-law, and only sibling have passed away but would have been ideologically attuned with Norma and me.) The problem exists with half my friends, half my social media contacts, almost half the country.

I simply refuse to engage any longer with those who do not even attempt to seek truth and fact. How can Trump supporters still exist now that everyone knows beyond any doubt what he stands for? They're not monolithically poorly educated — large portions are "smart" in other areas, college-degreed, highly educated.

Many are selfish. Donald purports to give them what they want (tax cuts and growing 401[k]s). Many are bigots. They like (covertly or overtly) his support of white hegemony while hiding it in plain sight. Finally, many just like that he spits in the eye of forces they disdain (politicians, pandemic "hoaxes," mask-wearing to save lives). Most are prone to conspiracy theories, suspending reason and empathy to feed their grievances. Whatever their motives, they're all essentially saying, "I want what *I* want and screw humanity."

Historians, theologians, mental health professionals, and educators will debate for decades what to do about this disdain for facts — which took hold strongly in the early 21st century, then exploded during the Trump era.

The solution is simple but couldn't take effect for a generation even if instituted today. Still, better late than never. The appreciation for reasoning, reality, and the search for truth — with a healthy-but-not-unhealthy dose of pathos — must be taught early and consistently, throughout primary and secondary education. Currently students are left to try and grasp these essential components of learning and thinking on their own. Currently about half have been unsuccessful.

Imagine if students were left on their own to learn arithmetic, to learn to read.

Delayed Response

When my nephew (whom we'll call) Josh was about 11 years old, his aunt and I took him shopping at the local mall. Norma stopped to browse women's clothing inside a Talbots. Josh and I dutifully waited outside. While sitting on a bench near the fountain, out of nowhere he asked me, "What makes a person a Democrat?"

I was taken aback, wanting to give him a thorough, thoughtful explanation, especially since I knew his parents were Republicans. At that point Norma emerged from the store, so I told my nephew I'd get back to him when I had a chance to explain it properly.

Then Josh's parents, in some fit of false superiority and mysterious resentment, kept him and his brother away from us for two years with no good rationale any reasonable person could discern.

The moment had passed, and I never did get to explain to Josh "what makes a Democrat." But I've given it a lot of thought since then and I'm ready to say my piece:

> "Today's Democrat, for all her party's faults, embraces a
> culture of life, that is, embraces a continuous moral support
> for equality, diversity, fairness, truth, the earth, the worker,
> the (biblical) stranger, freedom of (any) religion or no

religion, a cultural safety net, voting rights, and an ethical government that works for the people."

I might go on to explain that party identification has been ephemeral since America's founding. But liberal and conservative philosophies are consistent and that's what matters. Throughout history I might have been a Republican, Democrat, or some independent combination depending upon the decade. But I always would have been left-of-center, a liberal. And today, liberals are Democrats. Today Republicans are light-years of morality and integrity away from where they were in Abraham Lincoln's day. Today Republicans are the party of Trump corruptly trying to retain power and enrich themselves by falsely feeding people's grievances.

One Last Try

Though difficult now, I might still try to tell my nephew "what makes a Democrat," a decade and a half after he asked the question. I might also try to convince him that President Trump lost the election fair and square:

> "The Nov. 3rd election was the most secure in American history. Right now, across the country, election officials are reviewing and double-checking the entire election process prior to finalizing the result. ... There is no evidence that any voting system deleted or lost votes, changed votes, or was in any way compromised."

> ("Joint Statement From Elections Infrastructure Government Coordinating Council & the Election Infrastructure Sector Coordinating Executive Committees"; Election Infrastructure Government Coordinating Council [GCC] Executive Committee – Cybersecurity and Infrastructure Security Agency [CISA] Assistant Director Bob Kolasky, U.S.

Election Assistance Commission Chair Benjamin Hovland, National Association of Secretaries of State [NASS] President Maggie Toulouse Oliver, National Association of State Election Directors [NASED] President Lori Augino, and Escambia County (Florida) Supervisor of Elections David Stafford – and the members of the Election Infrastructure Sector Coordinating Council [SCC] – Chair Brian Hancock [Unisyn Voting Solutions], Vice Chair Sam Derheimer [Hart InterCivic], Chris Wlaschin [Election Systems & Software], Ericka Haas [Electronic Registration Information Center], and Maria Bianchi [Democracy Works]; 11/12/2020.)

"Please don't retweet wild and baseless claims about voting machines, even if they're made by the president. These fantasies have been debunked many times, including by @DHSgov @CISAgov on this excellent site/resource, Rumor Control.https://t.co/XUcOkrQUf6"

(Krebs, Christopher, Cybersecurity and Infrastructure Security Agency [CISA, part of DHS] director; retweet; 11/12/2020; as cited in Becker, David, election law expert, *CBS News* analyst; Twitter post; 11/12/2020.)

President Trump fired Chris Krebs Nov. 17, 2020, for protecting the 2020 election as director of CISA, then reassuring the American people of his agency's successful work. As *The Washington Post* columnist David Ignatius summed up brilliantly in his piece the evening of Kreb's tweet-firing: Trump — through his scorched-earth attempts to subvert the election, then challenge the results through multiple baseless court challenges — inadvertently has shown us "how hard it is to sabotage election results."

"Since the election, President Trump has axed his defense secretary and other top Pentagon aides, his second-in-command at the U.S. Agency for International Development, two top Homeland Security officials, a senior climate scientist, and the leader of the agency that safeguards nuclear weapons.

"Engineering much of the post-election purge is Johnny McEntee, a former college quarterback who was hustled out of the White House two years ago after a security clearance check turned up a prolific habit for online gambling.

"A staunch Trump loyalist, McEntee, 30, was welcomed back … February and installed as head of personnel for the Trump White House. Since the race was called for President-elect Joe Biden, McEntee has been distributing pink slips, warning federal workers not to cooperate with the Biden transition, and threatening to oust people who show disloyalty by job hunting while Trump is still refusing to acknowledge defeat. …

"More firings are expected. … Critics say the dismissals threaten to destabilize broad swaths of the federal bureaucracy in the fragile period during the handover to the next administration.

> (Dawsey, Eilperin, Hudson, & Rein; "In Trump's Final Days, a 30-Year-Old Aide Purges Officials Seen as Insufficiently Loyal; *The Washington Post;* 11/13/2020.)

Some pundits have speculated the firings are worse than score-settling and insufficient-loyalty retaliation. Some pundits fear Trump

is packing high-level government positions with loyalists who could
help him retain power — illegally.■

11/27/20 — We Give Thanks: Mass Homicide Voted Out – Integrity, Competence, Compassion In

COVID-19 Deaths

02/06/2020 — U.S.: 1 | World: 620
11/26/2020 — U.S.: 262,283 | World: 1,423,988

> • Conservatively estimated Trump malfeasance deaths: 131,142
> • U.S.: 4.2% of Earth's population, 18% of its pandemic deaths

> (Ibid.; Glanz & Robertson; 5/20/2020.)
> (Ibid.; Gupta, MD; 9/18/2020.)
> (Ibid.; *The New England Journal of Medicine;* 10/8/2020.)
> (Ibid.; Redlener, MD & Sachs, Ph.D. & Hansen, MPA & Hupert, MD, MPH; 10/21/2020.)
> (as conservatively extrapolated from COVID-19 Dashboard by the Center for Systems Science and Engineering at Johns Hopkins University; 11/27/2020.)

I have two things to discuss today.

1) Article Title

First, let me address this week's article title, "We Give Thanks: Mass Homicide Voted out — Integrity, Competence, Compassion In."

The latter phrase needs no explanation.

Regarding the "Mass Homicide" part, MAGA supporters, please don't give me your mindlessly reflexive *TDS* (Trump Derangement Syndrome — as in, I have it) argument that anti-Trumpers like me blindly condemn your messiah because "orange man bad." I speak in facts and I speak in truths albeit sometimes with a sharp edge.

> "homicide: the intentional and unlawful taking of another person's life"
>
> ("homicide"; *Merriam-Webster.com;* retrieved 11/27/2020.)

And MAGA supporters, please don't give me your guff about Donald's own CDC and U.S. medical facilities artificially bumping up coronavirus death numbers to "get more money," as Mr. Trump has lied to you. Frontline health care workers are overwhelmed, exhausted, and dying themselves. American hospitals aren't giving out any raises or stock dividends for inflated pandemic deaths.

Additionally, yes, many patients had other disorders when they passed away. But if they hadn't contracted the virus, they wouldn't have died *yet*. Some of the 168 victims of the 1995 Oklahoma City bombing committed by white supremacists probably had preexisting heart disease and lung cancer, too — but they *died* from a bomb.

Donald Trump — through his inaction on, and sabotage of, pandemic-fighting efforts — is responsible for a conservatively estimated 50% of U.S. COVID-19 deaths.

Since February, every time he played down the virus and broadcast disinformation about the pandemic's progression, he influenced more of his followers and other low-information citizens to ignore precautions, and more people died.

More people died:

> — Every time he said, "I feel great, I got better and so will you," ignoring the death toll

> — Every time he conducted a superspreader rally or government get-together

> — Every time he said, "Don't be afraid of Covid. Don't let it dominate your life"

> — Every time he said, "You're gonna beat it. … Get out there"

> — Every time he was without a mask in the White House, even while infected

> — Every time he called the pandemic narrative a "Democrat hoax"

More people died:

> — Every time he called safety guidelines "a Democrat plot to abolish church attendance"

> — Every time he mocked or discouraged mask-wearing by those around him

> — Every time he mocked Joe Biden for observing pandemic safety guidelines

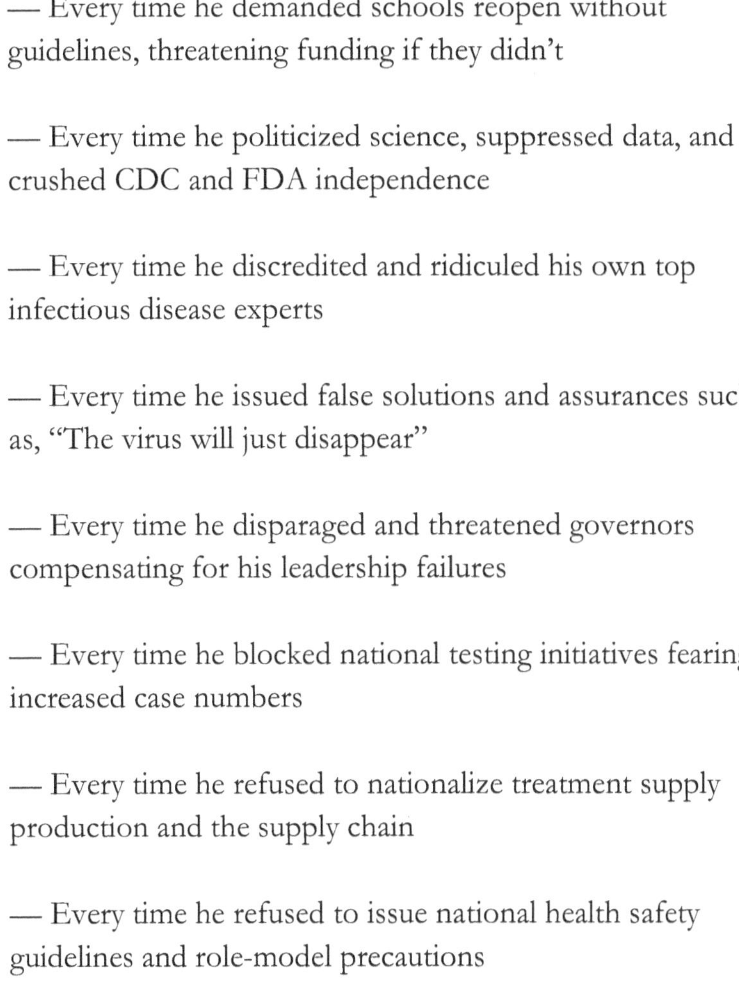

— Every time he demanded schools reopen without guidelines, threatening funding if they didn't

— Every time he politicized science, suppressed data, and crushed CDC and FDA independence

— Every time he discredited and ridiculed his own top infectious disease experts

— Every time he issued false solutions and assurances such as, "The virus will just disappear"

— Every time he disparaged and threatened governors compensating for his leadership failures

— Every time he blocked national testing initiatives fearing increased case numbers

— Every time he refused to nationalize treatment supply production and the supply chain

— Every time he refused to issue national health safety guidelines and role-model precautions

More people died.

For these reasons, half the country believes ignoring and fighting coronavirus safety guidelines is a Trump-supporting political statement. For these reasons, over 130,000 Americans — including many MAGA supporters — have fallen victim to COVID-19 and died needlessly.

And please don't tell me what President Trump *did* do. Yes, he instituted China travel restrictions in late January (40,000 Chinese still legally entered the U.S. in spite of restrictions). Contrary to his claims of brave action, however, he had little pushback — virtually all his advisers and others agreed with the move. And U.S. airlines and 38 other countries already had made the same decision. Since then the few times President Trump has given some lip service to pandemic health precautions — with a wink-wink to his followers that he didn't really mean it — he's immediately obfuscated or contradicted it through disinformation or belittlement, consistently playing down the danger.

Even Ted Bundy had some women friends.

Even David Duke is nice to some Black people.

Even Adolf Hitler had some Jewish relatives.

Final Bras D'honneur to Victims' Families

Over the past three weeks since the election, every day the incumbent president has refused to give vital pandemic data to the Biden transition team has been one more day's delay of urgent action for impeding the spread of a plague. Trump supporters still believe Donald's clear implications that the virus is not dangerous, not serious, probably a hoax, at least way overblown. This would be bad enough if only *they* became infected. But as all reasonable people know, infected Trump supporters also carry the virus to thinking and politically neutral people.

For all these reasons, the president's corrupt inaction has caused at least twice the deaths that were inevitable. It is continuing, indiscriminate mass homicide by a man who has the power to save lives but refuses to use it.

For what purpose? To convince the country — even as fatalities were piling up and hospitals were overwhelmed — that the virus should not require safety guidelines. Safety measures would slow the economy, thereby hurting the president's numbers in the one reelection polling category in which he was beating opponent Joe Biden, albeit by only a few points. Why no compassion even now that polling numbers are moot, now that he has lost the election? Because changing course would be a tacit admission of

error, something President Trump personally is incapable of —
even if it would save lives.

2) Malignant Intersection

OK, my second point of discussion is related to Trumpism because
it illustrates the malignant intersection of Trump-Republican
ideology and the selfish, hypocritical faction of white evangelicalism.
(As I've said, this is not meant to derogate the political morality of
all white evangelicals, about 18-19% of whom realize that the single
issue of abortion rights is far outweighed by harm to our
democracy, which ultimately would make issues such as abortion
rights moot.)

What kind of parents teach their kid that all the people in a
thousand-car food-bank line — most of whom are out of work due
to a pandemic, many visiting a food bank for the first time in their
lives — have only themselves to blame for "not planning ahead"?

What kind of father teaches his children that there is no basis
for BLM, no basis for considering the statistically high mistreatment
and killing of Black men by police, and therefore always responds
with "All Lives Matter," effectively teaching the child that racism is
inconsequential, not a serious issue?

What kind of mother says — when her young-adult son talks
about wanting to open his mind to "both sides of the argument,"
both sides of politics and current events — "Well, I don't know
about that; you need to do what *God* wants you to do"?

This upsets me to no end. I'm no theologian, but I've talked to
enough people to know that God — when she "speaks" — speaks
to everyone differently. Or they hear her differently. How else can
we explain The Crusades? How else can we explain many decades
of Middle East religious conflict? Slavery versus abolition? How else
can we explain the fight over a woman's right to control her own
body, with people of high integrity and equally sincere Christian
ideology on both sides of the issue?

No one has an absolute line on the Word of God for every issue that comes up in the world. Maybe God still cares about democracy. Maybe She prioritizes. Do the 81% of white evangelical Trump supporters ever think of that? Maybe God agrees we'll have to address abortion later — after we save the country and the world from Trumpian destruction — lest there be nothing left to fight for, lest abortion, premarital sex, and Christian "rights" become moot.

White evangelical MAGA followers, if you *were* convinced Trump was destroying democracy — if you were to admit that to yourselves — Would you still support him for the single issue of abortion? If "All Lives Matter," what about the 130,000 indiscriminate homicides? If you're pro-life, what about the *post-born* 5,400 migrant children psychologically tortured by caged separation from their parents in a strange land for months, many never to be reunited because of callous incompetence?

When your sons or daughters say they want to open their minds to "both sides of the argument," both sides of politics and current events, you better damn-well encourage them. What if it was a *Democratic* narcissistic psychopath in the Oval Office falsely using the Word of God to brainwash your children?■

12/03/20 — Losers Anonymous

COVID-19 Deaths

02/06/2020 — U.S.: 1 | World: 620
03/05/2020 — U.S.: 12 | World: 3,293
04/02/2020 — U.S.: 5,137 | World: 48,284
05/07/2020 — U.S.: 73,431 | World: 264,189
06/04/2020 — U.S.: 107,175 | World: 386,464
07/02/2020 — U.S.: 128,062 | World: 516,726
08/06/2020 — U.S.: 158,268 | World: 708,278
09/03/2020 — U.S.: 185,752 | World: 863,577
10/01/2020 — U.S.: 206,963 | World: 1,014,958
11/05/2020 — U.S.: 234,756 *(est.)* | World: 1,231,003 *(est.)*
12/03/2020 — U.S.: 273,847 | World: 1,495,311

• Conservatively estimated Trump malfeasance deaths: 136,924
• U.S.: 4.2% of Earth's population, 18% of its pandemic deaths

(Ibid.; Glanz & Robertson; 5/20/2020.)
(Ibid.; Gupta, MD; 9/18/2020.)
(Ibid.; *The New England Journal of Medicine;* 10/8/2020.)
(Ibid.; Redlener, MD & Sachs, Ph.D. & Hansen, MPA & Hupert, MD, MPH; 10/21/2020.)
(as conservatively extrapolated from COVID-19 Dashboard by the Center for Systems Science and Engineering at Johns Hopkins University; 12/3/2020.)

> *[NEW MEMBER:]* "Hi. My name's Donald and I'm a loser."
>
> *[GROUP:]* "Hi, Donald."
>
> Also, "Keep comin' back"; "One day at a time"; "Let go and let God"; and "Denial is not a river in Egypt."
>
> "[Donald Trump] just needs to go to Losers Anonymous. Like, he's really in a psychosis right now. ... [T]he people around him, like his daughter, like Jared Kushner ... I think that they need to stage some sort of intervention at this point."
>
> (Hostin, Sunny, attorney, journalist, co-host; *ABC's The View;* 11/30/2020.)

Damn. "Losers Anonymous." That should have been my line, my snarky metaphor, being a former alcoholism counselor and all.

(I know: The kinder, gentler terminology these days is "substance use disorder," but I'm a tough-love guy. I refuse to coddle in-denial alcoholics or drug addicts — or *losers* — with watered-down diagnoses that avoid "labeling" them. You got labeled when you groped the boss' wife in a blackout at the office holiday party. And Donald got labeled when the American people said, "Thanks but no thanks" to a second term.)

Besides being vengefully funny, the Losers Anonymous analogy has many parallels to where Mr. Trump finds himself now.

An alcoholic doesn't know, or won't admit, he's an alcoholic for the first major portion of his adult drinking career. Eventually after part of him comes to know, the larger part won't admit it until he hits his personal "bottom," if he ever does.

Denial — Not a River in Egypt

Donald has been a loser throughout his adult life. He just didn't know it. We've learned his father raised him to avoid a rigid-but-false version of loserism. Essentially Fred Trump taught his son that showing any of the common characteristics of humanity — empathy, kindness, emotional vulnerability, self-reflection, ability to apologize and admit mistakes and losses — made one a loser. By his father's metric Donald steadfastly avoided loserism. By any other standard, Donald always has been — a loser.

Like any good alky, Donald Trump had great enablers propping up his loserism. He claims to be a self-made billionaire, receiving only a "small" $1 million loan from Dad early in his career, which he purportedly paid back. In fact Trump the son inherited at least $413 million dollars over the years including through paternal bailouts (to cover up business failures) and unrepaid loans. In Fred's last year of life, Donald tried to manipulate his dementia-afflicted father's will to cheat siblings and other heirs out of their rightful bequests. He clearly participated in using likely fraudulent accounting tactics to hide inheritance tax liability for him and his siblings. (Ibid.; Barstow, Craig, & Buettner; 10/2/2018.)

Had Donald simply left his money in mutual funds, his current net worth would be much higher than it is. In other words, he's a failed businessman. Through the lessons learned from his father — lying, denying, obfuscating, never admitting, never apologizing — The Donald has covered up every financial and business bust he's experienced. And there have been many (Remember Trump Steaks? I didn't think so), to the point that not only is he possibly not a billionaire anymore, he probably has massive personal debt that could drown him financially.

Donald J. Trump fooled the other 49 states with the constant covering up of his losing. But his home-state New Yorkers knew, especially the New York business and society elite. To them he always was a loser and part of him knew it.

Hit Bottom?

Now Donald has experienced his biggest loss ever: being one of the few U.S. presidents to lose reelection after a first term. The people said, "Thanks but no thanks" to rehiring the guy.

You might think this would be Donald's bottom. You would be wrong. He's now attempting to cover up the un-cover-up-able.

Once more, many people thought (hoped?) Mr. Trump wouldn't respond to a loss in the worst destructive way — in this case by subverting American democracy through baseless election result protests, challenges, and wild conspiracy theories. Wrong. He's claiming fraud with no evidence and destroying faith in our electoral system, at least among his 74 million voters. Why? At first he psychologically could not accept the defeat. Now, ultimately, continuing the nonacceptance is 1) making him money through fundraising (by conning his working-class supporters), and 2) setting him up for future endeavors (i.e., cons).

Un-American? "Who cares." Damaging democracy? "Not my problem." Hurting our country and its citizens for years to come? "Screw them — It's helping me."

One more time, Trump has no bottom. He has no Losers-Anonymous-12-Step bottom, one that might provoke him to seek help for his devastating disorder. And he has no bottom, no nadir, for narcissistic depravity — he always can go lower in the quest to help himself even if at enormous cost to everyone else.

The Grifter's Grifter

So Trump continues to bespoil the integrity of American democracy while the courts consistently shut him down.

> "Free, fair elections are the lifeblood of our democracy. Charges of unfairness are serious. But calling an election unfair does not make it so. Charges require specific

allegations and then proof. We have neither here. … The campaign's claims have no merit. … And it never claims fraud or that any votes were cast by illegal voters."

(Bibas, Stephanos, Third Circuit Court of Appeals [Trump-appointed] judge; opinion in response to Trump campaign injunction request; 11/27/2020.)

This opinion from the Third Court of Appeals sums up the near-40 court challenges the Trump campaign has made — and lost — to election results in battleground states where Trump fell short. But the lame-duck president has demonstrated he'll never give up the lie, as illustrated by this vicarious message sent through his TV attorneys:

"The activist judicial machinery in Pennsylvania continues to cover up the allegations of massive fraud. We are very thankful to have had the opportunity to present proof and the facts to the PA state legislature. On to SCOTUS!"

(Ellis, Jenna & Giuliani, Rudy, Trump campaign lawyers; Twitter post; 11/27/2020.)

In the meantime, like any self-respected confidence artist, he doesn't let little things like truth and patriotism get in the way of making a buck, especially with an available pool of 74 million marks. Consider this recent fundraising email from the Master Grifter, himself.

VERBATIM: Trump 2020 Fundraising Email (12/2/2020)

Friend,

I can't defend this Election alone… I need YOUR help.

Making sure we have enough resources to protect the integrity of this Election is critical; especially when the Left and Fake News media are working overtime to try to STEAL IT.

I've decided to REACTIVATE your PERSONAL 1000% IMPACT OFFER.

This is it, Friend. This is where we step up and show the Democrats that REAL Americans want a FAIR and TRANSPARENT Election.

Please contribute $45 or MORE in the NEXT HOUR and you can increase your impact by 1000%.

I know I can count on you, Friend.

My team is sending me the FIRST list of donors soon and I'll be looking for your name. Make sure I see it.

Please contribute another $45 RIGHT NOW to get on the list and to increase your impact by 1000%.

Thank you,

Donald J. Trump
President of the United States

> (Trump, Donald, R-Fla., U.S. president; fundraising email; 12/2/2020.)

Donald Trump is sucking dry the poor working class bastards that hang on his every word. He's raked in $170 million so far. This money isn't going to "FAIR and TRANSPARENT Elections." Most of it is going straight into Mr. Trump's coffers to be used for future cons. But you'll want to make sure he sees "your name" on that "FIRST list of donors."

The Thing That Wouldn't Leave

Mr. Trump has indicated he won't attend his successor's inauguration, as all presidents have done since 1869. This always has been a tremendously important symbolic event demonstrating America's commitment to peaceful transfer of power through free and fair elections.

Mr. Trump has indicated he'll likely hold a 2024 campaign kickoff rally during Joe Biden's inauguration ceremony, though it's unclear if he'll follow through with another presidential run.

Mr. Trump is making lots of money off his refusal to accept defeat. He's setting himself up to maintain control over the consistently obsequious, sycophantic elected Republicans who never have spoken up, never have let him down. To their discredit, they're deathly afraid his influence over voters could end their careers. And to them, career and power trumps everything — integrity, honesty, morality, humanity — everything. Donald will maintain control of Trump Republicans with the threat of a 2024 run, through the dangling of endorsements (or reprobation), and possibly by establishing a far-to-the-right-of-*Fox-News* media empire.

As one pundit put it, the only thing worse than death to (the galactically, pathologically narcissistic) Trump is irrelevance.

And as I say, there is no bottom to Donald's depravity in his quest to avoid irrelevance and enhance self-dealing. Not preventable widespread pandemic death. Not active subversion of American democracy. No bottom.■

12/10/20 — Deep State Swallows SCOTUS, President

COVID-19 Deaths

02/06/2020 — U.S.: 1 | World: 620
12/10/2020 — U.S.: 289,450 | World: 1,571,890

> • Conservatively estimated Trump malfeasance deaths: 144,725
> • U.S.: 4.2% of Earth's population, 18% of its pandemic deaths

>> (Ibid.; Glanz & Robertson; 5/20/2020.)
>> (Ibid.; Gupta, MD; 9/18/2020.)
>> (Ibid.; *The New England Journal of Medicine;* 10/8/2020.)
>> (Ibid.; Redlener, MD & Sachs, Ph.D. & Hansen, MPA & Hupert, MD, MPH; 10/21/2020.)
>> (as conservatively extrapolated from COVID-19 Dashboard by the Center for Systems Science and Engineering at Johns Hopkins University; 12/10/2020.)

There's no way around it: If you *still* support Donald Trump in 2020, you support the following:

— Massive needless pandemic death allowed to support his reelection

— Psychological torture and subhuman mistreatment of thousands of innocent migrant children to "set an example"

— Systematic subversion of American democracy, using and inducing violence in the process

All to support an aspiring autocrat's hold on power. Donald Trump is a danger to America.

Deep State Now Owns SCOTUS, President

> "The [Trump Campaign] application for injunctive relief presented to Justice Alito and by him referred to the Court is denied."
>
> (U.S. Supreme Court; "Order in Pending Case: 20A98 — Kelly, Mike, et al. v. Pennsylvania, et al."; 12/8/2020.)

With that breathtakingly short order the United States Supreme Court — unanimously, definitively — shot down the Trump campaign's request to throw out Pennsylvania's Biden-friendly presidential election result. The 18-word judicial dis from the highest court in the land also made it clear: Don't try coming back with any more of this bull feces.

In other words: "[T]his ship has sailed," as U.S. District Judge Linda Parker wrote Monday.

In other words: "This is madness," as Sen. Mitt Romney (R-Utah) tweet-exclaimed Tuesday.

What does this mean?

It means the deep state has infiltrated the U.S. Supreme Court including President Trump's three appointees — whom he thought he owned. In fact the only logical conclusion is that the deep state conspired to take control of Mr. Trump's thoughts, causing him to fill his three high court vacancies with judges who would betray him. They looked good on paper but ultimately would not be complicit in Donald's plan to steal the election "legally."

That damn deep state. Its conspirators have been out to sabotage our 45th president from Day 1. They finally took over his brain to do it.

All Seriousness Aside

President Trump knows his delusory legal machinations to overturn the election will fail in court. His real goal is to keep the poor-me narrative front and center with his base of supporters, most of whom believe the fantasy. This is good for Trump on several levels: 1) fundraising (*yugely*) on the lie; 2) maintaining control over the GOP; 3) preparing for future cons; and 4) just on general screw-you principles toward political enemies *and* (any-less-than-100%-submissive) allies.

And who knows: Some cockamamie judge or Republican legislator might successfully introduce a significant monkey wrench into the process.

No Metaphor

This is no metaphor. Donald Trump is doing everything in his power to subvert American democracy while simultaneously ignoring the near-300,000 U.S. pandemic deaths. Trump represents the worst of both worlds: traitor *and* tacit mass murderer.

And Republican enablers are supporting these atrocities. All GOP members of the U.S. Congress were polled this week on Joe Biden's status as president-elect. Only 27 would acknowledge the truism publicly. The others (and their supporters) are undermining faith in the rule of law, American electoral integrity, and political morality (which doesn't have to be an oxymoron) for years to come. Like the president, they also represent betrayal of their oaths and tacit mass murder.

There's Still No Way Around It

To those former MAGA supporters who have seen the light, experienced an epiphany, realized the error of their ways, I salute you. I love you. Anyone can make a mistake. Those who can admit that mistake, admit having been conned and manipulated, are my heroes.

Mr. Trump has abandoned his presidential duties, ignored the COVID-19 pandemic, and distracted the country with 50-some frivolous, baseless lawsuits as part of an empty show of fighting his reelection loss. American coronavirus deaths are up to 2,000-3,000 daily. But the recalcitrant child in the Oval Office remains oblivious to all things not about him.

There's no way around it: If you *still* support Donald Trump, you support the following:

— Massive needless pandemic death allowed to support his reelection

— Psychological torture and subhuman mistreatment of thousands of innocent migrant children to "set an example"

— Systematic subversion of American democracy, using and inducing violence in the process

All to support an aspiring autocrat's base of support, reelection, then hold on power after his refusal to accept election loss. Donald Trump is a serious danger to America.

Admitting the problem is the first step.■

12/17/20 — Don't Think Twice, It's All Right (and Other Classic Songs)

COVID-19 Deaths

02/06/2020 — U.S.: 1 | World: 620
12/17/2020 — U.S.: 307,512 | World: 1,651,891

> • Conservatively estimated Trump malfeasance deaths: 153,756
> • U.S.: 4.2% of Earth's population, 19% of its pandemic deaths

> > (Ibid.; Glanz & Robertson; 5/20/2020.)
> > (Ibid.; Gupta, MD; 9/18/2020.)
> > (Ibid.; *The New England Journal of Medicine;* 10/8/2020.)
> > (Ibid.; Redlener, MD & Sachs, Ph.D. & Hansen, MPA & Hupert, MD, MPH; 10/21/2020.)
> > (as conservatively extrapolated from COVID-19 Dashboard by the Center for Systems Science and Engineering at Johns Hopkins University; 12/17/2020.)

(I Know) I'm Losing You

The bitter truth:

> "Today was a before-and-after moment in the life of the nation. One hundred [twenty-]six members of Congress broke faith with American democracy today. They did

something the fascists, the Nazis, the Confederate Army was unable to do. … A majority of elected officials of one of the two major parties in a federal house broke faith with the idea that the people are sovereign, that we're a government of the people, by the people, for the people. … [T]he competition in American politics is now between a democratic party, meaning a party that believes in democracy, versus an autocratic party. We've never seen that. … [W]e're one election away from losing the country to people who no longer believe in democracy."

> (Schmidt, Steve, I[formerly R]-N.J., 2008 McCain-Palin presidential campaign chief strategist; *MSNBC's The Last Word* with Lawrence O'Donnell; 12/10/2020.)

A little milquetoast but still, the most we've gotten from a sitting GOP senator:

"President Trump's efforts to try to overturn the will of the people … is terribly dispiriting to people all over the globe. … [N]ow you've had every court say that President Trump does not have a case. You have the Electoral College that has voted. It's very clear that President-elect Biden will become our next president. And it's time to move on."

> (Romney, Mitt, R-Utah, U.S. senator; *CBS' This Morning;* 12/15/2020.)

Succinct and to the point:

"Let's use the technical term for what's going on here, and it's 'batsh*t crazy.'"

> (Riggleman, Denver, R-Va., U.S. representative; *CNN's The Lead* with Jake Tapper; 10/15/2020.)

(describing President Trump's perpetuation of wild conspiracy theories to influence the election three weeks before Election Day)

They should have listened to Lindsey:

> "My party has gone batsh*t crazy."
>
> (Graham, Lindsey, R-S.C., U.S. senator; celebratory dinner after Graham's presidential primary withdrawal; 2/26/2016.) *(referring to the Republican Party's imminent nomination of Donald Trump for president)*

Go Your Own Way

No better singer for disillusioned, traditional Republicans:

> "I spent 29 years as a Republican, I've spent two and a half as an independent, and later this afternoon I will register as a member of the Democratic Party. Because in America today, it's only the Democratic Party — which is the oldest political party in the world — that stands for the ideas and ideals of American liberty."
>
> (Schmidt, Steve, D[formerly R]-N.J., 2008 McCain-Palin presidential campaign chief strategist; *Battleground* [podcast hosted by Schmidt]; 12/14/2020.)

Go Southeast Michigan:

> "I am withdrawing from my engagement and association with the Republican Party at both the national and state level. ... I am [changing] my party affiliation to Independent. ... It is unacceptable for political candidates to treat our

election system as though we are a third-world nation and incite distrust of something so basic as the sanctity of our vote. … If Republican leaders collectively sit back and tolerate unfounded conspiracy theories and 'stop the steal' rallies without speaking out for our electoral process, which the Department of Homeland Security said was 'the most secure in American history,' our nation will be damaged. … [W]ith the leadership of the Republican Party and our Republican Conference in the House actively participating in at least some of those efforts, I fear long-term harm to our democracy."

(Mitchell, Paul, I[formerly R]-Mich., U.S. representative; letter to Republican National Committee chair; 12/14/2020.)

Go West Michigan:

"Today, I am declaring my independence and leaving the Republican Party."

(Amash, Justin, I[formerly R]-Mich., U.S. representative; "Justin Amash: Our Politics Is in a Partisan Death Spiral. That's Why I'm Leaving the GOP."; *The Washington Post;* 7/4/2019.) *(after digesting President Trump's malfeasance laid out in the Mueller report)*

Just a few of the others on the Trump-era list of former Republicans:

— David Jolly (I) — *fmr. U.S. rep. (Fla.)*
— George Conway (I) — *Washington, D.C., attorney; spouse of Trump adviser Kellyanne Conway; Lincoln Project co-founder*
— George Will (I) — *author; political commentator*
— Gordon Humphrey (I) — *fmr. U.S. senator (N.H.)*

— Jennifer Horn (I) — *fmr. Log Cabin Republicans board member; fmr. N.H. GOP chair*

— Joe Scarborough (I) — *political commentator; fmr. U.S. rep. (Fla.)*

— Joe Walsh (I) — *fmr. U.S. rep. (Ill.); fmr. presidential candidate; Bravery Project head*

— Richard Painter (D) — *fmr. chief White House ethics lawyer (George W. Bush)*

— Stuart Stevens (I) — *political consultant; Mitt Romney presidential campaign manager*

R-E-S-P-E-C-T

Disillusioned non-Trump Republicans do not make up a majority of the GOP. But they're not nothin'. Let me reprise three of my paragraphs penned during Trump's reelection campaign:

"There is a historically unprecedented number of luminaries from the president's own party who support the opposition candidate in November 2020 to stop the frightening, horrendous damage President Trump is doing to our country. That's why there are more than a half-dozen well-organized groups of distinguished Republicans, conservative thinkers, and former GOP legislators who support aborting Trump's campaign to cripple American democracy. ...

"It doesn't matter if some on the list are Never Trumpers from 2016. It doesn't matter if some are GOP moderates. It doesn't matter if some are dead. What matters is that they are — hundreds of them — all from the president's own party, and they all desperately want him out of office. Unprecedented. ...

"Virtually all these Republicans are pro-life, anti-Roe-v.-Wade Christians who want more conservative federal and Supreme Court justices. They all dislike socialism. Virtually all of them hold traditional conservative policy values — which I generally disagree with but still respect. But they also all know that none of these things would matter if we allowed an aspiring autocrat a second term to continue tearing down the institutions and moral foundation of our country's government, until there was nothing left to fight for."

(Ersin, Tom; *GraniteWord.com;* July, October, 2020.)

"Help Me, Rhonda, Help Me Get 'Er out of My Heart"

The Republican Party has split into two factions: 1) the majority, Trump Republicans who will carry on Trumpism after the leader is out of power; and 2) the minority, traditional Republicans who still uphold democratic principles, still generally stand up for integrity and character even under threat of tweet-attack.

It's laudable that prominent Republicans such as Steve Schmidt and Richard Painter were willing not only to leave the GOP but join the Democratic Party out of sheer principle. Most other non-Trump Republicans, however, don't see that as a realistic option. Many of those also don't see themselves kissing and making up with Trump Republicans.

It appears there is only one option: for the minority to form a third party supporting the conservative principles of Ronald Reagan, George Will, and John McCain but denouncing the autocratic characteristics of Trumpism and the GOP's even pre-Trump gravitation toward self-dealing and mendacity.

"The Republican Party is an organized conspiracy for the purposes of maintaining power for self-interest and the self-interest of its donor class. There is no fidelity to the American ideal."

> (Schmidt, Steve, D[formerly R]-N.J., 2008 McCain-Palin presidential campaign chief strategist; *MSNBC's Deadline: White House* with Nicolle Wallace; 12/9/2020.)

Now we just need that new party name for the good Republicans. Whigs? Tories? Reform Party? Reborn Party?

Don't Think Twice, It's All Right

> "When your rooster crows at the break of dawn
> Look out your window, and I'll be gone
> You're the reason I'm a-traveling on
> But don't think twice, it's all right"

> (Dylan, Bob; "Don't Think Twice, It's All Right"; *The Freewheelin' Bob Dylan* [LP album]; 1963.)∎

12/23/20 — This Christmas I Ask: When Did My Evangelical Friend Become OK With Needless Death?

COVID-19 Deaths

02/06/2020 — U.S.: 1 | World: 620
12/23/2020 — U.S.: 322,849 | World: 1,719,436

> • Conservatively estimated Trump malfeasance deaths: 161,425
> • U.S.: 4.2% of Earth's population, 19% of its pandemic deaths

> > (Ibid.; Glanz & Robertson; 5/20/2020.)
> > (Ibid.; Gupta, MD; 9/18/2020.)
> > (Ibid.; *The New England Journal of Medicine;* 10/8/2020.)
> > (Ibid.; Redlener, MD & Sachs, Ph.D. & Hansen, MPA & Hupert, MD, MPH; 10/21/2020.)
> > (as conservatively extrapolated from COVID-19 Dashboard by the Center for Systems Science and Engineering at Johns Hopkins University; 12/23/2020.)

When Did My Evangelical Christian Friend Start Hanging out Online With Sociopaths?

When did my sweet, compassionate evangelical Christian friend become a conspiracy-theory-believing, white-supremacy-sympathizing, pandemic-denying mask opponent callously willing to support thousands of post-born

Americans dying needlessly because she thinks her "rights and liberties are being taken away"?

When did my friend start buddying up on social media with the likes of Tucson Two-Tone who claims to have worked at the Defense Department for 30 years and hails Trump as our military savior? (Two-Tone fancies himself a consummate military man but thinks the dozens of respected three- and four-star Trump-critic generals are insubordinate wimps.)

When did my friend begin commiserating with Diana Roseanna Diana who believes Romans 12:2 is her catch-all excuse for discounting every Trumpian outrage — and crime — inflicted upon America?

For the uninitiated:

> "And be not conformed to this world: but be ye transformed by the renewing of your mind, that ye may prove what is that good, and acceptable, and perfect, will of God."

> (Church of England; "Romans 12:2"; *Holy Bible, King James Version;* 1611.)

Plain English?

> "Do not conform to the pattern of this world, but be transformed by the renewing of your mind. Then you will be able to test and approve what God's will is — his good, pleasing, and perfect will."

> (Biblica [formerly International Bible Society]; "Romans 12:2"; *Holy Bible, New International Version;* 1978.)

We certainly can say that supporting Trumpism does "not conform to the pattern of this world." But is it "God's will"? Not *my* God's will.

There are other social media influencers brainwashing my evangelical friend. Joe Beam saw "in real time" the election being stolen from Trump in Detroit. And his brother, Jim, believes COVID-19 is a Democrat hoax to eliminate churches. And Williams Brian thinks coronavirus health guidelines are the greatest "socialist" plot to usurp our freedoms since *Mein Kampf* (which helped birth Hitlerian *fascism,* not socialism).

President Trump has made ignoring pandemic health guidelines — causing needless sickness and death — a pro-MAGA political statement. Isn't Christianity better than that?

White Evangelical Hypocrisy

There are various wings of Trump-supporting, pandemic-denying citizens. Today I'm addressing the white evangelical wing.

Personally I'm not religious, haven't even settled on a preferred deity (though many might consider me a casual cultural Christian by birth). But I will speak to the approximately 81% of white evangelicals, most of whom live and die MAGA, in the language they understand. And I ask: How could my kindhearted friend — a passionate pro-Bible, Ten Commandments-adhering ultra-pro-life Christian — How could she turn into a callous COVID-downplayer willing to hasten fatalities among innocent people because mask guidelines "violate her constitutional rights"?

If you're willing to picket abortion clinics and assault their clients with jeers and gory photos — or support those who *are* willing, or just support anti-choice legislation — How can you *not* be willing to encourage friends and family to take the compassionate (and really easy) steps of wearing a mask in public and socially distancing when possible for the good of all humanity? Instead you say, "We should consider both sides. It's only fair. After all, pro-choicers want their choice, to abort a fetus. Fair is fair."

In other words you're saying, "We should have our choice: to sicken and kill hundreds of thousands of the post-born simply because we think masks are a deep-state plot to take away our rights and liberties."

My God. What has happened to humanity? What kind of colossally selfish spell has Mr. Trump cast upon his followers?

My Ah-Ha! Moment

"Eureka!" (i.e., "Holy sh*t!"). I was lying in bed trying to fall asleep and it came to me. When most MAGA WASPs say they're losing their rights and freedoms, it's code for this: Non-WASPs finally are gaining *their* rights and freedoms. And the vast majority of MAGA WASPs damn-well are threatened and angered by that:

1) Gay people attaining the right to serve openly in the military (or marry) means MAGA WASPs have *lost* the right to serve in the military *not* next to *a gay* (or not have to think about a lesbian wedding cake being baked in their neighborhood).

2) Muslim, Sikh, Jewish, and nonreligious students gaining the right *not* to be forced to hear a Christian prayer in public school means MAGA WASPs have *lost* the right — lost the "religious freedom" — to impose their beliefs on others.

3) African Americans gaining the right to sit at the Woolworths lunch counter means MAGA WASPs have *lost* the right to avoid Blacks in public places. Or Hispanics. Or Native Americans. Or any other damn foreigners.

4) Black Lives Matter protests raising our cultural consciousness mean MAGA supporters have *lost* the right to ignore — or support without embarrassing explanation — institutional law enforcement bias resulting in statistically

sky-high rates of Black male mistreatment and murder at the hands of police.

FINALLY) Mask mandates or even guidelines to save innocent American lives and not overwhelm the health care system threaten MAGA followers' right to say screw you to humanity.

Whose Rights Are We Talkin' About?

In other words, as a MAGA WASP, religious freedom means my *Christian* religion. Civil rights means my *Caucasian* civil rights. Ignoring and opposing public mask guidelines means retaining my right to say to hell with society, to ignore the opportunity to save lives. Refusing to wear a mask in public (or excusing and supporting those who refuse) means retaining my freedom *not* to help my neighbors — my hundreds of thousands of American neighbors — with a really small sacrifice.

And to hell with United States democracy if my right to be disinformed is questioned. I have the right to believe a colossally mendacious autocratic demagogue who wants to take us back to the good old days — the 1950s when Negros, homosexuals, heathens, and foreigners knew their place. Re-embracing the repressive culture of the '50s is tacitly inherent in our slogan: "Make America Great Again." Don't try to guilt me into seeing the truth, seeing the good, even if ignoring it is completely counter to my core Christian principles. I have a right to my hypocrisy and depravity. Christian principles apply to me only when I *say* they apply.

These are the rights that some 81% of white evangelical Christians believe they're losing. And Mr. Trump gives them a giant Wizard-of-Oz curtain behind which to hide their bigotry and hypocrisy in the name of "freedom."

Repost Heard 'Round the Facebook

Here's what set me off originally. My sweet, compassionate Christian friend reposted the following missive for comment. You might recognize this repost as one of countless pieces — commissioned by pro-Trump, pro-QAnon, white-supremacist, anti-government, and other conspiracy-theory groups — that purport to be from an "average person" on social media.

The repost does not have a religious slant per se. But most MAGA white evangelicals such as my friend have attached themselves to its arguments and implications. So as mentioned, I decided to speak to her and her crowd in the language they understand. I might have overdone the God-themed takedown, but I was on a roll and hard heads require hard truths.

Play Ball!

(Top of the 1ˢᵗ Inning) — The Repost [VERBATIM: Letter Spread on Facebook]

SCARY....   ·

Didn't write this, but it is spot on........ It's not about masks. Open your mind to the POSSIBILITY......

In 4 months, the U.S. transformed into an obedient socialist country. The government dictated what events are acceptable to attend. Violent protests that instill fear are OK, but church services, family funerals, and patriotic celebrations are dangerous. And you bought it without a fight.

Standing in a graduation line is a "safety hazard." Small businesses were forced to close but crowds to support the corporate money machine at Walmart, Lowes, and Home Depot are OK.

Come on. It's "just a mask" and "safety precautions."

How about a little hush money? Here's $2,400 that we stole out of your paycheck in the first place. Enjoy. Buy something with it, from a big corporation.

Cash is dirty. We can't give change. There's a coin shortage. Use your card. In 4 months, they convinced you to use a traceable card for everything.

In less than 4 months, the government closed public schools then "restructured" education under the guise of "public safety." In less than 4 months, our government demonstrated how easily people assimilate to "guidelines" that have NO scientific premise whatsoever when you are fearful. In less than 4 months, our government successfully instilled fear in a majority of the population in America that allows them to control every aspect of your life. Including what you eat, where you go, and who you see.

And the most dangerous and terrifying part? People are not afraid of their freedoms being removed. They're afraid of their neighbors, family, and friends. And they hate those who won't comply.

It's absolutely terrifying to me that so many people don't question "why." They are willing to surrender their critical thinking skills and independence. They just... gave up without thinking. Without a fight.

Do you know what's coming next? "It's just a vaccine. Come on. It's for the greater good."

Wait until you're told that you can't enter any store or business without proof of the Covid-19 vaccine. Wait until you can't go to public events or get on a plane without proof of receiving the vaccine. To everyone that doesn't believe this is possible - DO YOU UNDERSTAND that the government successfully dictated to people WHEN they were allowed to be outside, where they were allowed to go, and how their children would be educated in less than 4 months? And that a majority of the population followed blindly because they were told to do so.

You're kidding yourself if you think this behavior won't be repeated with a vaccine. Or whatever the next step is.

But that couldn't happen here, right?

Try to See It Through God's Eyes

(Bottom of the 1ˢᵗ Inning) — My Response to the Repost

My friend, you introduced the letter with, "Didn't write this, but it is spot on." You've given it your full-throated endorsement. You can't now say you're just passing on food for thought.

This is the kind of disinformation that has been damaging our country for four years. There are so many logical fallacies, lies, and false sinister implications that it would take many times the space of your repost to refute the fraud being perpetuated.

It's called argumentum verbosium. This is one of many commissioned pieces written by QAnon and other Trump groups — in the guise of John Q. Citizen — for propaganda purposes.

But let me address just a few points:

1) The letter writer says people "surrendered their critical thinking skills." Yes, the people who believe this type of disinformation have.
God gave us the gift of critical thinking, the ability to sort lie from truth. But He leaves it up to the individual to choose to

use it. By misrepresenting its definition, the letter writer
wants to fool you into *not* using God's gift.

2) *God gave us the gift of masks* to be able to protect our
neighbors whom He urges us to love. So you're telling God,
"No, my right to an uncovered face in public places will not
be taken away, even for a short while, never mind how many
die." Somehow I think God comes down on the side of
protecting life.

3) *God gave us the gift of technical alternatives, temporary ways to
worship Him,* for those who are forgoing large gatherings such
as church services, temporarily, to protect fellow Christians
and other human beings. This is because God wouldn't ask
us to choose between worshiping Him and killing our
neighbors.

4) *God knows it's not too much to ask of us to make a small sacrifice*
— to wear a mask in public, to avoid large gatherings
temporarily — so that we can protect our neighbors from
dying. God knows this because He knows a thing or two
about sacrifice.

5) *God hates those who rush to evil and false witness.* He knows that
His gifts of masks, vaccines, science, critical thinking, and
love for humanity are not some sinister plot to take away
religious freedom or worse. They're simply tools He
provides his followers to show their love for others by
helping not to kill each other.

6) *Scientific understanding evolves with new information, and different
states and localities differ because they're independent of each other.*
This is why there was no national conspiracy to usurp your
rights. Were some mistakes made by conscientious leaders?
Yes, honest mistakes. But God gave these state and local

leaders the best information available at the time and most did their best with what they had. Sadly their job was made harder by disinformation and violence-inducing rhetoric such as is being spread by the letter writer and the president. Also sadly, many Trump-allied leaders ignored the scientific data God provided them.

FINALLY) If you do shun God's gifts, thinking they're part of a sinister government plot to steal your rights, then you must agree: that sinister government was *made* sinister and used by Donald Trump. And it was Mr. Trump's unwillingness to address the pandemic and role-model safety guidelines that killed tens of thousands of Americans unnecessarily. Therefore we must all thank God for the recent rights-saving, lifesaving election result.

"They Want Choice, We Want Choice. Fair Is Fair"

(Top of the 2ⁿᵈ Inning) — Then My Friend Says …

Then my friend said something about people should have the choice not to wear a mask in public because pro-choice (pro-women's-right-to-control-their-own-bodies) proponents want choice. So she's just sayin': "They want choice, we want choice. Fair is fair."

(Bottom of the 2ⁿᵈ Inning) — My Response to Her Response

The problem with that reasoning is your "choice" — not to wear a harmless mask in public — sickens and kills post-born humans unnecessarily. If you object to a woman's choice to end a pregnancy — a life-changing, devastating decision for that woman, causing all involved great anguish — How can you object to a harmless guideline to wear a mask in public, temporarily, to save the lives of God's *post-*

born children? How can you object to loving your neighbor by making a small sacrifice that hurts no one? God gave us the gifts of masks, science, and neighbor-loving compassion, a desire not to kill your neighbor. How can any Christian — or anyone — object to that?

My friend, I'm shocked that as the passionate Christian I know you to be, you can object to choice that kills the pre-born, but you don't object to choice (not to wear a mask in public) that kills the post-born.

To choose consciously not to wear a mask in public — just because — when it saves *others'* lives is galactically selfish. Is this what God commands? Deadly selfishness? Or is He simply requesting of us a small sacrifice to save lives?

The other problem is the perpetuating of the fraudulent conspiracy theories. As I said, this is one of many "everyman" pieces written by QAnon and white supremacist groups that have flooded social media. In fact this disinformation ultimately can bring down a country. At that point, pro-life judges and religious freedom will be moot.

"Both Sides of the Argument"

(Top of the 3rd Inning) — Then My Friend Says … Again

Then my friend said something about never intending to elicit this much commotion and we should all consider "both sides of the argument"; and some people who wear masks still get the virus so maybe masks don't really work; and we're losing our rights and freedoms so we should retain our "choice"; and if non-mask-wearers want to risk their own lives, that's their right, their choice, and we should pray for "the unbelievers who do not wear them."

You must know that an inflammatory letter like the one you reposted could get lots of passionate response. And even though you say you wear a mask "if really necessary," by reposting the letter on your page you obviously support its theme: that masks and other pandemic health guidelines are an abrogation of your rights, and that those who refuse masks and social distancing in public simply are choosing to uphold their rights.

We can consider both sides, but if one side is killing post-born lives, I choose life.

But OK, here is my last point-by-point response:

1) *By "masks work,"* scientists mean they drastically lower the odds of virus contraction, in very high percentages overall. But nothing can guarantee safety 100% — just like seat belts cannot. Wouldn't you still ensure that your geriatric mother or second grade son wore a seat belt in your car even with only an 80% effectiveness for reducing injury and death, though not a guaranteed 100%?

2) *The "choice" is in loving humanity.* Individual choice in this case affects others as much or more than the mask-wearer. And the choice — to love your neighbor with a small sacrifice — is sooooo easy. Why not make the easy choice to honor God by protecting our neighbors, especially the weak? I don't get it.

3) *Many still seem to think masks only protect the wearer.* If that were true I would say have your *choice* all day long and twice on Sundays (and maybe Wednesday night Praise Group). But 80% of a mask's purpose is to protect others. What I

pray for is that "the unbelievers who do not wear them" follow the ways of Christ by learning that their mask-wearing sacrifice is not so much for them but to protect *others* from dying.

FINALLY, AGAIN) President Trump and his supporters have made ignoring pandemic health guidelines — causing needless sickness and death — a political statement. Isn't Christianity bigger than that?

(Ball Game Called Because of [Cognitive] Darkness)

Did I lean too hard on the God angle?■

12/31/20 — Mr. President, Even Pat Robertson Says, "It's All Over"

COVID-19 Deaths

02/06/2020 — U.S.: 1 | World: 620
12/31/2020 — U.S.: 342,414 | World: 1,807,866

> • Conservatively estimated Trump malfeasance deaths: 171,207
> • U.S.: 4.2% of Earth's population, 19% of its pandemic deaths

> (Ibid.; Glanz & Robertson; 5/20/2020.)
> (Ibid.; Gupta, MD; 9/18/2020.)
> (Ibid.; *The New England Journal of Medicine;* 10/8/2020.)
> (Ibid.; Redlener, MD & Sachs, Ph.D. & Hansen, MPA & Hupert, MD, MPH; 10/21/2020.)
> (as conservatively extrapolated from COVID-19 Dashboard by the Center for Systems Science and Engineering at Johns Hopkins University; 12/31/2020.)

I was moved this week to reprise a bit from Dana Carvey's 1995 stand-up comedy special, *Critics' Choice*, in which he roasted the popular false conspiracy theory of the day: that the iconic National Football League veteran O.J. Simpson was framed, because of his ethnicity, for the gruesome 1994 slash-and-stab murders of his ex-wife, Nicole Brown Simpson, and her friend Ron Goldman. O.J. is African American and the victims were Caucasian (mentioned only as pertinent to the story).

It was clear then and is clear now: O.J. did it (notwithstanding his continuing vow "to keep looking for the real killer"). But his superstar legal team persuaded enough people to believe a wall of disinformation, obfuscation, and mendacity to win a not guilty verdict.

[*DANA CARVEY:*] "Well, we had to do it sooner or later: Let's talk a little about O.J., please, because I have to get it off my chest. … Now, they say he was framed. *(smirks)* OK. *(audience laughs)* They say he was framed. Now, I know, I've been watching. I know about Mark DER FURMAN! *(executes the finger mustache and Nazi salute in reference to the racist investigator accused of planting evidence against O.J.)* He's an idiot. But if you look at it technically, he just couldn't have acted alone. There's just too many things, too many people would have had to be involved.

"And it's hard to comprehend that *spontaneous conspiracy:* Five-thirty a.m. at South Bundy [site of the murders outside Nicole's front door], someone walks up to you and says: 'We're framin' O.J. You in?'" *(long pause)*

[*CARVEY, AS YOU:*] "Framing O.J.? I could go to prison. I'd risk my entire career. And I REALLY *like* O.J. But you're right, it's just too good. I'm in. Pass it along."

[*CARVEY, AS 1st CALLER:*] *(normal-pitched voice)* "Framin' O.J. You in?"

[*CARVEY, AS 2nd CALLER:*] *(high-pitched voice)* "Framin' O.J. You in?"

[*CARVEY, AS 3rd CALLER:*] *(low-pitched voice)* "Framin' O.J. You in?" …

[CARVEY, ON SHORT-WAVE RADIO:] "To all our ships at sea: We're framin' O.J., we're framin' O.J." …

[CARVEY, AS FOREIGN OFFICIAL:] "You're going to frame O.J.!? But I REALLY *like* O.J.: 2,000 yards, Buffalo Bill. But you're right, it's just too good. We're going to FRAME HIM!" …

[CARVEY, IN HIS BEST PRESIDENT BILL CLINTON DRAWL:] *(ring, ring)* "You're gonna frame O.J.? Well, hell, I really like those 'Naked Gun' movies. But you're right: It's just too good. I'm gonna put at your disposal the Marines, the Navy, the CIA, and the FBI, because we have got to get that son-of-a-*b*tch*."

[CARVEY AS CARVEY:] "Now, maybe he was framed, I don't know." *(Dana smirks; audience roars)*

(Carvey, Dana; *Critics' Choice* [stand-up comedy special]; 1995.)

Sound Familiar?

Mr. Trump believes the election was stolen from him. Well at least he believed that when the election was called, Nov. 7, by all major media networks (an unofficial but traditionally inarguable determination). Then the recounts and vote audits came in. Then Mr. Trump's legal team lost all 59-and-counting of its election-challenge cases in court. Within a few weeks Donald knew he had lost but decided to keep up the charade, which he believed would better position him for current fundraising, future business deals, and possibly another presidential run in 2024. Then after several weeks of that, he reverted to the darkest depths of his narcissistic pathology, *believing* his own conspiracy of mendacity.

"Now, maybe the election was stolen, I don't know." *(smirks)*

Which is where we are today. And depending upon the poll, approximately 50-70% of Republicans believe Trump believing himself: that he won the election — by a lot. But it was stolen by dead Democrats voting for Joe Biden multiple times. Along with deep-state operatives secretly carting off millions of Trump ballots in maintenance trucks. To be destroyed in Venezuela. By the ghost of Hugo Chavez.

Note that many of the down-ballot Republicans on those same stolen ballots won their races. Wait. Wha?!

Recap

To recap, Democrats stole the presidential election from Donald Trump. And government agencies and branches all controlled by Mr. Trump from top to bottom let them do it — even though they REALLY *like* Donald.

Federal judges conspired against Trump to get him out of office. These include the hundreds of conservative judges appointed and seated over the past four years, about whom Donald and Mitch (McConnell) regularly brag. The 59-and counting election-challenge cases and lawsuits brought by the president's legal team were *all* shot down, by Trump-appointed (and other) conservative judges as well as jurists from the other side.

The Supreme Court of the United States conspired against Trump to get him out of office even though the justices include his three appointees (whom he assumed were in his pocket) and three other conservative justices. The Court denied Donald's two challenges by unanimous votes.

The Department of Justice conspired against Trump to get him out of office by allowing the deep-state election-theft campaign to proceed unimpeded. The DOJ is led by Trump's hand-picked lackey Attorney General William Barr who's been seen universally, consistently as acting improperly: as Donald's personal lawyer and defender. After authorizing several improper investigations in the hopes of helping the president's reelection, AG Barr announced Dec. 1 that the DOJ has "not seen fraud on a scale that could have effected a different outcome in the election."

The Republican leadership in the important swing state of Georgia conspired to keep Trump out of office by rigging the election for Democrat Joe Biden. Georgia's governor is Brian Kemp (R), a Trump ultra-loyalist since Inauguration Day, who was especially helpful with the president's mendacious and deadly plan to downplay the pandemic. After two hand recounts and an absentee ballot signature audit, Gov. Kemp and well-respected GOP Secretary of State Brad Raffensperger declared their state's election results dead-accurate and beyond reproach.

The Department of Homeland Security allowed the deep state to rig the election for Biden. Trump appointee and lifelong Republican Chris Krebs, director of the Cybersecurity and Infrastructure Security Agency (a branch of the DHS), authorized a statement saying the 2020 presidential election was "the most secure in American history. … There is no evidence that any voting system deleted or lost votes, changed votes, or was in any way compromised."

The FBI looked the other way. The CIA took a nap. Senate Republicans were weak. Wisconsin and Michigan election board members all risked their careers and freedom:

"We're stealing the election from Trump. You in?"

"Stealing the election from Trump? I could go to prison. I'd risk my entire career. And I REALLY *like* Trump. But you're right, it's just too good. I'm in. Pass it along."

Even Pat Robertson Says You Live in an Alternate Reality

Donald Trump has no bottom. He has no integrity, no morality, no humanity. He'll destroy the country if it benefits him. Or he'll destroy the country out of spite. He respects no world other than his own, hence Pat's "alternate reality" assessment. And now Donald is the lowest form of human scum on Earth (per his dad): a loser.

We could hope that fear of further embarrassment might force him to do the right thing. Arguably two of his biggest, strongest supporting entities have told him it's time to go.

Pat Robertson:

> "I think it's all over. I think the Electoral College has spoken. … I don't think the Supreme Court is going to move in to do anything. And I think we're going to see a President Biden. … With all [Mr. Trump's] talents and the ability to raise money and draw large crowds, the president still lives in an alternate reality. He really does. People say he lies about this, that, and the other. But no, he doesn't lie. To him, that's the truth: 'He had the biggest crowd on Inauguration Day, he had more people than ever.' … 'He saved NBC with "The Apprentice."' You go down the line of things that really aren't true. … He's very erratic. … And I think it would be well to say, 'You've had your day, and it's time to move on.'"

> (Robertson, Pat, televangelist, *Christian Broadcasting Network* founder; *CBN's The 700 Club;* 12/21/2020.)
> *(Pat Robertson has been a staunch Trump supporter saying the president was put in office by God)*

New York Post:

> "Mr. President, it's time to end this dark charade. … Unfortunately, you're obsessed with … Jan. 6, when Congress will, in a pro forma action, certify the Electoral College vote. You have tweeted that, as long as Republicans

have 'courage,' they can overturn the results and give you four more years in office. In other words, you're cheering for an undemocratic coup.

"You had every right to investigate the election. But let's be clear: Those efforts have found nothing. To take just two examples: Your campaign paid $3 million for a recount in two Wisconsin counties, and you lost by 87 more votes. Georgia did two recounts of the state, each time affirming Biden's win. These ballots were counted by hand, which alone debunks the claims of a Venezuelan vote-manipulating Kraken conspiracy.

"Sidney Powell [one of your top election attorneys] is a crazy person. Michael Flynn [your former national security adviser and convicted Mueller investigation felon] suggesting martial law is tantamount to treason. It is shameful."

> (editorial board; "The Post Says: Give It Up, Mr. President — for Your Sake and the Nation's"; *New York Post*; 12/27/2020.) *(the New York Post was one of the first newspapers to endorse Trump and has been a staunch supporter)*

Even the *New York Post* says your top advisers' advice in supporting your "undemocratic coup" is "crazy" and "tantamount to treason."
Even *The 700 Club* says, "It's all over."
Even Pat Robertson says you "live in an alternate reality." ∎

2021

01/06/2021 — Insurrection of January 6

01/07/21 — December 7, 1941. September 11, 2001. January 6, 2021.

COVID-19 Deaths

02/06/2020 — U.S.: 1 | World: 620
03/05/2020 — U.S.: 12 | World: 3,293
04/02/2020 — U.S.: 5,137 | World: 48,284
05/07/2020 — U.S.: 73,431 | World: 264,189
06/04/2020 — U.S.: 107,175 | World: 386,464
07/02/2020 — U.S.: 128,062 | World: 516,726
08/06/2020 — U.S.: 158,268 | World: 708,278
09/03/2020 — U.S.: 185,752 | World: 863,577
10/01/2020 — U.S.: 206,963 | World: 1,014,958
11/05/2020 — U.S.: 234,756 *(est.)* | World: 1,231,003 *(est.)*
12/03/2020 — U.S.: 273,847 | World: 1,495,311
01/07/2021 — U.S.: 361,297 | World: 1,885,689

• Conservatively estimated Trump malfeasance deaths: 180,649

• U.S.: 4.2% of Earth's population, 19% of its pandemic deaths

(Ibid.; Glanz & Robertson; 5/20/2020.)
(Ibid.; Gupta, MD; 9/18/2020.)
(Ibid.; *The New England Journal of Medicine;* 10/8/2020.)
(Ibid.; Redlener, MD & Sachs, Ph.D. & Hansen, MPA & Hupert, MD, MPH; 10/21/2020.)
(as conservatively extrapolated from COVID-19 Dashboard by the Center for Systems Science and Engineering at Johns Hopkins University; 1/7/2021.)

Insurrection of January 6

On Jan. 6, 2021, an event occurred in the nation's capital that — forgive the well-worn cliché — will go down in infamy. I won't write a term paper about it here because multiple books will be written about it. A 9/11-style commission likely will be formed to prevent future occurrences. A Robert Mueller-style special counsel likely will be appointed to investigate the perpetrators and make criminal referrals.

But in a nutshell:

On Wednesday during the constitutionally required congressional session to certify the Electoral College presidential winner — in this case, Joe Biden — members of a pro-Trump crowd estimated to number between 8,000 and 40,000 mounted a well-planned insurrection. Far-right internet sites had been trading information for months regarding Jan. 6 occupation planning, illegal gun movement, avoiding authorities, and breaking into secure buildings. Much of the mob overwhelmed police and breached the Capitol building for the first time since British troops torched it in 1814.

> "We will never give up. We will never concede. ... We will not take it anymore. ... [W]e will stop the steal. ... And we're going to have to fight much harder. ... Because you'll never take back our country with weakness. You have to show strength, and you have to be strong. We have come to demand that Congress do the right thing. ... If you don't do that ... you will have an illegitimate president ... and we can't let that happen. ... The radical left knows exactly what they were doing. They are ruthless, and it's time that somebody did something about it. ... Make no mistake, this election was stolen from you, from me, and from the country. ... This is a criminal enterprise. ... So I hope Mike [Pence, my vice president,] has the courage to do what he

has to do [and refuse to certify the election]. ... [I]f you don't fight like hell, you're not going to have a country anymore. ... So we are going to walk down Pennsylvania Avenue ... to the Capitol! ... and give [Congress] the kind of pride and boldness that they need to take back our country!"

(Trump, Donald, R-Fla., U.S. president; speech to "protesters" gathered at "Stop the Steal" rally; Washington, D.C.; 1/6/2021.) *(shortly before the protesters-turned-rioters walked the 16 blocks to the Capitol building, then surrounded and breached it)*

[EDITOR'S NOTE:] The "radical left" nor any other entity stole the election. Joe Biden is the legitimate president-elect.

Many hundreds of rioters beat police, smashed windows, and broke down doors to enter the Capitol, holding the facilities for about four hours. Sen. James Lankford (R-Okla.) and House Speaker Nancy Pelosi (D-Calif.) were interrupted midsentence upon security officials ordering the evacuation of their respective chambers. Vice President Mike Pence, in the building presiding over the Senate, was rushed to safety by Secret Service agents just seconds before rioters would have come upon him, his wife, and his daughter.

The mob terrorized lawmakers and staff, forcing them into hiding and gas masks, for hours in some cases, causing many to call loved ones to say goodbye just in case. Insurrectionists waved MAGA banners and Confederate colors and replaced American flags with Trump flags. They took pictures of themselves occupying the Senate dais. One infamous photo emerged of a rioter leaning back in House Speaker Nancy Pelosi's office chair flashing an excrement-eating grin with his feet atop her desk.

They ransacked many other congressional offices leaving floors covered in piles of strewn documents. They destroyed furniture and media equipment, stole and vandalized historical exhibits, discharged firearms inside the building, and smeared feces on the walls.

Rioters were recorded yelling angrily, "Where's Nancy?" Chants of "Hang Mike Pence" took on literal meaning when juxtaposed with images of the noose and makeshift gallows constructed on the grounds outside.

Let me say this again: Pro-Trump insurrectionist thugs smashed into the U.S. Capitol building to find the United States vice president and speaker of the House of Representatives — likely to kill them and stop the certification of Electoral College votes thinking this would keep President Trump in office after Jan. 20.

"Let's have trial by combat!"

> (Giuliani, Rudy, R-N.Y., top Trump attorney; speech to "protesters" gathered at "Stop the Steal" rally; Washington, D.C.; 1/6/2021.) *(shortly before the protesters-turned-rioters breached the Capitol building)*

During the insurrection even Trump allies and congressional supporters became frightened. Many called on the president to speak publicly, to quell passions. He refused — for two-to-three hours after the violence began. President-elect Joe Biden went on national television urging peace and calm, but obviously he lacks sway over MAGA supporters. Eventually Mr. Trump did send a few half-hearted tweets and issued one video wishy-washingly calling on his rioting supporters to "Stay peaceful," while he passionately performed his greatest hits of election-fraud lies. He rounded out his message with, "Go home," "We can't play into their hands," "I feel your pain," "We love you," "You're very special."

Twitter and Facebook took down the president's video almost immediately for "promoting disinformation" and "inciting violence." Within hours they blocked his accounts temporarily — a first in social-media-company reactions to Trump tweets and posts.

"This gathering should send a message to [the GOP in Washington]: This isn't their Republican Party anymore. This is Donald Trump's Republican Party. … If you're gonna be the zero and not the hero, we're coming for you and we're going to have a good time doing it!"

(Trump, Donald, Jr., R-N.Y., president's son; speech to "protesters" gathered at "Stop the Steal" rally; Washington, D.C.; 1/6/2021.) *(shortly before the protesters-turned-rioters breached the Capitol building)*

Capitol Finally Secured

Ultimately the National Guard was deployed though woefully late by most all security experts' accounts. And President Trump didn't even want to do it — reportedly Vice President Mike Pence had to persuade Donald forcefully, then make the call, himself. The Capitol was retaken and secured at about 5:40 p.m., three and a half hours after the initial breach. The building underwent a brief security sweep, and Congress resumed Electoral College vote certification shortly after 8 p.m.

That evening and the next morning, condemnation of the president grew deafening. He had been egging on his supporters for many weeks urging them to "protest" the Electoral Vote count at the Capitol on Jan. 6, issuing multiple tweets and statements such as, "Be there, it's going to be wild." It's widely believed that he got exactly the result he wanted: violence.

Many generals and admirals began calling for his ouster through the 25th Amendment or impeachment, as impractical as those two remedies would be within the 13 days left in Trump's presidency. Many lawmakers including some Republicans began calling on the president to resign.

As of Thursday morning Donald Trump still is president, rage-bingeing on cable news in the White House, plotting his next move. He did, however, issue a statement overnight intended to keep the 25th Amendment wolves at bay. Though not a concession, it was his first acknowledgement that his presidency would be ending Jan. 20, 2021:

> "Even though I totally disagree with the outcome of the election, and the facts bear me out, nevertheless there will be an orderly transition on Jan. 20th. I have always said we would continue our fight to ensure that only legal votes were counted. While this represents the end of the greatest first term in presidential history, it's only the beginning of our fight to Make America Great Again."

> (Trump, Donald, R-Fla., U.S. president; White House statement; 1/7/2021.)

"It's only the beginning of our fight." Crazy, right?

The strong determination by an increasing number of experts and pundits is that Mr. Trump's psychological incapacity to accept his election loss leaves the country in grave danger — even graver danger than an insurrection and attempted coup — over the next 13 days.

> "There's no question the president formed the mob, the president incited the mob, the president addressed the mob. He lit the flame. ...

> "What he has done and what he has caused here is something that we've never seen before in our history. It's been 245 years, and no president has ever failed to concede or agree to leave office after the Electoral College has voted. And I think what we are seeing today is the result of that, the result of convincing people that somehow Congress was going to overturn the results of this election, the results of suggesting that he wouldn't leave office."

Drowned out by the Insurrection: Two Georgia Senate Runoffs

There was an election Tuesday. Two Georgia U.S. Senate runoffs should have been sleepy foregone conclusions: Both Republicans should have won easily in this traditionally conservative state. These contests, one regular and one special senatorial election, were warranted because neither Nov. 3 general election race produced a winner with over 50% of the vote as required in Georgia.

But things are changing. In 2020 a Democrat (Joe Biden) won the state's presidential race for the first time since 1992 (when Bill Clinton won it).

Things are changing. Instead of Republicans keeping their suffocating hold on the U.S. Senate, Majority Leader Mitch McConnell (R-Ky.) must turn over the gavel to Senate Democratic Leader Chuck Schumer (D-N.Y.) Jan. 20. After seating the two new Georgia Democratic senators the body will be split 50-50, which means Vice President-elect Kamala Harris will become the tie-breaking vote. This throws control of the Senate — with its inherent powers of choosing legislation to consider, appointing committee chairs, conducting hearings, and launching investigations — back to the Democrats.

This is monumental.

Things are changing. Granted, Biden won Georgia by only 11,779 votes (out of nearly 5 million cast). And the two Senate vote-winning margins were only 1.2% and 2.0%. But even slim Democratic victories are a testament to changing demographics and the voter-suppression-fighting efforts of Stacey Abrams (D) (who narrowly lost the state's 2018 gubernatorial race) and other get-out-the-vote activists.

Lost in the Insurrection: Another Trump Mob-Boss Phone Call

How do we know the exact victory margin for Biden in Georgia? Besides being readily available on the internet (I hear that internet thing is really set to take off), President Trump has memorialized the number in one of his final impeachable, criminal acts (notwithstanding inciting another insurrection, another coup attempt, and other possible MAGA shenanigans arising before Jan. 20, 2021, 12:01 p.m.). An hourlong-plus secret recording has been released in which Mr. Trump called Georgia Secretary of State Brad Raffensperger (R) to cajole, pressure, and ultimately threaten him, wanting Brad to find "11,780 votes, one more than we need." Trump mentioned the number *11,779* nine times, I kid you not (with 10 other mentions of "around 11,000 votes" and "11,780 votes — one more than we need").

Everyone should listen to the entire call. The highlights in the media don't do it justice. Despite the tendency of succumbing to Trump-outrage fatigue, it exposes some of the most damning criminal evidence ever seen against an American president (notwithstanding inciting insurrection), including President Richard Nixon's suite of Watergate crimes. As always, the simple question hanging in the air for Republicans and all other MAGA supporters: "What if (former President) Obama had done this?"

> "We only lost the state by that number: 11,000 votes, and 779. ... So what are we gonna do here, folks? I only need 11,000 votes. Fellas, I need 11,000 votes. Give me a break! ... What's wrong with you, Brad? Why don't you want to find this? Why do you keep fighting this thing. ... I think you're gonna have to say you want to reexamine it. ... There's nothing wrong with saying, you know, that you've recalculated. ... [Not reporting fraud is] a criminal offense. And you can't let that happen. That's a big risk to you and to

Ryan, your lawyer. … And it's going to be very costly in many ways … very dangerous."

> (Trump, Donald, R-Fla., U.S. president; phone call to
> Brad Raffensperger, R-Ga., secretary of state;
> 1/2/2021; as cited in Gardner, Amy & Firozi,
> Paulina; "Here's the Full Transcript and Audio of the
> Call Between Trump and Raffensperger"; *The
> Washington Post*; 1/5/2021.)

But Donald's supporters hang on.

Trump Republicans still thought they could help themselves politically by disrupting yesterday's pro forma tabulation of each state's Electoral College votes. At their planned symbolic, bothersome act of congressional "drama" (as in drama-queen drama), 140-plus GOP House representatives and 12 Republican senators had expected to display their disdain for American democracy and the Constitution by objecting to several swing states' electors. This move would do nothing but drama-queen delay for several hours the inevitable: President-elect Joe Biden's Electoral College victory certification.

To their credit, several representatives and four senators reversed their plan after the weight of the insurgency mere hours before changed their minds. Astonishingly 139 GOP representatives and eight senators decided to retain their membership in Tom Nichols' aptly named *Sedition Caucus*.

Blame to Go 'Round

The Republicans' loss of Senate control was put into motion Tuesday, Jan. 5 (Georgia's run-off election day), and confirmed Wednesday, Jan. 6 — during the pro-Trump rioters' occupation.

The blame game started even before the second winner was called. Republican leaders and lawmakers — some publicly, many privately — are blaming the president. And it's true: Mr. Trump's constant attacks on general election legitimacy and specific attacks on Georgia's GOP governor and secretary of state likely stifled Republican turnout even though the *overall* turnout rate shattered previous records for that state's runoff elections. Many pundits are noting the global ignominy with which Donald is leaving office: He's overseen the loss of the House, the White House, and now the Senate, and he's split his party possibly irreparably. In other words he leaves as a *yuge* loser. A morally bankrupt joke of a loser.

But who put Mr. Trump in power? Who enabled him for over four years? Who allowed the man-child of a president to empower himself more with each tantrum and outrage? Who made the deal with Beelzebub and created a Frankenstein monster they long ago lost control of?

Republican lawmakers.

Who has dragged out faux objections to a legitimate presidential election solely for perceived future political advantage? Who turned off their own voters in Georgia causing the colossal dual senatorial election upset and loss of Senate control? GOP lawmakers: including 139 U.S. representatives and eight U.S. Senators.

Remember these senators' names. They've been identified as members of the "Sedition Caucus" by prominent (reasonable) Republican Tom Nichols in his *The Atlantic* article "Worse Than Treason: No Amount of Rationalizing Can Change the Fact That the Majority of the Republican Party Is Advocating for the Overthrow of an American Election."

Remember these senators' names:

    Sen. Cindy Hyde-Smith (R-Miss.)
    Sen. Cynthia Lummis (R-Wyo.)
    Sen. John Kennedy (R-La.)
    Sen. Josh Hawley (R-Mo.)
    Sen. Rick Scott (R-Fla.)
    Sen. Roger Marshall (R-Kan.)

Sen. Ted Cruz (R-Texas)

Sen. Tommy Tuberville (R-Ala.)

Never vote for them again. Never watch an interview with any of them again. Never buy a used car from any of them. Erase them from American consciousness.

> "We need to look infinitely harder at who we elect to any office in our land — at the office-seeker's character, at their morals, at their ethical record, their integrity, their honesty, their flaws, what they have said about women, and minorities, why they are seeking office in the first place, and only then consider the policies they espouse."
>
> (Kelly, John, Gen., former [Trump] White House chief of staff, former [Trump] Department of Homeland Security secretary; statement issued to *CNN* reporter Jim Acosta; 1/7/2021.)∎

01/13/2021 — Impeachment No. 2 (Inciting Insurrection): House Votes "Aye," Sends Article to Senate

01/14/21 — It Might Finally Be Happening: Supporting Trump Might Be More Costly Than Not

COVID-19 Deaths

02/06/2020 — U.S.: 1 | World: 620
01/14/2021 — U.S.: 384,784 | World: 1,980,885

> • Conservatively estimated Trump malfeasance deaths: 192,392
> • U.S.: 4.2% of Earth's population, 19% of its pandemic deaths

> > (Ibid.; Glanz & Robertson; 5/20/2020.)
> > (Ibid.; Gupta, MD; 9/18/2020.)
> > (Ibid.; *The New England Journal of Medicine;* 10/8/2020.)
> > (Ibid.; Redlener, MD & Sachs, Ph.D. & Hansen, MPA & Hupert, MD, MPH; 10/21/2020.)
> > (as conservatively extrapolated from COVID-19 Dashboard by the Center for Systems Science and Engineering at Johns Hopkins University; 1/14/2021.)

It might finally be happening. In the wake of the pro-Trump riots in Washington, D.C., last week, some Republican lawmakers and influencers are determining that maintaining support for Donald might be more costly to their careers, financial well-being, and country club standing than *not* supporting him.

It only took an insurrection at the U.S. Capitol and an attempted coup to convince them to reconsider.

It's been a week since the Trump-instigated Insurrection of January 6 during which many thousands of "protesters" cheered on the many hundreds of rioters who overwhelmed and beat police, breached and ransacked the Capitol building, terrorized congressional members and staff, hunted and threatened to kill the vice president and House speaker, and caused at least five deaths and hundreds of injuries. Since then Republicans cautiously have begun peeling off from Trump. Early in the week House Republican leader Kevin McCarthy told his caucus members that — though he believed the president was responsible for the violence, he would prefer a House censure — he would not lobby or pressure them to oppose impeachment. Rep. Liz Cheney (R-Wyo.), third-highest ranking GOP House member, announced along with five other representatives from her caucus that she would vote in favor of impeachment.

And Wednesday she — and they — did.

Impeachment

President Donald J. Trump was impeached by the House Jan. 13 for the high crime and misdemeanor of "incitement of insurrection." The vote was 232-197 with 10 Republicans siding with Democrats to impeach. Here are some notable points:

> — Mr. Trump is the first president in U.S. history to be impeached twice.

> — Mr. Trump has been the subject of half of all U.S. presidential impeachments (two of four).

> — Mr. Trump's second presidential impeachment was the most bipartisan in U.S. history.

Senate Leader Mitch McConnell (R-Ky.) has determined that he will not reconvene the Senate early (it currently is in recess). But here is the good news:

> — McConnell has blessed the House's impeachment and has floated the possibility that he might vote to convict at the Senate trial (giving tacit permission for other GOP senators to follow).

> — The Senate is scheduled to come back Jan. 19 anyway, only six days after the House impeachment.

> — Democrats will control the Senate starting Jan. 20, which will ensure fairness and efficacy.

> — Though Trump remains in office until his term ends in six days, Jan. 20, it's believed the threat of Senate conviction will encourage him to stay on his best behavior.

Why hold a Senate impeachment trial after the president already is out of office?

> — Accountability, accountability, accountability. All future presidents must know there will be severe consequences for illegal Trumpian behavior. Citizens must see that Congress acts in accordance with the American ideal that "no person is above the law."

> — Did I mention accountability? A conviction likely would lead to barring Trump from holding public office ever again (you'd think this would be a relief to aspiring 2024 GOP presidential candidates, of which there are several in the Senate). It also would strip him of his lifetime pension, secret service protection, and generous travel allowance.

— Even with an acquittal it's important to get all senators on record as we now have in the House: Who supports democracy and who supports autocracy?

The Awakening

In a miraculous cognitive awakening, many more Republicans now are admitting that, yes, Joe Biden did beat Donald Trump in the 2020 presidential election fair and square. Remember that believing President Trump's "big lie" — that the election was stolen from him by widespread deep-state voting fraud — is what prompted MAGA Nation seditionists, including seven distinct white supremacy groups, to commit 20-year felonies by planning and attempting to take over Congress.

The dam incurred a major crack Tuesday, Jan. 12, when all-powerful Senate Majority Leader Mitch McConnell (R-Ky.) let leak (and Mitch never leaks) that he may support impeachment:

> "Senator Mitch McConnell has concluded that President Trump committed impeachable offenses [suborning insurrection] and believes that Democrats' move to impeach him will make it easier to purge Mr. Trump from the party, according to people familiar with Mr. McConnell's thinking. The private assessment of Mr. McConnell, the most powerful Republican in Congress, emerged on the eve of a House vote to formally charge Mr. Trump with inciting violence against the country for his role in whipping up a mob of his supporters who stormed the Capitol while lawmakers met to formalize President-elect Joseph R. Biden Jr.'s victory."

> (Martin, Jonathan & Haberman, Maggie & Fandos, Nicholas; "McConnell Privately Backs Impeachment as House Moves to Charge Trump"; *The New York Times;* 1/12/2021.)

This move by McConnell could be a personal bet-hedging ploy, or it could grow more serious amid the surging river of anti-Trump sentiment, ultimately giving GOP senators permission to break from the president and vote to convict when the House's one article of impeachment reaches their body. It's an open question whether there will be enough of them to convict; 17 are needed if the Senate has perfect attendance on the day of the vote.

At least three Republican senators already have called for President Trump to resign. Senate staffers have said anonymously that possibly 20 GOP senators eventually could support impeachment conviction; though realistically, 20 likely is wildly optimistic.

I'm Sorry but Liberals Were Right All Along

"Boy, do I hate being right all the time."

> (Dr. Ian Malcolm, played by Jeff Goldblum; Spielberg, Steven: director; Crichton, Michael: writer; *Jurassic Park* [motion picture]; 1993.) *(spoken at the first sighting of a dangerous escaped cloned dinosaur — the colossally huge and terrifying T. Rex that had breached the confines of its dinosaur zoo "cage" — about to wreak havoc and death upon its island habitat; Dr. Malcolm had warned against toying with nature)*

As I was researching this quote from the 1993 movie *Jurassic Park* to get the citation correct, I discovered that citing it is not as novel as I thought it would be. Turns out there are T-shirts, coffee cups, golf tees, video games, clubs and other organizations, and even museums associated with or eponymously named for "Boy, do I hate being right all the time."

Nevertheless: Boy, do I hate being right (even if not all the time).

I take no I-told-you-so comfort in the death and destruction caused by a President Trump. But I respectfully welcome the end of the "American carnage." I'm proud of myself and the many other liberals who have been sounding the alarm since Donald descended the escalator at Trump Tower amid the cheers of supporters, many paid actors, "and some, I assume, are good people" to announce his candidacy for president in 2015.

There are, and will be many more, volumes written on the early Trumpian red flags that signaled white supremacy and authoritarianism. Examples of his corruption, incompetence, and amorality occurred daily from the start. Donald consistently showed us he always was capable of a new nadir, that he had no bottom.

And in my optimistic naiveté, at every frequent peak of perversion and debauchery since his campaign began, I thought, "Surely the time is now": that maintaining support for Donald Trump is more costly to Republicans' livelihoods, financial health, and social standing than *not* supporting him.

I consistently was wrong.

Even Current Supporters Knew Early On

"Before they were sycophants, they were psychics."

(Keilar, Brianna, news anchor; *CNN's Newsroom;* 1/11/2021.)

CNN's Brianna Keilar was referring to people like Sen. Lindsey Graham (R-S.C.), Sen. Ted Cruz (R-Texas), former [Trump] U.S. ambassador to the United Nations Nikki Haley (R-S.C.), Sen. Marco Rubio (R-Fla.), Sen. Rand Paul (R-Ky.), Sen. Mike Lee (R-Utah), former [Trump] Secretary of Energy Rick Perry (R-Texas), and White House press secretary Kayleigh McEnany, who all sounded our same liberal alarm *before* Mr. Trump won the 2016 Republican presidential nomination.

On *CNN's Newsroom* last Monday, Ms. Keilar put together a greatest hits montage of the aforementioned prominent Republicans' 2015-2016 pre-nomination quotes blasting warnings that a President Trump would be a disaster and a danger. I've noted many of these before but here are some nuggets: Lindsey Graham called Mr. Trump a "kook" and "unfit for office"; Ted Cruz said, "Nominating Donald Trump would be a train wreck" and "He's a pathological liar."

All politicians are concerned about their careers. But only Republicans, as a group, turned on a dime, ate their words, shed all integrity, and became blind to depravity and ineptitude after Donald Trump took over their party and the White House. By *taking over their party* I mean he demagogued his way to attaining an ironclad base of voting support that became completely immune to truth and reason. Trump lied to supporters daily, hourly, with the expertise of a consummate confidence artist.

Note that one only can be a persistent expert liar, a professional fabulist, through corrupt and total forfeiture of integrity. For (almost all) Republican lawmakers that knew better, it took that same forfeiture of integrity to ignore, excuse, and support the universe of mendacity and outrageous action.

Autopsy

Why did Republicans allow the most heinous of presidents and presidential behavior to flourish unchecked? Because they cravenly determined that maintaining support for Donald Trump was far less costly than standing up to him.

Ultimately 100% personal fealty was required. Any single crack in support for Donald, no matter how obsequious and sycophantic that Republican might have been up until that moment, could have doomed that party member's career. That's because Donald Trump had attained the power and backing to threaten to "primary" GOP officeholders. That is, he could muster his supporters to support that officeholder's further-to-the-Trumpian-right opponent in his or her next primary election. Whether aimed at an elected official or not, a simple series of tweet-attacks from Donald had the potential to ostracize anyone from the pack.

And he followed through with that powerful threat several times (think run-out-of-office Republicans Jeff Flake, Bob Corker, Mark Sanford, et al.), which kept the rest in line.

You Were Warned: Adam Schiff Tried to Tell You

As reported, President Trump faced impeachment proceedings once before beginning December 2019 but ultimately was acquitted in the Senate Feb. 5, 2020. He had tried to extort a U.S. ally, Ukraine, for false dirt on Joe Biden (Trump's then-likely 2020 presidential opponent) in exchange for desperately needed, already congressionally authorized foreign aid to defend against Russian incursion. Lead House impeachment manager Adam Schiff was downright clairvoyant in his closing arguments:

> "We must say enough — enough! He has betrayed our national security, and he will do so again. He has compromised our elections, and he will do so again. You will not change him. You cannot constrain him. He is who he is. Truth matters little to him. What's right matters even less, and decency matters not at all.

> "Can we be confident that he will not continue to try to cheat in [the 2020] election? … The short, plain, sad, incontestable answer is no, you can't. You can't trust this president to do the right thing. Not for one minute, not for one election, not for the sake of our country. You just can't. He will not change and you know it.

> "What are the odds if left in office that he will continue trying to cheat? I will tell you: 100%. A man without character or ethical compass will never find his way."

(Schiff, Adam, D-Calif., lead House impeachment manager, House Intelligence Committee chair; closing arguments, President Donald J. Trump first Senate impeachment trial; 2/3/2020.)

"Boy, do I hate being right all the time."

And Here We Are

It might finally be happening. Some Republican lawmakers and influencers might be determining that continued support for Donald could be more costly than *not* supporting him.

Too bad the good of the country had so little to do with their possible reconsideration.

As many pundits and historians have said, Trumpism is bigger than Trump, and its roots in white supremacy and misplaced grievance run deep. Why didn't his party stand up to him? More importantly, how do we avoid electing future corrupt, incompetent, amoral aspiring autocrats?

A K-12 critical thinking curriculum. And more humanities in high school.■

01/20/2021 — Inauguration Day: Joe Biden Sworn in as 46th U.S. President

01/21/21 — "Democracy Has Prevailed"

COVID-19 Deaths

02/06/2020 — U.S.: 1 | World: 620
03/05/2020 — U.S.: 12 | World: 3,293
04/02/2020 — U.S.: 5,137 | World: 48,284
05/07/2020 — U.S.: 73,431 | World: 264,189
06/04/2020 — U.S.: 107,175 | World: 386,464
07/02/2020 — U.S.: 128,062 | World: 516,726
08/06/2020 — U.S.: 158,268 | World: 708,278
09/03/2020 — U.S.: 185,752 | World: 863,577
10/01/2020 — U.S.: 206,963 | World: 1,014,958
11/05/2020 — U.S.: 234,756 *(est.)* | World: 1,231,003 *(est.)*
12/03/2020 — U.S.: 273,847 | World: 1,495,311
01/07/2021 — U.S.: 361,297 | World: 1,885,689
01/21/2021 — U.S.: 406,384 | World: 2,078,315

• Conservatively estimated Trump malfeasance deaths: 203,192
• U.S.: 4.2% of Earth's population, 20% of its pandemic deaths

(Ibid.; Glanz & Robertson; 5/20/2020.)
(Ibid.; Gupta, MD; 9/18/2020.)
(Ibid.; *The New England Journal of Medicine;* 10/8/2020.)
(Ibid.; Redlener, MD & Sachs, Ph.D. & Hansen, MPA & Hupert, MD, MPH; 10/21/2020.)
(as conservatively extrapolated from COVID-19 Dashboard by the Center for Systems Science and

Engineering at Johns Hopkins University;
1/21/2021.)

This is the last weekly installment of my commentative real-time history of the Trump presidency. (I will do an epilogue down the road, tying up some loose ends.) I can hear the cheers through my keyboard as I type, including from all of MAGA Nation (at least the seven followers who sometimes read my articles online over the past four years) and friends who simply are sick of all-things Donald.

The as-of-yesterday-former president has been mostly quiet this past week making no public appearances except his poorly attended end-of-presidency send-off performance Wednesday morning at which he crooned his predictably mendacious greatest hits. Aides had kept him from interacting with reporters before his final exit, fearing his extreme "volatility." The primary White House news of the week falls under the media-dubbed "pardon watch." And late on the eve of President Joe Biden's inauguration, Mr. Trump did not disappoint:

> "President Trump on Tuesday granted clemency to 143 people, using a final act of presidential power to extend mercy to former White House strategist Stephen K. Bannon, well-connected celebrities, and nonviolent drug offenders — but he did not preemptively pardon himself or his family.

> "Among those who were pardoned or who had their sentences commuted on Trump's final full day in office were the rapper Lil Wayne and former Detroit mayor Kwame Kilpatrick, who has been serving a 28-year prison sentence on corruption charges. Trump also pardoned two former Republican members of Congress, Rick Renzi of Arizona and Randall 'Duke' Cunningham of California. Both had completed prison terms that stemmed from corruption convictions. A third, Robert 'Robin' Hayes of North

Carolina, was also pardoned after finishing a probation sentence for making a false statement during a federal investigation."

(Helderman, Rosalind S. & Dawsey, Josh & Reinhard, Beth; "Trump Grants Clemency to 143 People in Late-Night Pardon Blast"; *The Washington Post*; 1/20/2021.)

[FUN FACT:] Steve Bannon had not been convicted yet but was under indictment for fraudulently collecting and stealing contributions to a "Build-the-[southern border]-Wall" fund.

Note that Trump's long clemency list of overwhelmingly Caucasian corrupt politicians and businessmen — "scores of crooks and cronies," per columnist Dana Milbank — reflects the very crimes of which Donald is guilty as sin, the same types of indictments and convictions he'll be fighting off for the rest of his life. The cherry? Many of these crooks and cronies paid Trump allies high fees for access to those pardons. How is this not illegal!?!

Then he wraps it all up at the last minute by letting one of his tippy-top swamp creatures off the hook: Bannon, the guy that fleeced Trump's own working-class supporters by conning them out of money they thought was going to "Build That Wall."

Other than that, I thought I'd lay out a few notable Trump administration-defining recent occurrences and a few era-defining firsts.

Trump Presidency Firsts

— 147 Republican members of Congress feigned belief that the 2020 election was stolen from their president and backed up their fake belief by voting to overturn the Electoral College Vote — even *just hours after* the Insurrection of January 6.

— Donald Trump is the first president in 152 years to boycott his successor's inauguration.

— The Trump administration handoff of the presidency is the first non-peaceful transfer of power since the Civil War.

— Donald Trump is the first U.S. president to be impeached twice (and only the third to be impeached even once).

Biden Presidency Firsts

— Joe Biden is the oldest president ever to be inaugurated (78).

— Joe Biden is the first son (or daughter) of Delaware ever to be inaugurated.

— Kamala Harris is the first women to be inaugurated vice president (or president).

— Kamala Harris is the first African American to be inaugurated vice president.

— Kamala Harris is the first person of South Asian descent to be inaugurated vice president.

Pandemic Firsts

— The U.S. COVID-19 death count surpassed 400,000 Jan. 19, 2021.

— President-elect Biden oversaw a national memorial service on the eve of his inauguration to honor and mourn pandemic victims. This is the first memorial, or even offering of condolences to families, from anywhere near the White House since President Trump began playing down the first American coronavirus death Feb. 6, 2020.

End of Trumpism?

President Joe Biden took the oath of office, administered by Chief Justice of the Supreme Court John Roberts, 12 minutes before the constitutionally designated time of power transfer (noon) in a seemingly symbolic show of national anxiousness to move on from Trumpism.

President Biden gave a soaring 22-minute speech. *Fox News'* last-remaining respectable journalist, Chris Wallace, called it the greatest presidential inauguration speech of his lifetime. Later that night other *Fox* hosts couldn't wait to begin building their wall of fallacy and ad hominem, from belittling the way Joe walks to asserting that "Biden's not mentally well and everyone in Washington knows it but they won't report it."

What's that? "The slime — oozin' out — from your T-V — set"? *(— thanks to Frank Zappa).*

Can we make an agreement to boycott the Laura Ingrahams and Tucker Carlsons of the world?

When they deny what they know and wish not to be true, they're a waste of time. If they're *Fox News* talk show hosts with high ratings, they're also *dangerous* to the country. When they deny the veracity of legitimate information sources, they're *dangerous*. By their standards, all truth is deniable. Once they've been exposed, any further attempt at critically thoughtful debate is a colossal waste of time. But they're still dangerous.

New President

Newly inaugurated President Joseph R. Biden Jr. means business. Just a few hours after being sworn in, he signed 17 presidential executive orders and directives prepared by his legal team in the preceding weeks to reverse Trumpian policies that have caused our country the "greatest damage." The following actions were taken:

— Initiated many pandemic-related steps to begin — yes, aggressively *begin* — confronting the devastation from COVID-19, such as giving authority and credibility back to scientists, establishing prevention guidelines with teeth, activating the Defense Production Act, and organizing and expediting the vaccination response with experts instead of political lackeys
— Rejoined World Health Organization, aka WHO
— Reinstated Deferred Action for Childhood Arrivals, aka DACA
— Called for path to citizenship for immigrants
— Softened aggressive deportation efforts
— Ordered prompt reunification of remaining separated migrant children with their parents
— Rescinded order to exclude noncitizens from census count
— Rescinded Muslim travel ban
— Stopped (southern border) "Build That Wall" construction
— Rejoined Paris climate agreement
— Revoked Keystone XL pipeline permit
— Reinstated effective vehicle emission standards
— Established moratorium on oil and gas leases in Arctic National Wildlife Refuge
— Established top-level task force to root out systemic racism
— Killed (historical) 1776 Commission, which altered, softened role of slavery in American history
— Reinstituted permission for diversity and inclusion training at government-related entities
— Reinforced Civil Rights Act of 1964, with focus on sexual orientation and gender identity

— Moved to extend moratorium on evictions and foreclosures

— Moved to extend moratorium on student loan payments and interest

— Established government ethics rules and pledges

— Froze all other last-minute "midnight regulations" Trump signed until after careful review

Secretary of State Mike Pompeo's Parting Words

"Woke-ism, multiculturalism, all the -isms — they're not who America is. They distort our glorious founding and what this country is all about. Our enemies stoke these divisions because they know they make us weaker. ... Censorship, wokeness, political correctness, it all points in one direction — authoritarianism, cloaked as moral righteousness."

(Pompeo, Mike, R-Kan., U.S. secretary of state; Twitter post; 1/19/2021.)

No, it's Mike Pompeo's and Donald Trump's authoritarianism that is cloaked as *these* -isms: Republicanism, conservatism, anti-PC-ism, and (phony) patriotism.

"Multiculturalism [is] not who America is." The now-former Secretary of State Pompeo thinks the iconic "American melting pot" of cultures (the very definition of *multiculturalism*) is a fondue warmer scientists use for creating vaccines to insert chips and spread autism. It's like this guy never had an elementary school history lesson.

And let's put this term *woke* to bed. It's been around apparently since World War II and recently has resurfaced. I don't like the term, for some reason I can't put my finger on, but it simply refers to raised consciousness — which is a great and wonderful thing.

Raised consciousness brought us the Founding Fathers who created American representative democracy (imperfect though it remains). Raised consciousness is the force behind constantly striving to create "a more perfect union," as long and uneven as that road has been. Raised consciousness brought the fight for anti-child-labor laws, abolition, Reconstruction, women's suffrage and women's rights, the Black vote and anti-Jim Crow laws, LGBTQ rights, and so many more cultural justice issues.

And it solidified the fight against Trumpism.

The road to raised consciousness has many hills and dips but it never ends. In honor of Martin Luther King Jr.'s birthday week: "The arc of the moral universe is long, but it bends toward justice."

So Mr. Former Secretary, take your slams against multiculturalism and woke-ism and place them in your white supremacist-sympathizing anal cavity. As for your condemning of political correctness — another road to raised consciousness — we know this simply is an anti-PC skirt behind which your crowd hides while continuing bigoted and sexist language, behavior, and policies.

Trump's Legacy

> "More than 30,000 falsehoods and lies. Nearly 400,000 coronavirus deaths. Rising white nationalism. Financial self-dealing. A social media ban. Two impeachments. A deadly attack on the U.S. Capitol.

> "President Trump's four years in office come to a close Wednesday after a reign defined by constant chaos, corruption, and scandal, a tenure that numerous scholars predict is destined to rank him among America's worst presidents. …

> "To Leah Wright-Rigueur, associate professor of American history at Brandeis University, Trump's presidency has been a case study in the 'naked, unadulterated pursuit of power

and self-interest, at the cost of 400,000 lives and at the cost of the American union.'"

(Nakamura, David; "As Trump's Presidency Recedes Into History, Scholars Seek to Understand His Reign — and What It Says About American Democracy"; *The Washington Post*; 1/18/2021)

Trump's Inner Thoughts

"In the [May 2020] video, [Otero County, N.M., Commissioner Couy] Griffin said, 'The only good Democrat is a dead Democrat.' He qualified in the video that he was only speaking metaphorically about politics. … [Now he] has been arrested in the [insurrectionist] riot.

"Trump promoted the video by saying, 'Thank you Cowboys [for Trump]. See you in New Mexico!' *(Twitter suspended Trump's and the Cowboys for Trump accounts this month.)*

"But while Griffin qualified his comments in the video, he later indicated to the Daily Beast that he wasn't speaking entirely figuratively. He suggested Democratic governors who locked down their states amid the coronavirus pandemic could be guilty of treason and might face the death penalty. 'You get to pick your poison: You either go before a firing squad, or you get the end of the rope,' Griffin said."

(Blake, Aaron; "Trump Promoted N.M. Official's Comment That 'The Only Good Democrat Is a Dead Democrat.' Now the Man Is Arrested in the Capitol Riot."; *The Washington Post*; 1/18/2021.)

Jesus H.!

Impeachment No. 2

Mr. Trump's impeachment trial in the Senate is scheduled to start within days. He's been impeached in the House on a single article for promoting violence toward political opponents and the government: "Incitement of Insurrection." Though already out of the White House, accountability and possible exclusion from future public office are key factors in pursuing the charges. The Griffin video retweet by the then-president might just be Exhibit A.

Inauguration Day — Our National Nightmare Has Ended

You might have heard about a certain recent past president who liked to exaggerate his inaugural crowd size while comparing it to that of his predecessors. This year former President Trump ensured that pictures of his successor's inaugural crowd size definitely would reflect a far smaller number than his own.

Inauguration Day ceremonies in 2021 were far different from the usual fare. As president, Mr. Trump effectively ignored a world pandemic that has killed over 400,000 Americans since early 2020. Half or more of those could have been avoided with competent, non-corrupt leadership.

Then the Insurrection of January 6 happened. Former President Trump called his supporters to Washington, D.C., the day of the normally perfunctory Electoral College vote certification (his perceived last chance to retain power). He incited them to breach and ransack the Capitol building. They brought guns, zip ties (for handcuffs), high-powered mace, bear spray, Tasers, bats, hockey sticks, and all manner of other tactical gear. They terrorized members of Congress and chanted "Hang Mike Pence!" and "Where's Nancy?!" (i.e., Nancy Pelosi, Democratic House speaker) while rampaging through halls and offices.

Consequently, for security and public health reasons, Inauguration Day ceremonies were trimmed back to a few hundred attendees instead of, for example, Barack Obama's 2009 estimated

1.8 million people. Yesterday the National Guard deployed 25,000 troops to ensure safety, and everyone at the festivities wore masks.

Instead of Trump lying about the photo comparisons showing his relatively sparse crowd of an estimated 300,000 to 600,000, he'll forever be remembered for 2021 Inauguration Day National Mall photos of 400 solemnly lighted columns framing the reflecting pool — one for each 1,000 U.S. COVID-19 deaths — near a forest of 200 American flags, one for each 1,000 canceled official invitations.

Speaking of Canceled Invitations

Norma and I got our official Inauguration Day invitations last week, all glossy and formal-like. We'd made the nonrefundable-hotel-room commitment a week after the election (four nights at triple the normal D.C. Hampton Inn prices, a five-minute walk from the White House). We had hoped we weren't too late and we weren't, snagging some of the last available reservations. Then we requested inaugural tickets from our congressperson as required.

In early December the COVID-19 travel warnings started blaring. Since my partner and I are somewhat older than 25, we made the painful decision not to go to Washington. After a fight with the hotel (Norma is really good at this type of thing) we did get a refund on the rooms.

Then came Jan. 6, the Trump-provoked riots at the Capitol building, and the subsequent security lockdown of government row (still in effect).

Per *SNL*'s Roseanne Roseannadanna (aka Gilda Radner), it's always somethin': If it's not a once-in-a-century pandemic, it's an armed insurrection. So no regular people got to go to the swearing-in ceremony, only a couple hundred elites. What a week on-site it could have been. Anyway, I took the day off work and we watched the festivities on television.

But we'll always have our official glossy Inauguration Day invitations (and Paris).■

The Presidential Inaugural Committee

is honored to announce the

inauguration of

Joseph R. Biden, Jr.

as President of the United States of America

and

Kamala Devi Harris

as Vice President of the United States of America

on Wednesday, the twentieth of January
Two thousand and twenty-one

GET READY FOR INAUGURATION DAY

On Wednesday, January 20, 2021, Americans across the country
will unite to celebrate the inauguration of
President-elect Joseph R. Biden, Jr.
and Vice President-elect Kamala D. Harris.

Official inaugural events will begin with a National Day of Service on Monday, January 18, 2021. In honor of the legacy of Dr. Martin Luther King Jr., the President-elect and the Vice President-elect will participate in community service projects and be joined by Americans in service to their local communities.

As safety is our top priority, Inauguration Day ceremonies, celebrations, and events will be virtual. The Presidential Inaugural Committee will be releasing additional details and information on how to virtually participate in the coming weeks.

As you celebrate this historic inauguration from home, share photos on social media using the hashtag **#InaugurationDay** or **#Inauguration2021**.

Follow **@BidenInaugural** on all social media platforms to stay up to date on official Inauguration Day events, including the swearing-in ceremony and celebrations.

Go to **BidenInaugural.org/Invite** or use the custom QR code below to receive access to the Biden-Harris Inaugural social media toolkit, additional links, and further information on how to get involved.

02/13/2021 — Impeachment No. 2 (Incitement of Insurrection): Senate Acquits

— Senators Voted 57-43 to Convict (67 Were Needed); 7 Republicans Sided With All Democrats

02/21/2021 — U.S. Hits 500,000 COVID-19 Deaths

— U.S.: 4.2% of Earth's population, 20% of its pandemic deaths
— At Least Half of All U.S. Deaths Could Have Been Prevented With Competent, Non-Corrupt Presidential Leadership Throughout 2020

Final Word

I give the final word to Mike Fanone, Washington, D.C., Metropolitan PD officer. He was attacked with a Taser multiple times, was beaten severely, suffered a heart attack, and thought he was going to die while defending the Capitol building, and legislators from both parties, from Trump-inspired insurrectionists Jan. 6, 2021. Before that day, Fanone described himself as a redneck cop, not particularly political, who voted for Donald Trump.

Since that day, Mr. Fanone has become an outspoken, congressionally testifying voice in opposition to Republicans' and former President Trump's attempts to recast the insurrection as an act of peaceful patriotic protest. His mission, which has changed his life, has been to let the country know: This was an attack on the Capitol, the seat of democracy, and there "needs to be a reckoning."

"For most Americans, Jan. 6 keeps getting further away. For Fanone, it's still the only thing — the day his life stopped. And yet, as awful as it was, he's grateful for it. 'That's like, difficult to come to terms with. What if I had not gone through that?' he says. 'I'd be the same dumb*ss that I was on Jan. 5. Not evil in my motivations. But ignorant to the truth.'"

(Ball, Molly; "What Mike Fanone Can't Forget"; *Time.com;* 8/5/2021.)

"The greatest trick in history was Donald Trump convincing redneck Americans [including me] that he somehow speaks for them. He will destroy this country simply for the sake of his ego, just because he can't accept that he lost an election."

(Fanone, Mike; as cited in Ball, Molly; "What Mike Fanone Can't Forget"; *Time.com;* 8/5/2021.)∎

The Author

Tom Ersin holds an advanced degree from Trump University, having risen to its most enlightened (and expensive) Operating Thetan Levels. No, wait — that's his Scientology training. Common mix-up. All seriousness aside, Ersin is a Macomb County, Michigan, long-time political observer, communications professional, and editor of online magazine *GraniteWord*. He's written a half-dozen nonfiction books on 21st century U.S. politics. His turn-ons are running his dog, Bob Barker, and railing about the lack of critical thinking. Find out more at GraniteWord.com. Email him at tom@graniteword.com.

<div align="center">~~~</div>

Please Make This Author Happy

I hope you got as much of a kick out of reading this book as I did writing it. I'd be forever appreciative if you would post a review on Amazon. Just a sentence or two and a rating would be great. Reviews are lifeblood for authors and they help readers find my books.

(https://www.amazon.com/dp/B09WHSGVG1)

Thanks a lot,
Tom

The Series

This is the third in my subseries comprising the three books:

> *Trumpism: Why Traditional Republicans Should Withdraw Support [2017-2021: A Primer]*

> *Trump's First Year in Office: The Awakening*

> *Trump's Last Year in Office: Two Impeachments and 400,000 Funerals*

All three books listed above are carve-outs from my exhaustive 1,400-page history:

> *Trump's Presidency: A Real-Time Commentative History [2017-2019]*

> *Trump's Presidency: A Real-Time Commentative History [2019-2021]*

This book, *Trump's Last Year in Office: Two Impeachments and 400,000 Funerals,* is the third book in the subseries, all drawn from the perspective of a long-time avid political observer. Think of the histories as an in-depth every-Thursday recap of all the news you were too busy to consume because you had a life and didn't realize the gravity of the dysfunction and disinformation. When you see my opinion you'll know it. Much more often, when you see facts, quotations, and details, I'm assuring you that I've backed up their accuracy with careful research and citation.

Milestones in the Trump Presidential Era

06/16/15 – ELECTION 2016: Donald **Trump announces candidacy**

07/mid/15 – GRU (RUSSIAN MILITARY INTELLIGENCE) GAINS ACCESS TO DNC COMPUTER NETWORK: **maintains access until at least June 2016**, when hacking plot was reported

05/03/16 – ELECTION 2016: Donald **Trump clinches Republican nomination**

06/09/16 – MEETING BETWEEN TRUMP CAMPAIGN, RUSSIANS: **Trump Tower meeting**, including Donald Trump Jr., Jared Kushner, Paul Manafort, Russian lawyer Natalia Veselnitskaya, et al. *(prompted by offer of "dirt on Hillary" from Russia)*

06/14/16 – 1ST REPORT OF HACKERS ACCESSING DNC SERVERS: next day, computer security firm **CrowdStrike identifies Russia as perpetrator**

07/05/16 – HILLARY CLINTON STATE DEPT. EMAIL CONTROVERSY: FBI Director James **Comey publicly closes Clinton (misuse of State Dept.) email investigation** with no charges; states Clinton team was "extremely careless" but not criminal

07/22/16 – WIKILEAKS' 1ST RELEASE OF (20,000) DNC, HILLARY CLINTON CAMPAIGN EMAILS: ultimately it would **release more than 44,000 emails, 17,000 attachments**

07/25/16 – RUSSIA ELECTION INTERFERENCE INVESTIGATION: **FBI publicly confirms opening investigation into hacking of DNC** *(4 days later, DCCC announces it has been hacked)*

07/31/16 – TRUMP-RUSSIA INVESTIGATION BEGINS: **FBI secretly initiates counterintelligence investigation, regarding possible Trump campaign collusion with Russia**, after learning Trump aide George Papadopoulos bragged to an Australian diplomat, *before* WikiLeaks' surprise DNC email dump, that Russians had obtained Clinton campaign "dirt": "thousands of emails" *(this and other evidence suggested to FBI that Trump could be a witting or unwitting Russian asset; also, NYT reports Trump Campaign Chair Paul Manafort's "business dealings with prominent Ukrainian and Russian tycoons")*

10/28/16 – HILLARY CLINTON STATE DEPT. EMAIL CONTROVERSY: FBI Director James **Comey publicly reopens Clinton (misuse of State Dept.) email investigation** based on new emails found on Clinton aide's laptop

11/06/16 – HILLARY CLINTON STATE DEPT. EMAIL CONTROVERSY: FBI Director James **Comey publicly re-closes Clinton (misuse of State Dept.) email investigation**; states FBI's original conclusions have not changed

11/08/16 – ELECTION DAY: **Donald Trump defeats Hillary Clinton**; Trump wins Electoral College 306-232; Clinton wins popular vote 65.9M-63.0M, 48.2%-46.1%

11/9/16 – 1/19/17 – FLURRY OF CONTACTS BETWEEN RUSSIANS, TRUMP TRANSITION TEAM: including presumptive national security adviser Gen. Michael **Flynn asking Russian ambassador not to retaliate** over President Obama's sanctions, **assuring him Trump will lift sanctions** after inauguration; Putin obliges

01/20/17 – INAUGURATION DAY: Donald **Trump takes office** as 45th president

01/27/17 – MUSLIM TRAVEL BAN: **instituted by Trump administration, causes chaos** due to total lack of warning to, coordination with airlines and government agencies involved *(blocked by several courts, eventually superseded by other executive orders)*

01/31/17 – SUPREME COURT: President **Trump nominates Neil Gorsuch,** Trump's 1st nominee *(after Senate Majority Leader Mitch McConnell, R-Ky., had denied President Barack Obama's nominee a hearing to fill March 2016 opening)*

02/13/17 – TRUMP FORCED TO FIRE NATIONAL SECURITY ADVISER: **president fires Gen. Michael Flynn** after 22 days in office, only upon public reporting that DOJ warned White House much earlier that Flynn was security risk *(Flynn lied to FBI, denied discussions with Russian ambassador during transition, to lift Russian sanctions after inauguration)*

02/14/17 – TRUMP MEETS PRIVATELY WITH FBI DIRECTOR JAMES COMEY: **president asks Comey to stop investigation of Gen. Michael Flynn:** "I hope you can see your way clear to letting this go, to letting Flynn go." *(Comey did not agree to comply)*

04/10/17 – SUPREME COURT: **Senate confirms Neil Gorsuch,** Trump's 1st justice

05/09/17 – TRUMP FIRES FBI DIRECTOR: **president fires James Comey,** ostensibly for mishandling of Clinton email investigation; 2 days later, Trump discloses to *NBC*'s Lester Holt, "When I decided [to fire Comey], I said to myself, I said, 'You know, this Russia thing with Trump and Russia is a made up story.'"

05/17/17 – TRUMP-RUSSIA INVESTIGATION — SPECIAL
COUNSEL APPOINTED: Trump's firing of FBI director prompts
appointment of Robert Mueller as special counsel to investigate
1) Russian 2016 U.S. election interference, 2) possible Trump
campaign conspiracy with Russia to help elect Trump, and 3)
Trump obstruction of justice to block FBI investigation of these
issues *(appointed by Deputy Attorney General Rod Rosenstein because
Attorney General Jeff Sessions had recused himself from all-things Russia due to
his false statements during his confirmation hearings)*

07/08/17 – TRUMP-RUSSIA INVESTIGATION: President
**Trump dictates statement in Don Jr.'s name covering up real
reason** (which was to collect dirt on Hillary Clinton) **for June 9,
2016, Trump Tower meeting between Trump campaign and
Russians**

08/11-12/17 – UNITE THE RIGHT RALLY: **Charlottesville,
Va.; large white supremacist rally** protesting removal of Gen.
Robert E. Lee statue and other Confederate monuments; included
infamous Tiki-torch marchers chanting, "Jews will not replace us!"
*(a neo-Nazi protester intentionally rammed his car into group of
counterprotesters, killing 1, injuring 35; Trump later said there are "very fine
people on both sides")*

08/late/17 – HURRICANE HARVEY: affected Texas, La;
Category 4, sustained winds of 130 mph, 100-plus deaths, $125B
damage

09/early/17 – HURRICANE IRMA: affected northeastern
Caribbean including Puerto Rico; Category 5, sustained winds of
180 mph, 80-plus deaths, $77B damage

09/late/17 – HURRICANE MARIA: affected northeastern
Caribbean including Puerto Rico; Category 5, sustained winds of
175 mph, 3000-plus deaths, $90B damage

10/01/17 – MASS SHOOTING: **Paradise**, Nev., outside
Mandalay Bay resort and casino on Las Vegas Strip, Route 91
Harvest outdoor country music festival; shooter: Stephen Craig
Paddock, 64, Caucasian American terrorist *(60 killed, 867 injured)*

10/31/17 – TRUCK ATTACK: **New York**, N.Y., Hudson River
Park bike path; driver: Sayfullo Habibullaevich Saipov, 29,
Uzbekistani jihadist terrorist *(8 killed, 11 injured)*

11/02/17 – ASIA TOUR: President Trump leaves for **12-day tour**
of Asian countries

11/05/17 – MASS SHOOTING: **Sutherland Springs**, Texas, First
Baptist Church; shooter: Devin Patrick Kelley, 26, Caucasian
American terrorist *(26 killed, 22 injured)*

11/07/17 – OFF-YEAR ELECTIONS: **Democratic wave**
(Democrats, diversity enjoy many big wins)

12/08/17 – TRUMP-RUSSIA INVESTIGATION: **Michael
Flynn**, former Trump national security adviser and top campaign
aide **pleads guilty** to lying about Russian contacts before
inauguration *(enters into plea agreement [flips] with special prosecutor Robert
Mueller)*

12/12/17 – ALA. SPECIAL ELECTION FOR U.S. SENATE:
long shot **Doug Jones (D) beats former Ala. Supreme Court
Chief Justice Roy Moore (R)** by 1.7% *(Jones replaces former Sen., now
U.S. Attorney General, Jeff Sessions [R] to be 1ˢᵗ Democratic Ala. senator
since 1997)*

01/02/18 – AL FRANKEN (D-MINN.): **resigns Senate seat** *(due to sexual misconduct allegations)*

02/14/18 – MASS SHOOTING: **Parkland**, Fla., Marjory Stoneman Douglas High School; shooter: Nikolas Cruz, 19, Caucasian American white supremacist terrorist *(17 killed, 17 injured)*

04/mid/18 – MIGRANT CHILD SEPARATION: Trump administration **begins "zero tolerance" policy for illegal immigration** at southern border; policy discontinued in June after national outrage *(5,400 children separated from families for weeks, months, with no communication, in subhuman conditions; hundreds never were reunited due to administration incompetence) (2017 pilot program ultimately revealed)*

05/18/18 – MASS SHOOTING: **Santa Fe**, Texas, Santa Fe High School; shooter: Dimitrios Pagourtzis, 17, Greek American terrorist *(10 killed, 13 injured)*

06/18/18 – TRUMP-KIM SUMMIT: **Sentosa, Singapore**; 1st-ever meeting between U.S.-North Korean leaders; near-meaningless milquetoast joint statement signed *(Trump highly criticized for giving parity to Kim Jong Un on world stage with no preconditions; Trump falsely boasted that "nuclear threat has ended")*

07/09/18 – SUPREME COURT: President **Trump nominates Brett Kavanaugh**, Trump's 2nd nominee *(after "swing-vote" Justice Anthony Kennedy announced his retirement effective July 31, 2018)*

07/11-12/18 – NATO SUMMIT: **Brussels, Belgium**; Trump embarrasses self, U.S. by disrupting proceedings, chastising other members *(many prominent Americans slam Trump's behavior)*

07/16/18 – TRUMP-PUTIN SUMMIT: **Helsinki, Finland**; Trump embarrasses self, U.S. by accepting Putin's 2016 election-interference denials over U.S. intelligence *(many prominent Republicans slam Trump's statements, several invoke the word "traitorous")*

08/25/18 – SEN. JOHN MCCAIN (R-ARIZ.) DIES: succumbs to brain cancer at 81; **McCain chastises Trump** with posthumous statement *(and disinvites Trump to funeral)*

09/27/18 – SUPREME COURT: Brett **Kavanaugh Senate confirmation hearings reopened specially for Christine Blasey Ford** to testify (extremely credibly) about alleged Kavanaugh drunken attempted rape of her while teenagers; Kavanaugh also testified, rebutting the allegations in emotional, combative, mendacious, highly partisan performance

10/02/18 – TRUMP FINANCES EXPOSED: *The New York Times* prints 14,000-word article exposing **Trump's tax fraud, inheritance theft, and self-made-man myth** *(Trump calls NYT "enemy of the people")*

10/02/18 – JAMAL KHASHOGGI MURDERED: Saudi expatriate and dissident, U.S. resident, and *The Washington Post* journalist was **tortured, strangled, and dismembered** in Istanbul, Turkey, Saudi embassy by Crown Prince Mohammed bin Salman-ordered hit squad *(Khashoggi's Apple Watch recorded entire event; Trump refused to hold Saudis accountable)*

10/06/18 – SUPREME COURT: **Senate confirms Brett Kavanaugh**, Trump's 2nd justice

10/27/18 – MASS SHOOTING: **Pittsburgh**, Pa., Tree of Life synagogue; shooter: Robert Gregory Bowers, 46, Caucasian American white supremacist terrorist *(11 killed, 6 injured)*

11/06/18 – MIDTERM ELECTIONS: **Democrats take House** in landslide, pick up 41 seats, win by record-setting national generic margin of 8.6%; Republicans retain Senate, pick up 2 seats

11/07/18 – MASS SHOOTING: **Thousand Oaks**, Calif., Borderline Bar and Grill college country-western bar; shooter: David Long, 28, Caucasian American terrorist *(13 killed, 1 injured)*

11/30/18 – FORMER PRESIDENT GEORGE H. W. BUSH (R-TEXAS) DIES: at 94; **Trump attends funeral** with all former living presidents (Obama, George W. Bush, Clinton, Carter) *(but clearly stands as an uncomfortable outsider)*

12/22/18 – GOVERNMENT (TRUMP) SHUTDOWN BEGINS: **Trump shuts down government for a record 35 days** after reneging on promise to sign border security bill without border wall funding *(he reneged after conservative pundits criticized him for "giving in to the Democrats"; ultimately Trump got nothing, but caved to national pressure)*

02/14/19 – NEW ATTORNEY GENERAL: **William Barr confirmed by Senate, takes office**; Barr was appointed by Trump after sending unsolicited memo to DOJ criticizing the special counsel Trump-Russia investigation *(Barr also served as attorney general under President George H. W. Bush in early 1990s)*

02/27/19 – MICHAEL COHEN TESTIFIES: Trump former personal lawyer-"fixer" **testifies (this time truthfully) before Congress** *(exposes Trump hush-money payoffs to paramours, tax fraud, etc.)*

03/15/19 – MASS SHOOTING: **Christchurch**, New Zealand, two neighboring mosques; shooter: Brenton Harrison Tarrant, 28, Caucasian Australian white supremacist terrorist *(51 killed, 40 injured)*

03/22/19 – TRUMP-RUSSIA INVESTIGATION: **Mueller report completed**, submitted to DOJ *(not publicly released)*

03/24/19 – TRUMP-RUSSIA INVESTIGATION: Attorney General William **Barr sends 4-page "summary" of Mueller's report to Congress** (made public immediately, intentionally); Barr's conclusions essentially state "no collusion, no obstruction" *(Mueller's team is furious that its report was misrepresented and that Barr refused to release the report's own [accurate] summaries)*

04/18/19 – TRUMP-RUSSIA INVESTIGATION: **Mueller report released publicly**; AG Barr's March 24 "summary" exposed as intentionally misleading (many say, "lying") attempt to create false Trump-exoneration narrative for 25 days to soften impact of Trump's crimes and malfeasance exposed in report

04/25/19 – ELECTION 2020: Joe **Biden announces** candidacy

05/31/19 – MASS SHOOTING: **Virginia Beach**, Va., municipal building; shooter: DeWayne Craddock, 40, Caucasian American terrorist *(12 killed, 4 injured)*

07/24/19 – TRUMP-RUSSIA INVESTIGATION: Special counsel Robert **Mueller testifies before Congress** to: 1) widespread Russian election interference; 2) Trump welcoming, encouraging, using, covering up illegal Russian election help; 3) Trump obstruction of justice during investigation, at least 10 instances *("If the president clearly did not commit a crime, we would have said so")*

07/25/19 – TRUMP EXTORTS UKRAINE: **Trump phone call to extort** Ukrainian President Volodymyr Zelenskyy *(for phony dirt on likely presidential opponent Joe Biden in exchange for already congressionally authorized U.S. military aid to fight off Russian incursion)*

08/03/19 – MASS SHOOTING: **El Paso**, Texas, Walmart retail store; shooter: Patrick Wood Crusius, 21, Caucasian American white supremacist terrorist *(23 killed, 23 injured)*

08/04/19 – MASS SHOOTING: **Dayton**, Ohio, Oregon Historic District; shooter: Connor Betts, 24, Caucasian American terrorist *(9 killed, 17 injured)*

09/01/19 – SHARPIE-GATE: **Trump errs in Hurricane Dorian tweet**; spends 12 days trying to prove he didn't, including redrawing an official weather map with childlike Sharpie markings, which he displayed in news conference

09/24/19 – IMPEACHMENT NO. 1 (EXTORTION OF UKRAINE): House Speaker Nancy Pelosi begins **"official impeachment inquiry"**

09/25/19 – IMPEACHMENT NO. 1 (EXTORTION OF UKRAINE): **Trump releases transcript of call** to Ukrainian President Zelenskyy *(Trump thinks it exonerates him, though clearly it implicates him; he famously asked Zelenskyy, "We'd like you to do us a favor though.")*

12/18/19 – IMPEACHMENT NO. 1 (EXTORTION OF UKRAINE): **House votes to impeach** President Trump *(2 articles)*

12/mid/19 – PANDEMIC: COVID-19 **coronavirus first identified** in Wuhan, China

01/09/20 – HILLARY CLINTON CLEARED OF EVERYTHING: Trump **DOJ clears Hillary Clinton** of all charges, accusations, allegations ever lodged at her *(news is buried)*

01/30/20 – PANDEMIC: **WHO declares "Public Health Emergency** of International Concern"

01/31/20 – PANDEMIC: Trump institutes porous **China travel ban**, follows U.S. airlines and 38 other countries

02/05/20 – IMPEACHMENT NO. 1 (EXTORTION OF UKRAINE): **Senate acquits** President Trump *(1 Republican, Mitt Romney, joins all 47 Democrats in vote to convict, 48-52; 67 were needed)*

02/06/20 – PANDEMIC: **1ˢᵗ U.S. COVID-19 death** *(in northern California)*

03/15/20 – PANDEMIC: Trump institutes nationwide **social distancing guidelines to last 2 weeks** *(critics, scientists, doctors say this should have been done weeks sooner and lasted much longer)*

05/25/20 – BLACK LIVES MATTER: **George Floyd murdered** by on-duty Minneapolis police officer during routine encounter involving minor infraction *(national record-large protests begin over succeeding days including people of all ethnicities)*

05/27/20 – PANDEMIC: **U.S. hits 100,000 COVID-19 deaths;** Trump universally panned for mishandling pandemic; he's played down, belittled, and politicized dangers and refused to nationalize prevention recommendations, supply manufacturing, and supply chain, all in the belief that these moves will hurt economy, thereby hurt his reelection chances *(expert estimates determine Trump malfeasance responsible for half of all U.S. COVID-19 deaths to date)*

06/01/20 – TRUMP BIBLE PHOTO OP: **Trump orders federal forces to clear legal, peaceful D.C. protesters** — using rubber bullets, tear gas, flash-bang shells — for photo op in front of church, to display his "toughness" in handling BLM protests *(Trump is excoriated by multiple top generals, other national luminaries)*

06/05/20 – ELECTION 2020: Joe **Biden clinches Democratic nomination**

07/mid/20 - PANDEMIC: **U.S. hits 150,000 COVID-19 deaths**; expert estimates determine Trump malfeasance responsible for half of all U.S. COVID-19 deaths to date *(U.S.: 4.3% of Earth's population, 22% of its pandemic deaths)*

08/11/20 – ELECTION 2020: Joe **Biden chooses Sen. Kamala Harris (D-Calif.) as vice presidential** running mate

08/18/20 – TRUMP-RUSSIA INVESTIGATION: GOP-controlled **Senate Intelligence Committee report confirms extensive Russian 2016 U.S. election interference, collusion** between Trump campaign and Russia

09/18/20 – SUPREME COURT – Justice **Ruth Bader Ginsburg (liberal) dies** at 87; *(Senate Majority Leader Mitch McConnell, R-Ky., vows to fill seat before election, ignoring "McConnell Rule" established upon Justice Gorsuch's confirmation: no hearings in last year of presidential term)*

09/26/20 – SUPREME COURT: President **Trump nominates Amy Coney Barrett**, Trump's 3rd nominee

10/02/20 – TRUMP CONTRACTS COVID-19: President Trump **hospitalized for 3 days**, leaves hospital against medical advice *(exposes aides, contacts to virus; still plays down dangers, refuses to role-model and nationalize prevention guidelines)*

10/08/20 – KIDNAPPING PLOT – GOV. GRETCHEN WHITMER (D-MICH.): **FBI foiled white supremacist militia plan**, hatched over previous 5 months, to "kidnap … and hold for ransom and reward" the Mich. governor *(white supremacist militia group was angry about state's COVID-19 stay-at-home restrictions, and partially were inspired after President Trump tweeted April 17, 2020: "LIBERATE MINNESOTA! … LIBERATE MICHIGAN! … LIBERATE VIRGINIA, and save your great 2nd Amendment. It is under siege!")*

10/27/20 – SUPREME COURT: **Senate confirms Amy Coney Barrett**, Trump's 3rd justice *(conservative majority now at 6-3)*

11/03/20 – ELECTION DAY: **Joe Biden defeats Donald Trump**; Biden wins Electoral College 306-232; Biden wins popular vote 81.3M-74.2M, 51.3%-46.9% *(results not confirmed for 4 days due to late counting of deluge of Biden-friendly mail-in ballots)*

12/mid/20 – PANDEMIC: **U.S. hits 300,000 COVID-19 deaths**; expert estimates determine Trump malfeasance responsible for half of all U.S. COVID-19 deaths to date *(U.S.: 4.2% of Earth's population, 19% of its pandemic deaths)*

01/06/21 – INSURRECTION OF JANUARY 6: **Trump-supporting seditionists attempt to stop congressional pro forma certification of Electoral College votes** overseen by Vice President Mike Pence *(Trump supporters breach, terrorize, ransack Capitol building for several hours, causing 7 deaths, 140 police injuries; Trump watched on TV, refused to take any action, for approximately 3 hours)*

01/13/21 – IMPEACHMENT NO. 2 (INCITEMENT OF INSURRECTION): **House votes to impeach** President Donald Trump *(1 article)*

01/20/21 – INAUGURATION DAY: Joe **Biden takes office** as 46th president

02/13/21 – IMPEACHMENT NO. 2 (INCITEMENT OF INSURRECTION): **Senate acquits** former President Trump *(7 Republicans join all 50 Democrats in vote to convict, 57-43; 67 were needed)*

02/21/21 – PANDEMIC: **U.S. hits 500,000 COVID-19 deaths**; expert estimates determine Trump malfeasance responsible for half of all U.S. COVID-19 deaths to date *(U.S.: 4.2% of Earth's population, 20% of its pandemic deaths)*

For detailed Trump-Russia timeline, visit:
https://www.factcheck.org/2017/06/timeline-russia-investigation/

"Had racism been toxic to the American electorate, Trump's candidacy would not have been viable."

(Serwer, Adam; "The Nationalist's Delusion"; *The Atlantic*; 11/20/2017.)